Critical Essays on

THOMAS HARDY'S POETRY

CRITICAL ESSAYS
ON
BRITISH LITERATURE

Zack Bowen, General Editor
University of Miami

Critical Essays on

THOMAS HARDY'S POETRY

edited by

HAROLD OREL

G. K. Hall & Co. / New York
Maxwell Macmillan Canada / Toronto
Maxwell Macmillan International / New York Oxford Singapore Sydney

G. K. Hall & Co.   Maxwell Macmillan Canada, Inc.
Macmillan Publishing Company   1200 Eglinton Avenue East
866 Third Avenue   Suite 200
New York, New York 10022   Don Mills, Ontario M3C 3N1

Library of Congress Cataloging-in-Publication Data

Critical essays on Thomas Hardy's poetry / edited by Harold Orel.
        p.   cm.—(Critical essays on British literature)
    Includes bibliographical references and index.
    ISBN 0-8161-8768-1
    1. Hardy, Thomas, 1840-1928—Poetic works.   I. Orel, Harold.
1926-   . II. Series.
PR4757.P58C75   1994
821'.8—dc20   94-27561
                                                            CIP

MAY   1995

The paper used in this publication meets the minimum requirements of
American National Standard for Information Sciences—Permanence of
Paper for Printed Library Materials. ANSI Z3948-1984. ⊚™

10   9   8   7   6   5   4   3   2   1

Printed in the United States of America

To Dudley and Marian Mills,
with love.

Contents

◆

General Editor's Note

◆

The Critical Essays on British Literature series provides a variety of approaches to both classical and contemporary writers of Britain and Ireland. The formats of the volumes in the series vary with the thematic designs of individual editors, and the nature of the published criticism, augmented, where appropriate, by original essays by recognized authorities. It is hoped that each volume will be unique in developing a new overall perspective on its particular subject.

Harold Orel's introduction deals with the relationship between Thomas Hardy's life and his poetry. Beginning with Hardy's struggle for recognition as a poet despite his fame as a novelist, Orel traces the evolution of the criticism of Hardy's poetry from slighting condemnation through the New Critical discovery of his poetic genius to the biographical recovery of Hardy's poetic subjects and the late, informed appreciation of his poetry. Orel's tripartite selection of essays covers an overview of Hardy's poetry, Hardy's relation to other writers, and a series of detailed criticisms of specific works.

ZACK BOWEN
University of Miami

Publisher's Note

◆

Producing a volume that contains both newly commissioned and reprinted material presents the publisher with the challenge of balancing the desire to achieve stylistic consistency with the need to preserve the integrity of works first published elsewhere. In the Critical Essays series, essays commissioned especially for a particular volume are edited to be consistent with G. K. Hall's house style; reprinted essays appear in the style in which they were first published, with only typographical errors corrected. Consequently, shifts in style from one essay to another are the result of our efforts to be faithful to each text as it was originally published.

Introduction

♦

HAROLD OREL

Thomas Hardy came late to the business of being a professional novelist. He began his career as an architect's apprentice in Dorchester in 1856 at the age of sixteen, but he wanted, at various times and always in a vague, unfocused way, to do other things: to become an actor, a man of the cloth, a journalist who reported on different kinds of cultural activity. By 1862 he was working as an assistant architect for Arthur Blomfield in London, but after a siege of ill health he returned to Dorchester and to the office of Arthur Hicks, his first employer. Not until 1868 did he send his first novel, *The Poor Man and the Lady*, to the publisher Alexander Macmillan. Hardy was, by then, twenty-eight years old. The failure to place *The Poor Man and the Lady*, followed by a series of very small successes with the three novels that he did get into print (*Desperate Remedies* in 1871, *Under the Greenwood Tree* in 1872, and *A Pair of Blue Eyes* in 1873), led him to postpone making a decision to leave his work as a school designer, church restorer, and general handyman/architect. Hardy was also keenly aware that he was working for people who had superior social connections and greater capital than he could ever realistically accumulate; he had small chance of founding his own architectural firm.

Emma Gifford, the woman Hardy loved, supported his decision, made in the early 1870s, to consider literature his "true vocation," and to devote full time to the writing of fiction. But making up his mind to move away from a career in architecture was not an easy thing to do. In 1872 he helped the architect T. Roger Smith design schools for a London School Board competition, and Smith was sufficiently pleased by the fact that one of his entries had won in the competition that he refused to consider as final Hardy's departure from London to work on *A Pair of Blue Eyes*. Hardy had to consider very seriously Smith's offer to take him on again before he decided that Emma's advice and his own inclination should be acted on.

He married Emma on 17 September 1874. He was now in his thirty-

2 ♦ HAROLD OREL

fourth year. There was no certainty that what he had written thus far had taught him how to win a larger audience, or that he had learned how to persuade publishers to pay more substantial advances for his work. Even the popularity of *Far from the Madding Crowd* (1874) could not be considered a reliable indicator of his future fortunes. He was launching himself and Emma into the unknown, and he knew that not all of his friends were convinced that he was acting prudently.

Nevertheless, Hardy had assessed accurately the likely degree of success that he might achieve as an architect in someone else's firm. Moreover, he was a better judge of his own story-telling talents than the publishers, editors, and reviewers who were watching his career; he knew that he could become "a good hand with a serial" (Hardy's own wording), and for twenty years he was to take pride in his ability to turn in commercially valuable product—that is, his novels—on time. His belated choice of a true vocation turned out to be fully justified. By 1880 he was recognized internationally as one of the best Victorian novelists; within two decades he was undergoing a transformation into the Grand Old Man of English letters, a position that he guaranteed for himself by living another thirty years.

Hardy began writing poetry long before 1866, the year in which he made a serious effort to place some poems in various magazines. No editor would accept any of them. He continued writing new poems for more than sixty years, putting some away in desk drawers, taking them out occasionally for revision and polishing, and ultimately arranging a table of contents for each one of what was to add up to eight published volumes of poems. He was in the process of revising the poems of *Winter Words*, which he planned to publish on his next birthday, when death intervened on 11 January 1928. Not until 2 October—some four months past the birthday he did not live to see—did *Winter Words* make its appearance in bookstores.

HARDY'S POETRY

It is fitting, therefore, that a *Critical Essays* volume should begin by acknowledging the justice of Hardy's observation, made more than once in the 1920s, that he had devoted more years of his life to writing poetry than to writing prose fiction. Even if we start the clock with the publication of *Wessex Poems* (1898), his first published book of poetry, we will want to remember that he had been composing and polishing several of the poems therein for up to thirty years.

Hardy preferred to be judged as a poet than as a novelist, and his slighting remarks about his own novels were made with greater sincerity than was conceded by even those personal friends who recorded them. Hardy was not simply expressing pique at the judgment of contemporary critics and reviewers who much to his chagrin, kept calling for a new *Tess*: he genuinely believed that a poet who earned a place in "a good anthology like the *Golden Treasury*" (edited by Francis Turner Palgrave) had achieved a lasting success, perhaps the only success that really counted. (So wrote Florence Emily Hardy, his second wife, in the final poignant pages of *The Later Years of Thomas Hardy, 1892–1928*, published by Macmillan in 1930.)

Perhaps in some afterlife Hardy's restless spirit can find solace. His *Collected Poems* (1930), which printed 918 poems, has been almost continuously in print for more than six decades. The number of poems has been augmented by previously uncollected verse, now published in James Gibson's edition, *The Complete Poems of Thomas Hardy* (1976). No anthology of either Victorian or modern poetry can be considered worth its price if it fails to print a substantial selection of Hardy's poems.

The epic-drama *The Dynasts*, published in three volumes between 1904 and 1908, invited readers to contrast Hardy's accomplishments with those of the greatest of poets from the past. As he wrote in his preface, "The wide prevalence of the Monistic theory of the Universe forbade, in this twentieth century, the importation of Divine personages from any antique Mythology as ready-made sources or channels of Causation, even in verse, and excluded the celestial machinery of, say, *Paradise Lost*, as peremptorily as that of the *Iliad* or the *Eddas*." Hardy, conscious of the problems inherent in his unusual crossing of literary genres, was too diffident to suggest that his modernity in any way implied an artistic superiority to Homer or Milton. More important, he was asking his public to apply to his work the highest literary standards. He believed in the hierarchy of literary forms, over which the epic reigned.

THE STAGES OF CRITICISM

For a full three decades (1898 to 1928), the reactions of reviewers, critics, and even his admirers to his determination to write poetry instead of novels or short stories might be summarized as a puzzled, and at best a grudging, willingness to allow him his bent.[1] The publication of *Wessex Poems* provided the first opportunity for these opinions to cloud, in many readers' minds, the view that Hardy had always been satisfied to be recognized as a novelist, and that he would continue to write novels for the rest of his life. (Even so, Hardy, whenever interviewed prior to the publication of *Jude the Obscure*, had made no secret of his love of poetry.)

For example, W. B. Columbine, in the *Westminster Review*, thought that Hardy's first book of verse had virtues, sufficient in number "to give him an honourable place amongst the minor poets of our time."[2] Other critics were less willing to be even that sympathetic toward what they saw as Hardy's dereliction of duty. W. M. Payne seemed to hope that Hardy's poems could be written off as "evidently nothing more than literary diversions."[3] The reviewer for *Literature* scolded Hardy for failing to observe the requirements of form in verse.[4] Another reader, disappointed by Hardy's "want of style," recorded his opinion that Hardy's Wessex poems were "not as excellent technically" as the poems of the Poet Laureate, Alfred Austin.[5] An anonymous reviewer, writing in the *Saturday Review*, a periodical that Hardy always read carefully, denounced *Wessex Poems* as a "curious and slipshod volume," filled with "slovenly" and "uncouth verses, stilted in sentiment, poorly conceived and worse wrought," and added that Hardy should have burned most of them.[6]

Two observations recurred: the first was that Hardy might reasonably be compared to George Meredith, a novelist who also dallied with the Muse (a comparison that often turned out to Hardy's disadvantage); and the second was that the verse was less interesting than the doctrine. Lionel Johnson, who spoke admiringly of the variety contained in Hardy's first collection, thought that *Wessex Poems* was "cruel" to the land it described, which he felt should not be thought of as wholly "Leopardian."[7] May Kendall stressed the gloominess of Hardy's "verdict on life," but added that his poetry showed the need for Christian strength as the new century approached.[8] The *Athenaeum* reviewer admired the poems that focused on Hardy's "curiously intense and somewhat dismal vision of life"; these provided a reader with "the most poetically successful moments," even though the range of vision was rather narrow.[9]

The more galling observation, so far as the Man from Wessex was concerned, was that the verses of all of his collections were so often characterized as, "in great part, translated prose."[10] This attitude persisted right through the issuance of the three volumes of *The Dynasts*. A comment made by the reviewer for the *Academy and Literature* (London) may be taken as representative: "While there are numerous passages which rise to the level of a poetised rhetoric, not unworthy of the subject-matter, and occasional passages which exhibit Mr. Hardy's gift of romantic description, as a whole the dialogue is the prose of the novelist cut into lengths. . . . We can only say, with a sigh, that we would give many such dramas for one *Return of the Native*." Combining realism and abstraction had proved unsuccessful: "If it were worked out in that medium of the novel wherein he is a master, we might have an imposing and enthralling trilogy of novels."[11]

To be sure, there was much generous praise and a recognition, widening as the years went by, that the writing of poetry was not a passing fancy of Thomas Hardy, but rather a conversion of sorts, or, more precisely, a reaffirmation of long-held poetic ideals. But it is fair to say that Hardy never enjoyed, during his final three decades, the esteem that Tennyson and Browning had won as professional poets, and that he recognized the fatal influence exerted by the success of his novels over the possibility of his recognition as a first-rate, full-time, practicing poet.

This stage in the reception of Hardy's poetry may be accounted as the first of three. It lasted at least until the summer of 1940, when the Thomas Hardy Centennial Issue of the *Southern Review* was published. In this season, while England fought for survival in World War II, the seemingly endless, and occasionally arid, debate about whether Hardy was a Victorian poet or a transitional poet who anticipated the principles of modernist poetry ended in W. H. Auden's ringing declaration in the journal that Hardy was both his Keats and his Carl Sandburg: that is, that Hardy was important as an expression of "the Contemporary Scene." The majority of essays printed in this special issue of the highly influential periodical concentrated not on Hardy's novels but on his poems, and specifically on their art; they were written by John Crowe Ransom, R. P. Blackmur, Howard Baker, Delmore Schwartz, F. R. Leavis, Allen Tate, and Morton Dauwen Zabel. To this collection Bonamy Dobrée contributed an analysis of *The Dynasts*, by 1940 a half-forgotten poem, which praised the epic as "a grand performance, solidly conceived, and quite firm in structure,"[12] and declared that it "strikes our awareness with as sharp an impact as it did at the beginning of the last war" (Dobrée, 109).

These critics hit several new notes. They were not examining the thought or philosophy of Hardy's poems so much as the craft and particularity of his images. They found matter for praise in Hardy's idiosyncrasies where earlier critics had discovered reasons for denunciation. Hardy's avoidance of formula was seen as a strength. The personal experiences that served as inspiration compelled him to write; there may be found in his canon far more "occasional" poems than one at first recognizes, and those not merely the poems about the *Titanic*, Leslie Stephen, Swinburne, and the Boer War. These critics enjoyed Hardy's variety of meters, and responded gallantly to the difficulty of his lyrics. They recognized the limitations of his meliorism (they unanimously rejected the older view of Hardy as a pessimist), and expressed dismay that so often Hardy had felt himself called upon to re-spond—in his poems—to the arguments of theologians, social scientists, and philosophers.

Blackmur went so far as to argue that Hardy's sensitivity to these issues "was all loss in his work: a loss represented by what we feel as the privation of his humanity."[13] Like Wordsworth, Hardy "found substance for poems in the everyday histories of simple people,"[14] but he only began there; he did not rest content with recounting those histories.

"What I valued most in Hardy, then, as I still do," Auden wrote,

was his hawk's vision, his way of looking at life from a very great height, as in the stage directions of *The Dynasts*, or the opening chapter of *The Return of the Native.* To see the individual life related not only to the local social life of its time, but to the whole of human history, life on the earth, the stars, gives one both humility and self-confidence. For from such a perspective the difference between the individual and society is so slight, since both are so insignificant, that the latter ceases to appear as a formidable god with absolute rights, but rather as an equal, subject to the same laws of growth and decay, and therefore one with whom reconciliation is possible.[15]

The fact that these views have become commonplace today should not cause us to forget that they reintroduced Hardy to an audience long grown weary of the self-importance of much Victorian poetry. Hardy's voice, these critics reminded readers, was distinctive, personal, and consistently interesting, despite all the faults with it that others had discovered (and the existence of which they themselves often reaffirmed). And it was no accident that this issue of the *Southern Review* appeared when it did. Hardy, who had written often about the barbarism of war, had foreseen the futility of Versailles and the certainty of still another world conflict, and much of his poetry seemed as timely as ever.

1940 was also the year in which Carl Weber, an enthusiastic collector of Hardyana at Colby College, Maine, published his biography, *Hardy of Wessex: His Life and Literary Career.* It became a standard reference because much of its information was more judiciously proportioned and more clearly set forth than that of earlier works. The book did not regard the poems as an unfortunate experiment; but Weber, whose sympathy for the various difficulties that beset Hardy led him to minimize or omit unpleasant aspects of Hardy's character, seemed temperamentally unable to cope with the burning, bitter self-reproach that haunted practically all the poems dealing with Emma. Hardy, in Weber's treatment, was very much an idealized man of letters, and a long-suffering paragon who had to cope with a partially demented and increasingly unpleasant wife.

Weber gave wide currency to the story that Emma made a special trip to London and "applied to Dr. Richard Garnett at the British Museum for aid in inducing her husband to burn his vicious manuscript [*Jude the Obscure*]. She had already written Garnett to no avail; now she implored him; she wept. . . . In the end Mrs. Hardy returned, defeated, to Max Gate [Hardy's home in Dorchester]."[16] This anecdote was repeated verbatim in Weber's introduction to *Hardy's Love Poems* and in his *"Dearest Emmie": Thomas Hardy's Letters to His First Wife* (both published in 1963): "Emma's 'general unbearableness' . . . was much greater than any reader of Hardy's poems might have supposed. Her abrupt departures for Calais, her unannounced return home in 1900, her aches and pains, her lame knee and sprained ankle, her chills and influenza, her failing eyesight and her 'shingles,' her general unpredictability, are clearly brought out by the searchlight of these letters" (*"Dearest Emmie,"* 102).

Robert Gittings, some thirty-five years later, investigated the story, found no factual basis for it, and identified its source as Ford Madox Ford, who he said is "recognized as one of the great literary liars." Perhaps the most astonishing nugget turned up by Gittings's research was the willingness of Ford to concede that the truth of the anecdote could not be vouched for: "If even that arch-romancer Ford Madox Ford was so sceptical, it is all the more astonishing that biographers have accepted the story."[17]

This difference of opinion between biographers should not be dismissed as a small matter. Hardy wrote more than two hundred love poems—a quarter of his total production, if we put *The Dynasts* aside. The majority of them (which are by no means limited to "Poems of 1912–13," the famous sequence included in *Satires of Circumstance, Lyrics and Reveries*) record important aspects of Hardy's changing emotions and attitudes toward Emma. By any critical standard, many of these poems are among Hardy's finest productions. Weber's blaming Emma almost entirely in 1940 for the division of hearts that led to the poems being written caused an entire generation of critics to misunderstand the biographical realities of Hardy's marriage (Weber, with good intentions, had obfuscated them).

In brief, two linked lines of argument became important during this second period. The first was that Hardy was a major poet, an artist in tune with changing times, perhaps (as Ezra Pound said, with characteristic belligerency) one of the two Victorian poets, the other being Browning, who deserved respectful consideration in the twentieth century; and the second maintained that although the circumstances of Hardy's life were more interesting than had hitherto been suspected, they did not have much bearing on the subject matter or the tone of most of the poems. The net effect of these schools of thought was to encourage close textual analyses. Notes on the meanings of dialectal expressions and word coinages proliferated in the anthologies used in classrooms, and sometimes it even looked as if the fate of the poet William Barnes—one of Hardy's heroes, who had stubbornly persisted in incorporating the expressions of Dorset dialect into his poetry, and whose literary fame had suffered as a consequence—might overtake a poet who also employed the Wessex *r* and *z* to vivify the speech of his rural characters. Hardy's experiments with metrical schemes were laboriously plotted; one critic counted more than thirty of them in *The Dynasts* alone.[18]

It would be an overstatement to call a majority of the writings on Hardy's poetry New Criticism, but something very much resembling the New Criticism of the early 1930s enjoyed a field day in Hardy studies for a full quarter century, right up to the appearance of a new spate of biographical studies in the 1960s, when the third (and current) phase began. In fairness to the intelligence animating those discussions, critics who employed the tenets of New Criticism enhanced Hardy's reputation as a craftsman, and made him eminently respectable as a poet.[19] They championed Hardy in ways that Hardy, who had jealously guarded his own privacy while at the same time submitting volume after volume of autobiographically based poems to the judgment of his peers, doubtless would have approved. Among his admirers were G. Wilson Knight, who identified affinities between Hardy and Shelley;[20] Elizabeth Bowen, who believed that "a philosophic consciousness of the future" was no less important in Hardy's thinking than an awareness of the past;[21] Herbert Read, who saw Hardy as having descended from a "specifically English tradition" of poetry;[22] Yvor Winters, who admired the feeling (and nonparaphrasable content) in Hardy's poetry, while condemning his use of "satires of circumstances" to prove a point;[23] Babette Deutsch, who aligned Hardy with A. E. Housman and Robinson Jeffers, and who wrote appreciatively of Hardy's "paradox" and "grim humor";[24] Randall Jarrell, who could scarcely find language enthusiastic enough to describe Hardy's poetic achievement;[25] and Mark Van Doren, who argued that Hardy surpassed Yeats in both the inherent interestingness of his poems and the quality of his human concerns.[26]

I do not mean to suggest that Hardy's poetry became more important than his novels for most readers, or that, for a full quarter century after 1940, the battle for the establishment of Hardy's credentials as a major poet was turning into an unimportant issue. The discussions of Hardy's pessimism continued, and—sometimes subtly, sometimes crudely—interfered with many readers' understanding of the poet's intention and deepest conviction.

But readers, in general, were looking more closely at individual poems than most critics of the first phase had bothered to. Brief articles on sharply defined issues appeared in the *Explicator, Modern Language Notes, Modern Philology, Notes and Queries*, and *Colby Library Quarterly*, to name only American periodicals, and English criticism pursued parallel paths. V. H. Collins, concentrating on the "340 love poems" of Hardy's *Collected Poems* (more than one-third, by his count), was duly impressed by Hardy's ability to dramatize the woman's point of view.[27] Henry Reed studied "the making of *The Dynasts*" as if no one had read the epic-drama properly before he had.[28] Cecil Day-Lewis praised Hardy's experiments with stanzaic form, and the deliberate roughness of Hardy's diction.[29] Marguerite Roberts, reassessing Hardy's contribution to drama, felt obliged to note the importance of the dramatic element in the shorter poems.[30] Almost everyone in the literary Establishment, it seemed, thought well of Hardy's poetry: C. M. Bowra believed that Hardy might well be the most tragic poet since Shakespeare, but quickly added that pessimism should not be regarded as the key to his greatness;[31] John Laird argued that Hardy's skill as a poet accounted for the impact of Hardy's ideas on the reader;[32] James G. Southworth's study of Hardy's poetry was widely read;[33] Vivian de Sola Pinto, in the course of an extended comparison between Hardy and Housman, found that Hardy was by far the more subtle artist, and much more sophisticated in his use of the subconscious;[34] Samuel Hynes made a strong case for the art behind a large number of Hardy's lyrics that had barely been noticed before;[35] David Perkins identified Hardy's major theme as isolation, and the problems inherent in the attempt to escape from it;[36] and Mark Van Doren proclaimed Hardy's poetry the work of a "genius."[37]

And there was high praise, too, for Hardy's longest poetical work: Annette B. Hopkins's study of Hardy's use of historical sources in *The Dynasts*;[38] E. A. Horsman's sympathetic analysis of Hardy's unconventional language (for example, scientific words and negative prefixes);[39] the review in the [*London*] *Times Literary Supplement* that suggested readers look again at the neglected, underestimated epic drama,[40] Louis Morcos's investigation of Hardy's use of Scripture;[41] and J. O. Bailey's *Thomas Hardy and the Cosmic Mind*, which united a deep sympathy toward Hardy's philosophical views with Bailey's own alert critical sensibility.[42]

Misreadings of Hardy's poetical texts often developed as a consequence of the thinness of the biographical materials available to critics prior to the 1960s. Moreover, important documents were scattered in various libraries and special collections, and these needed to be consulted. The treasure trove at the Dorset County Museum in Dorchester, rich as it was (and is), was only one of several important repositories of Hardy material. Not enough was known about Hardy's life, or indeed the circumstances of the environment into which he had been born in 1840, to enable readers to assess fairly the uses to which Hardy put his own experiences in his lyrics, his occasional poems, his philosophical musings, and even his dramatic ballads, which were often cast in dialogue form.

Thomas Hardy is unique—certainly among Victorians, and perhaps among all English writers of the past two centuries—in terms of the number of discoveries biographers and scholars have made, in the very recent past, about the relationship between his life and his art. The task of assessing the astonishing richness of the materials made available to interested readers since the mid-1960s still challenges biographers and critics. Here follows a list of the more significant publications:

Evelyn Hardy and Robert Gittings's *Some Recollections by Emma Hardy with Notes by Evelyn Hardy Together with Some Relevant Poems by Thomas Hardy with Notes by Robert Gittings* (London and New York: Oxford University Press, 1961).

C. J. P. Beatty's *The Architectural Notebook of Thomas Hardy* (Dorchester, England: Dorset Natural History and Archaeological Society, 1966; Philadelphia: George S. Macmanus, 1966).

Harold Orel's *Thomas Hardy's Personal Writings: Prefaces, Literary Opinions, Reminiscences* (Lawrence: University Press of Kansas, 1966; London: Macmillan, 1967).

J. Stevens Cox's *Monographs on the Life, Times and Works of Thomas Hardy* (Guernsey: Toucan Press, 1961–1972).

Lennart A. Björk's *The Literary Notes of Thomas Hardy* (Göteborg, Sweden: Acta Universitatis Gothoburgensis—Gothenburg Studies in English

No. 29, 1974; New York: Humanities Press, 1975); subsequently revised, expanded, and printed in two volumes as *The Literary Notebooks of Thomas Hardy* (London: Macmillan, 1985).

Richard H. Taylor's *The Personal Notebooks of Thomas Hardy* (London: Macmillan, 1978).

Richard Little Purdy and Michael Millgate's seven-volume edition of *The Collected Letters of Thomas Hardy* (Oxford: Clarendon, 1978–1988).

James Gibson's edition of *The Complete Poems of Thomas Hardy: A Variorum Edition* (London: Macmillan, 1979).

Samuel Hynes's *The Complete Poetical Works of Thomas Hardy*, 3 vols. (London: Oxford University Press, 1982–1985).

Richard H. Taylor's edition of the *Emma Hardy Diaries* (Ashington: Mid-Northumberland Arts Groups; and Manchester: Carcanet New Press, 1985).

These books and monographs contain primary materials written by Hardy, or by men and women who knew Hardy, and they have made available the kinds of information that critics want and need to use in order to reach considered judgments. When Walter F. Wright wanted to amass the documents he needed for his pioneering work, *The Shaping of "The Dynasts": A Study in Thomas Hardy* (Lincoln: University of Nebraska Press, 1967), he had to spend more than a year in the Dorset County Museum, the Hardy Memorial Library, and the British Museum; but now a researcher in a well-stocked library can assemble the same materials, and more, within a few days. In addition, in the past fifteen years there have appeared several brilliantly edited editions of Hardy's creative work by Dale Kramer, Juliet Grindle, Simon Gatrell, and Robert Schweik, among others, and more are in the offing; Samuel Hynes's edition of *The Dynasts* is scheduled for publication in 1994.

Biographies of some importance in completing a reshaped picture of Hardy's life have also been published. Among these works, which provide readers with complex and thought-provoking reassessments of Hardy's reasons for turning away from prose fiction, are Harold Orel's *The Final Years of Thomas Hardy, 1912–1928* (London: Macmillan, 1976) and *The Unknown Thomas Hardy: Lesser Known Aspects of Hardy's Life and Career* (Brighton, England: Harvester Press, 1987); Robert Gittings's *Young Thomas Hardy* and *The Older Hardy* (London: Heinemann Educational, 1978); Michael Millgate's *Thomas Hardy: A Biography* (London: Oxford University Press, 1982); and Frank B. Pinion's *Thomas Hardy: His Life and Friends* (New York: St. Martin's, 1992). In addition, Michael Millgate's editing of Florence Hardy's *The Early Life of Thomas Hardy, 1840–1892* (London: Macmillan, 1928) and *The Later Years of Thomas Hardy, 1892–1928* (London: Macmillan, 1928–1930) restored Hardy's original wording, and corrected the distortions introduced by Florence's changes to the text, which were made after Hardy's death, but prior to publication; this new edition has become indispensable as *The Life and Work of Thomas Hardy by Thomas Hardy* (London: Macmillan, 1985). Biographies of Hardy's two wives must also be consulted, since in several valuable ways they supplement the data recorded in the biographies of Hardy: Denys Kay-Robinson's *The First Mrs. Hardy* (London: Macmillan, 1979) and Robert Gittings and Jo Manton's *The Second Mrs. Hardy* (London: Heinemann, 1979).

Thus, it has become increasingly difficult, and most likely impossible, for knowledgeable critics to sustain any of the old myths in their discussions of the poetical half of Thomas Hardy's career. The notion, for example, that Hardy the autodidact versified half-baked pronouncements about religion, philosophy, or science because his thinking suffered from gaps in his reading of Victorian authorities (Hardy was extraordinarily well informed, and kept a very careful record of what he thought important or striking in books, magazines, and newspaper cuttings); or the idea that Hardy's notorious "pessimism" was a fundamental part of his character; or the line of argument that belittled Hardy's quarrels with critics on the ground that they originated from an excessive pride of authorship rather than from legitimate concern about being misunderstood on substantive matters, have all been defused by the recent biographical scholarship. We are now able to understand better the lasting impact of Hardy's fifteen years in the architectural profession on vocabulary, choice of subject matter, and tone in his poetry. We are also better informed about Hardy's creative editing. The drafts of Hardy's poems were published in James Gibson's *The Complete Poems of Thomas Hardy: A Variorum Edition* (London: Macmillan, 1979). Many scholars have since used this book as the basis of their own work. Two detailed studies by Dennis Taylor may be cited: *Hardy's Poetry, 1860–1928* (London: Macmillan, 1981) and *Hardy's Metres and Victorian Prosody* (Oxford: Clarendon Press, 1988). We can identify connections between a very large number of poems and Hardy's friendships and travels, both within England and on the Continent, because of the superbly edited *Collected Letters*. And because we know so much more about Emma Hardy than any biographer (including Edmund Gosse, a close friend of Hardy and an influential critic for more than four decades) knew during Hardy's lifetime, we are reading the love lyrics and meditations on remembered passion with a firmer grasp of underlying biographical realities. In brief, we are well into the middle of the liveliest and most provocative period of an entire century of criticism of Hardy's poetry.

THE ESSAYS

This *Critical Essays* volume concentrates, for several reasons, on the writings about Thomas Hardy's poetry that have appeared during the third (and still-current) phase. Most of the essays from the first phase are very dated. Many of the best essays of the second phase have already been reprinted in various anthologies of criticism; these are readily available. But the third phase may be illustrated by so many first-rate examples that I have not deemed it necessary, desirable, or useful to reprint the essays collected in volumes edited by Lance St. John Butler (*Thomas Hardy after Fifty Years*, 1977); Annie Escuret (*Cahiers Victoriens et Edouardiens*, vol. 12, 1980); R. G. Cox (*Thomas Hardy: The Critical Heritage*, 1970); Margaret Drabble (*The Genius of Thomas Hardy*, 1976); Albert J. Guerard (*Hardy: A Collection of Critical Essays*, 1963); Frank B. Pinion (*Thomas Hardy and the Modern World*, 1974, and *Budmouth Essays on Thomas Hardy*, 1976); and Norman Page (*Thomas Hardy Annual* 1–5, 1982–1987); or those that appear in the special Hardy issue of *English* 22 (1973). Hardy, within relatively recent times, has become a poet of enormous interest to our best critics, and I believe that the essays reprinted here will provide a reasonably representative picture of their concerns.

I have grouped these selections, which are arranged chronologically by dates of publication, under three headings. The first set of essays offers overviews that relate Hardy to both the art and the traditions of poetry; the second set considers Hardy's relationships to other writers; and the third set provides a closer look at specific poetical texts. Although the writers of these essays do not always refer to the Hardy documents—letters, notebooks, various texts—that have so recently come into print, they are fully aware of the weight that such documentation carries.

Tom Paulin's emphasis on Hardy's reportage reminds us of what "the real" meant to Hardy. The essay provocatively raises the question of how Hardy, who admired the Romantics (especially Shelley and Wordsworth), measured their interest in "visible objects." Feelings, of course, counted for a great deal, and memories, doubtless, for even more; but Hardy was also concerned with facts. Paulin, like Hardy, distrusts windy rhetoric, and his admiration for "Shut Out That Moon," a poem that "brings the blinds firmly down on the pathetic fallacies of romantic moonlight and dark, Keatsian scents," identifies one of the ways in which Hardy's poetry has served to guide the lyrical practice of younger poets.

Geoffrey Harvey, seeing in Hardy's poetry a new form of Wordsworthian concern with the natural world, rightly stresses the astonishing determination of poem after poem to make nature's defects the basis of art. Harvey joins a growing number of critics who question the view (put forward most recently by J. Hillis Miller) that Hardy thought of the mind as a prisoner—or a "puppet"—of the "Immanent Will." The manner in which Hardy defines the role of the imagination is subtly argued here. "For Hardy," Harvey writes, "the neutral objects of the material world are given meaning as they are stamped by people's creative existence," and this necessary connection between what we see and what we truly know serves, in its own way, to pinpoint the *fons et origo* of Hardy's moments of vision.

William H. Pritchard, like practically everyone else, feels obligated to consider the reasons why Hardy renounced the writing of novels, though he so obviously excelled as a creator of fiction that appealed to large audiences. Pritchard focuses on the issue of voice, which many critics have ignored. High praise of Ezra Pound's insights (such as, Hardy's poems at their best remind the reader of forgotten moments in his or her own life; Hardy's fullness and clarity of expression leave no room for "the explaining critic") suggests that Hardy's poetry, for Pritchard no less than for Pound, bears important emotional resonances. Perhaps the gracefulness of Pritchard's writing will lure us—if only for a moment—into assenting to the proposition that our knowledge of Hardy's deteriorating marriage need not affect our understanding or appreciation of the poems. (Pritchard admits that he finds the separation between life and art in this case "difficult and uneasy.") The title of his essay, "Hardy's Winter Words," may be misleading, since Pritchard examines Hardy's entire career as a practicing poet.

The case argued by Samuel Hynes—that Hardy is a major poet, but that his serious faults must not be ignored by his admirers—remains as controversial among some readers today as when he first advanced it in *The Pattern of Hardy's Poetry* (1961). Before this judgment can be refuted, one must deal with the examples that Hynes cites: Hardy's erratic categorizing of his own poems; his delight in being a "poet" in a conventional and self-conscious way; metrical clumsiness; a mechanical use of sound effects. "The poems of the public, literary Hardy are mostly bad poems," Hynes writes. (The case for "badness" can be argued at even greater length than it is here.) Even though we wish to reduce the number of such poems that Hynes identifies as unworthy of Hardy's talent, we are nagged by the thought that Hardy, in collecting his poems, might well have rendered a greater service to his own posthumous reputation if he had been more self-critical.

The second grouping of essays deals with the important issue of Hardy's intellectual and emotional ties to other poets. Hardy, who respected and on occasion borrowed from his predecessors, loved the Romantic poets more than the poets of any earlier period; in his imagination, they loomed larger than Tennyson, Browning, and Arnold. His habits of composition, and his basic philosophy of life, were too well established by the early years of this century for him to borrow from younger poets. (Hardy's interest in T. S. Eliot is still in need of examination. Christopher Ricks, in "Hardy's Spellbound Palace," an essay published in the *Critical Review* (no. 32 [1992]: 106–13), hints that Hardy, in "A Spellbound Palace [Hampton Court]," may have copied Eliot deliberately, and there is additional evidence that Hardy was paying attention to the development of Eliot's career.)

Frank Pinion's claim that Shelley's influence on Hardy was tremendously important—"greater than that of any other writer"—is buttressed by examination of Hardy's interest in the topics treated in *Queen Mab, Prometheus Unbound, Hellas,* and *The Revolt of Islam.* The correspondences between Shelley's themes and the subjects of Hardy's poems are not simply evidence of an abiding interest of reform-minded poets in perennial problems of society, such as divorce or war, though major currents of history significantly help to determine what any serious poet, troubled by the pains of humanity, will write about. Deep called unto deep when Hardy, even before the 1860s, read Shelley. Hardy fully and candidly admitted his admiration for Shelley's fearless stance on all kinds of issues, although Hardy found himself forced to temper the radical tendencies of his youth in order to secure the approval of more conservative publishers, who relied on the judgment of worldly-wise readers such as George Meredith. Pinion has here touched on subject matter that would make a fascinating full-scale book.

The essay by James Persoon is a careful examination of how Hardy rethought Matthew Arnold's "Dover Beach," and I have debated with myself whether it belongs, more suitably, in the final section of this anthology. But Persoon's investigation of the reasons why Hardy had so little to say about his eminent contemporary goes well beyond a study of the indebtedness of a single poem to a universally admired model. A reader who follows Persoon's weighing of the evidence may well conclude (as Persoon did) that Hardy was, characteristically, wrestling with the best wording for "Going and Staying" as part of a larger effort to define his relationship to a poet and thinker whose ideas continually challenged his own. It is helpful to remember that Hardy was a careful reader of the poetry written by his contemporaries, even if he grumbled about its inadequacies when compared to the poetry of the great Romantics.

The final classification provides, for the reader who wants to see how Hardy achieved some of his most striking effects, four examples of critical readings of specific poems. A variety of Hardy's interests and categories of poems is represented here. In particular, it has seemed vital to include a first-rate analysis of *The Dynasts*, the epic drama that loomed so large in Hardy's imagination for fully half his lifetime. Though not attempting deliberately to paint a landscape in which critics are seen talking mostly to one another rather than to the general public, I commend to my reader a consideration of the inevitable linkages between essays and the recurring arguments over kinds of excellence that make Hardy criticism so lively.

The first essay, which concentrates on Hardy's treatment of ballads and narratives, is part of a 1974 study that Paul Zietlow named after one of Hardy's collections of poetry, *Moments of Vision*. One might expect that little profound will be said about such poems, intended for a quick reading by a large and undifferentiated public, and often overinsistent about their own suitability for musical treatment. But Zietlow shows that "the tragic scrupulosity of the moral imagination" dominates here, as elsewhere in Hardy's canon, and that the conscience of one man or woman can be more unforgiving than any external force. Zietlow's insistence that the telling of a tale in any particular poem not be regarded as neutral forces us to reconsider the whole line of argument, so popular during the second phase of Hardy criticism, that technique and texture are far more important than message.

Vern Lentz considers the odd fact that Hardy, a self-declared rationalist, employed ghosts and "disembodied voices" in at least forty-six poems. The speaking ghost proved a convenient way of offering a superior judgment on the ever-present delusions of human life (Hardy often imagined himself as a spectre); but, as Lentz shows, it performed multiple functions, and the scattering of such poems throughout the canon indicates that Hardy remained true to his "aesthetics of disjunction": The world of the living and the world of the dead may be separate in fact, but the poet who sees the relationship between the two can comment freely, to ironic effect. The voice of the ghost, by the way, is not necessarily that of Hardy; some questions are intractably stubborn, and cannot be answered, no matter what the ghost knows.

U. C. Knoepflmacher begins with a challenging proposition: for Hardy, "the recovery of the feminine was the propelling force behind his finest lyrics." Poem after poem seeks to annul gender, even as Hardy indicates that it is very difficult for a woman to find a "feminine space" that is "capable of annulling gender and rendering sexual difference immaterial." Knoepflmacher offers some acute observations on the illustrations Hardy drew for "Heiress and Architect" and "Her Death and After." (These, regrettably, are almost never reprinted in modern editions of Hardy's poems.) Of particular interest are some poignant remarks dealing with Hardy's ambivalent views toward his mother, Jemima Hardy.

Kenneth Millard, who treats *The Dynasts* as "a response to the problem of poetry in the early twentieth century," suggests provocatively that Hardy shares a great deal with such Edwardian poets as Henry Newbolt, John Masefield, Edward Thomas, A. E. Housman, John Davidson, and Rupert Brooke. This interpretation does not necessarily conflict with the readings of an older generation of literary critics, who thought of Hardy as more a transitional poet than a Victorian poet in the line of Tennyson and Arnold. More challenging is Millard's proposition that Hardy "put his imagination at the service of history." It is based on an assumption that the research Hardy conducted prior to the writing of his epic-drama, and the importance Hardy assigned to the factual documentation he had amassed, damaged the quality of the poetry contained in that important work. Millard's view confronts head-on, in an exhilarating way, the view of several modern critics that Hardy has produced, in *The Dynasts*, the best long poem in English written during this century. Perhaps Millard himself is troubled by the thesis, though others have certainly subscribed to it. Despite Hardy's repeated exaltation of the Immanent Will as the force that directs our destinies, Millard believes that Hardy ultimately reaffirms his faith in human character. Indeed, Hardy's failure to insist on humankind's total insignificance and lack of freedom of choice helps to create the "poetry" of the epic-drama.

The last word has not been written about Hardy's poetry. We can be sure, however, that the generation after our own will continue to be fascinated by the creative work of his last three decades. In it one may find rich materials that evoke admiration, respect, and, often enough, the love that binds poet to reader for a lifetime of reading pleasure.

Notes

1.   A dismissive attitude toward significant numbers of Hardy's poems—whole categories, in fact—may be found throughout the secondary literature of this century. In more recent times one of Hardy's staunchest admirers, Samuel Hynes, in his Oxford Authors edition of Thomas Hardy's poetry (1984), writes, "If one reads through all the poems that Hardy dated before 1895 (the year of *Jude the Obscure*, his last novel), it becomes clear not only that there are not many of them, as compared to the 900-odd that he was still to write, but that they are not very good poems, and that they are not, on the whole, characteristically Hardyesque, either in style or in subject. An honest critic would have to admit that if the whole lot were lost he would regret at most two or three. . . ." (xxi). The problem complicating one's reaction to Hynes's disdain is related to the knowledge that Hardy did not consistently date the composition of his poems, and that poems from any period of his life might be pulled from a desk drawer and added to the latest volume going to press. We simply do not know how many of Hardy's poems were written before 1895, whether he dated them or not. Nor are most critics apt to be persuaded by Hynes's argument that "to be a great poet [Hardy] had to be an *old* poet" (xxiv). Time, to be sure, is both a theme and an organizing principle in much of Hardy's poetry, but the joy of experiences being lived and relished presently is also there, in numerous poems, and competes seriously with poems about "the pastness of the past" (xxvii).

2.   W. B. Columbine, "The Poems of Thomas Hardy," *Westminster Review* 152 (August 1899): 180–84.

3.   W. M. Payne, "Recent Poetry," *Dial* 26 (16 April 1899): 274–75.

4.   "Form in Poetry," *Literature* 4 (4 March 1899): 217–18.

5.   "The Lounger," *Critic* (New York) 34 (February 1899): 127. Austin held the post from 1896 to 1913, and was succeeded by Robert Bridges. By then Hardy had published three collections of poems, as well as *The Dynasts*, and, according to Edmund Gosse, "secretly hoped for the appointment"; however, he believed that his poem "God's Funeral" had disqualified him from consideration. See Michael Millgate, *Thomas Hardy: A Biography* (Oxford: Oxford University Press, 1982), 475n.

6.   "Thomas Hardy as Poet," *Saturday Review* (London) 87 (7 January, 1899): 19.

7.   Lionel Johnson, "Mr. Hardy's Poems," *Outlook* (London) 3 (28 January 1899): 822–23.

8.   May Kendall, "Pessimism and Thomas Hardy's Poems," *London Quarterly Review*, n.s., 91 (April 1899): 223–24.

9.   "Literature," *Athenaeum*, no. 3716 (14 January 1899): 41–42.

10.   F. Y. E., "Afterthoughts in Verse," *Speaker* (London), n. s., 5 (21 December 1901): 342–43.

11.   "Reviews: A Vast Venture," *Academy and Literature* (23 January 1904): 95.

12.   Bonamy Dobrée, "*The Dynasts*," *The Southern Review* 6, no. 1 (Summer 1940): 121. Hereafter cited in text as Dobrée.

13.   R. P. Blackmur, "The Shorter Poems of Thomas Hardy," *Southern Review* 6 no. 1 (Summer 1940): 23.

14.   Howard Baker, "Hardy's Poetic Certitude," *Southern Review* 6, no. 1 (Summer 1940): 58.

15. W. H. Auden, "A Literary Transference," *Southern Review* 6, no. 1 (Summer 1940): 83.

16. Carl J. Weber, *Hardy of Wessex: His Life and Literary Career* (New York: Columbia University Press, 1940), 167.

17. Robert Gittings, *The Older Hardy* (London: Heinemann, 1978), 81.

18. See Elizabeth Hickson, *Versification of Thomas Hardy* (Philadelphia: Privately printed, 1931). This study, not significantly revised from its original form as a dissertation written at the University of Pennsylvania, remains an authoritative reference for students of poetry interested in Hardy's experiments with rhyme, meter, and diction. Only recently has a superior study been published: Dennis Taylor's *Hardy's Metres and Victorian Prosody* (Oxford: Clarendon, 1988), which prints "A Metrical Appendix of Hardy's Stanza Forms" on pages 207–66.

19. Some practitioners of the New Criticism (which, by the 1980s, had aged, not always gracefully) have argued forcefully that theirs is still the best way to appreciate the art of poetry. See, for example, William Buckler, *The Poetry of Thomas Hardy: A Study in Art and Ideas* (New York: New York Univ. Press, 1983), and in particular his chapter "Critical Perspectives: An Introductory Statement," with its high praise of the "positive influence" and "wholesome guidance" of New Criticism. Buckler concedes that it is "not as methodologically prescriptive as more recent scholastic systems have tended to be, and . . . not as deeply invaded by extra-literary developments in anthropology, linguistics, psychoanalytical theory, and physics as they have been" (12). But Buckler believes that this is all for the good.

20. G. Wilson Knight, *The Starlit Dome: Studies in the Poetry of Vision* (London: Oxford University Press, 1941).

21. Elizabeth Bowen, *English Novelists* (London: Collins, 1947), 40.

22. Herbert Read, *A Coat of Many Colours: Occasional Essays* (London: Routledge, 1945), 239–44.

23. Yvor Winters, "The Morality of Poetry," in *In Defense of Reason* (Chicago: Swallow Press, 1947), 26–29.

24. Babette Deutsch, *Poetry in Our Time* (New York: Holt, 1952).

25. Randall Jarrell, *Poetry and the Age* (New York: Knopf, 1953).

26. Mark Van Doren, *The Autobiography of Mark Van Doren* (New York: Harcourt, Brace, 1958).

27. V. H. Collins, "The Love Poetry of Thomas Hardy," *Essays and Studies by Members of the English Association* 28 (1942): 69–83.

28. Henry Reed, "The Making of *The Dynasts*," *Penguin New Writing*, no. 18 (July–September 1943): 136–47.

29. Cecil Day-Lewis, "The Shorter Poems of Thomas Hardy," *Bell* (Dublin) 8 (September 1944): 513–25. These views were expanded in Day-Lewis's *The Lyrical Poetry of Thomas Hardy* (London: Cumberledge, 1957), which insisted on the close linkage between Hardy's poems and Hardy's character.

30. Marguerite Roberts, "The Dramatic Elements in Hardy's Poetry," *Queen's Quarterly*, 51 (Winter 1944–1945): 429–38.

31. C. M. Bowra, *Inspiration and Poetry* (London: Macmillan, 1955).

32. John Laird, *Philosophical Incursions into English Literature* (London: Cambridge University Press, 1946).

33. James G. Southworth, *The Poetry of Thomas Hardy* (New York: Columbia University Press, 1947).

34. Vivian de Sola Pinto, *Crisis in English Poetry* (London: Hutchinson House, 1951).

35. Samuel Hynes, *The Pattern of Hardy's Poetry* (Chapel Hill: University of North Carolina Press, 1961).

36. David Perkins, "Hardy and the Poetry of Isolation," *Journal of English Literary History* 26 (June 1959): 253–70.

37. Mark Van Doren, "The Poems of Thomas Hardy," in *Four Poets on Poetry*, ed. Don Cameron Allen (Baltimore: Johns Hopkins Press, 1959), 83–107.

38. Annette B. Hopkins, "*The Dynasts* and the Course of History," *South Atlantic Quarterly* 44 (October 1945): 432–44.

39. E. A. Horsman, "The Language of *The Dynasts*," *Durham University Journal*, n.s., 10 (December 1948): 11–16.

40. "Hardy after Fifty Years," [*London*] *Times Literary Supplement*, 15 January 1954, 33–35.

41. Louis Morcos, "*The Dynasts* and the Bible," *Bulletin of English Studies* (Cairo, Egypt; 1955): 29–65.

42. J. O. Bailey, *Thomas Hardy and the Cosmic Mind* (Chapel Hill: University of North Carolina Press, 1956).

HARDY AND THE ART
OF POETRY

◆

Observations of Fact

TOM PAULIN

Hardy's sensitivity to the cadences of actual speech is matched by his insistence throughout his work on what is authentically visible. Like Leslie Stephen and Frederic Harrison—both positivists and friends of his—he followed Comte in accepting that all real knowledge is based on observed facts, and this ruled out religious faith almost automatically: the "quick, glittering, empirical eye" is "sharp for the surfaces of things" but for nothing beneath them. It can never penetrate beyond surfaces and know things in themselves. For Ruskin this keen sight is essentially religious, and in a passage in *Modern Painters* which Hardy knew (he copied it into one of his commonplace books) he resembles any agnostic positivist when he insists that we must observe things closely:

> the greatest thing a human soul ever does in this world is to *see* something, and tell what it *saw* in a plain way. . . . To see clearly is poetry, prophecy, and religion,—all in one.

Hardy made this note in 1900, but he first read *Modern Painters* during the 1860s and throughout his life he acted on Ruskin's recommendation to observe closely. Like the architect in his early poem, "Heiress and Architect," he developed a "cold, clear view" of things, though for him this faculty of conscious, deliberate observation seldom, if ever, combined "prophecy and religion" with poetry. He trained his eyes to seize the most distinctly visible feature in his field of vision and then he described it.

This is what happens in this description of Gladstone at the time of the Home Rule Bill:

> Saw Gladstone enter the Houses of Parliament. The crowd was very excited, not only waving their hats and shouting and running, but leaping in the air. His head was bare, and his now bald crown showed pale and distinct over the top of Mrs. Gladstone's bonnet.

Tom Paulin: "Observations of Fact," *Thomas Hardy: The Poetry of Perception*, Chapter Four (London: Macmillan, 1975), pp. 91–106. Copyright, Macmillan Press, England, 1975. Reprinted by permission.

Another note from this period shows the same insistence on the visibility of things:

> Cold weather brings out upon the faces of people the written marks of their habits, vices, passions, and memories, as warmth brings out on paper a writing in sympathetic ink. The drunkard looks still more a drunkard when the splotches have their margins made distinct by frost, the hectic blush becomes a stain now, the cadaverous complexion reveals the bone under, the quality of handsomeness is reduced to its lowest terms.

Here, he obeys Ruskin, observes closely and clearly and tells what he sees. Similarly, in his description of Gladstone he quaintly concentrates on one of the scene's most *distinct* features and touches it into life by using Gladstone's bald head as a focal point. For Hardy this type of accurate seeing is absolutely essential. The poet's task is "to find beauty in ugliness" and this means that any and every object—no matter how prosaic—is worth noticing. In some ways this opens up a whole new poetic territory, in others, because it's a reflex action prompted by disillusion, it simply binds and restricts the eye to the dead surfaces of fact:

> Brush not the bough for midnight scents
>   That come forth lingeringly,
> And wake the same sweet sentiments
>   They breathed in you and me
> When living seemed a laugh, and love
>   All it was said to be.
>
> Within the common lamp-lit room
>   Prison my eyes and thought;
> Let dingy details crudely loom,
>   Mechanic speech be wrought:
> Too fragrant was Life's early bloom,
>   Too tart the fruit it brought!

"Shut out that Moon" brings the blinds firmly down on the pathetic fallacies of romantic moonlight and dark, Keatsian scents. The eye is imprisoned by drab contemporary fact, and behind this positivistic commitment to a prosaic ugliness lies Hardy's rejection of conventionally beautiful landscapes in favour of the greater—because more modern—reality of waste heaths and barren mountains. And yet it's not as simple as this. "Afterwards," one of his finest poems, is about just this compulsive positivism (noticing *things*), but these perceived objects are not "dingy details" or dead facts:

> When the Present has latched its postern behind my tremulous stay,
>   And the May month flaps its glad green leaves like wings,

Delicate-filmed as new-spun silk, will the neighbours say,
  'He was a man who used to notice such things'?

It would be wrong to insist that the green leaves or the other "things" in the poem—hawk, hedgehog, stars, passing-bell—exist simply as observed facts. The act of observation becomes a kind of vision here (this is the last poem in *Moments of Vision*) and deliberate scrutiny, the cold clear view of things, passes into a reverence for what is observed. The fresh green leaves are like butterflies hatching from their chrysalids, their texture is like fresh silk, and here, because of a hint of mulberry-feeding silkworms, there is a suggestion of a process that is both natural and man-made. In order to make such a comparison Hardy has obviously had to give spring leaves more than a casual glance, but his precise observation of them doesn't result in a coldly accurate description. The way he matches their sheens and also compares the fluttering leaves to one of the most wonder-inducing of natural processes—the hatching of a butterfly—means that his attitude to them is more than one of merely scientific interest. The butterfly is an ancient symbol of the soul and the poem is about survival after death, but it realises immortality in physical, visible terms. Resurrecting angels and winged souls are naturalised as fluttering leaves, as things. This also happens in "Voices from Things Growing in a Churchyard":

These flowers are I, poor Fanny Hurd,
    Sir or Madam,
A little girl here sepultured.
Once I flit-fluttered like a bird
Above the grass, as now I wave
In daisy shapes above my grave,
    All day cheerily,
    All night eerily!

Again, immortality is realised as an observed fact.

Hardy's matching of filmy leaves with fresh silk in "Afterwards" is particularly curious in that he's joining a natural fact with a process that involves leaves, silkworms and spinning wheels and so suggests a co-operation between nature and human skills. He knew that Paleyan natural theology with its Great Designer is bunk, but there are moments when its basic idea seems feasible on an aesthetic level. What I mean by this is best shown by Arthur Koestler's descriptions in *The Act of Creation* of "the new landscapes seen through an electron microscope":

They show the ultra-structure of the world—electric discharges in a high voltage arc which look like the most elaborate Brussels lace, smoke molecules of magnesium oxide like a composition by Mondrian, nerve-synapses inside a muscle suspended like algae, phantom-figures of swirling heated air, ink molecules travelling through water, crystals like Persian carpets, and ghostly mountains inside the micro-structure of pure Hafnium, like an illustration to Dante's Purgatorio. What strikes one is that these landscapes, drawn as it were in invisible ink, possess great intrinsic beauty of form.

These shapes are not meant to be seen, and yet, once seen, they look like designs (Paley would interrupt here and say a design presupposes a Designer). The structure of matter, then, resembles certain man-made patterns, fresh leaves are like new-spun silk, electric discharges like Brussels lace. So hidden, natural forms appear to be echoed in human designs. This is what I mean by suggesting that Hardy's positivistic observation has passed into vision— the kind of vision found in Hopkins. (The common influence is Barnes, who delighted to match and contrast colours and shades: snow-white washing against a clear blue sky is one of the examples [Geoffrey] Grigson cites). For Hopkins "inscape" is perceived or "stressed" by looking at nature very closely. It's as though Crabbe, down on his knees examining a saltwort, changes into Coleridge and starts to see visions. By "instress" Hopkins means the perception of a unique beauty, an individually distinctive pattern, and in a brief journal-entry he also compares an observed natural phenomenon to silk:

> Waterfalls not only skeined but silky too—one saw it fr. the inn across the meadows: at one quain of the rock the water glistened above and took shadow below, and the rock was reddened a little way each side with the wet, wh. sets off the silkiness.

Unusually for Hopkins, this sounds bogus. We can accept that certain natural colours and shades match, but to insist that the texture of the water here is "set off" by the wet rock is to suggest that nature is displaying a tasteful colour-sense. Hopkins is responding as an aesthete and transforming a water-fall into an ornamental prop in a private landscape garden. In this instance the metaphysical intentions behind his aestheticism are unpersuasive, and doubtless Hardy would have disclaimed having any such intention when he wrote the first stanza of "Afterwards." His aim is to objectify himself in the details he describes. This will be achieved through the association which he has with these objects in the minds of people who themselves used to observe his habit of noticing "such things." In this way his perception is reified and becomes as much a fact as its objects.

Hume's principle of "custom," which he defines as "the effect of repeated perceptions," illustrates what Hardy is doing in "Afterwards": as a positivist who also wants to represent an idea of immortality he must make it convinc-ing, and to be convincing it must be visible. Custom, for Hume, enables us to attribute a "continued existence" to objects which otherwise have no obvious connection with each other; "nor is it," he says, "from any other principle but custom operating upon the imagination, that we can draw any inference from the appearance of one to the existence of another." So each time Hardy's neighbours notice certain things they will immediately associate him with them, remembering that they were once a "familiar sight" to him, and so will necessarily make him spring back into a kind of existence in their memories. His "constant conjunction" with certain objects—the phrase is Hume's—will ensure that they will always associate him with them and so will always remember him. For Hume, we make sense of the world by seeing certain things again and again, and in this way we link a series of familiar impressions together and construct an apparently solid and durable world for ourselves. Hardy's stress on habitual sight echoes this: he will be the missing term which his neighbours will introduce into a familiar equation. In other words, his inseparable connection with certain objects will not be broken by his death and disappearance from his neighbours' sight. However, there are a series of short breaks in the poem's perceptual sequences:

> If it be in the dusk when, like an eyelid's soundless blink,
>   The dewfall-hawk comes crossing the shades to alight
> Upon the wind-warped upland thorn, a gazer may think,
>   'To him this must have been a familiar sight.'

One of the functions of the comparison between the bird's flight and "an eyelid's soundless blink" is to remind us of that act of perception which is taking place and which is part of the poem's subject. Like the filmy leaves and spun silk this curious simile is a fitting of man to nature, and it's also an enactment of the nightjar's swiftness, its almost instantaneous flight to the thorn. Hearing and sight are both momentarily closed off.

There are two other examples of occlusion in the poem. In the first line where the Present latches its postern behind his "tremulous stay," Hardy identifies his being shut off from sight and life by death with the back door of a house closing behind him. But no sooner have we read this line than the next introduces spring, and because he is associated with the flapping leaves his memory is freshly revived. The last stanza contains another example of this idea of disappearance and reappearance:

> And will any say when my bell of quittance is heard in the gloom,
>   And a crossing breeze cuts a pause in its outrollings,
> Till they rise again, as they were a new bell's boom,
>   'He hears it not now, but used to notice such things'?

There is a hiatus, a break in a visible or audible sequence, a "soundless blink." And in the third stanza he says that even if it should be pitch dark when he dies there will still be a dimly visible object—a hedgehog—to recall him to mind, or:

If, when hearing that I have been stilled at last, they stand at the door,
  Watching the full-starred heavens that winter sees,
Will this thought rise on those who will meet my face no more,
  'He was one who had an eye for such mysteries'?

Despite this reverence for the mysteries of nature the poem's notion of immortality is decidedly agnostic and humanist. There is a neat religious reference in: "Till they rise again, as they were a new bell's boom." The phrase "rise again" is familiar—"and the third day he shall rise again"— while the word "new" also holds familiar biblical connotations: "Therefore if any man be in Christ, he is a new creature; old things are passed away; behold, all things are become new." The immortality which the agnostic poet anticipates is compared gently and with sad irony to the Christian's expectations of the resurrection of the dead and the life everlasting. We are back with the winged, new leaves.

"The Occultation," which is also in *Moments of Vision*, similarly describes a hiatus and then applies it to the possible survival of something which has disappeared. The verb "to occult" is a term used in astronomy and it means "to cut off from view by passing in front":

When the cloud shut down on the morning shine,
  And darkened the sun,
I said, 'So ended that joy of mine
  Years back begun.'

But day continued its lustrous roll
  In upper air;
And did my late irradiate soul
  Live on somewhere?

In "Afterwards" he will survive after death as a kind of percept, a memory that will be activated when his neighbours look at certain objects associated with him. There, a sequence of observations is only apparently and temporarily interrupted by the death of the principal observer, while in this poem the observer wonders whether he may not infer the survival somewhere of his "late irradiate soul," his vanished "joy," just as he infers the continued existence of the sun when it's concealed by a cloud. Though the reference is probably as much to the end of a love affair as to the woman's death, the principle is the same as it is in "Afterwards": an abrupt closing-off followed by a reminder that the perception of a thing, rather than the thing itself, has disappeared. The bell of quittance is still tolling in the gloom even though the occluding breeze makes it impossible to hear it for a moment.

In "The Occultation" survival is presented as a metaphysical possibility but in "Afterwards" it's rendered in human, secular terms: the poet will be remembered after his death. Both in this and the setting of "Afterwards" are reminiscent of the moment in Gray's Elegy (another of Hardy's favourite poems) when the "hoary-headed Swain" relates how he and the other villagers often used to see the poet out on one of his customary walks:

> 'One morn I miss'd him on the custom'd hill,
>   Along the heath and near his fav'rite tree;
> Another came; nor yet beside the rill,
>   Nor up the lawn, nor at the wood was he;
> 'The next with dirges due in sad array
>   Slow through the church-way path we saw him borne.

There are a number of minor verbal echoes of the Elegy in Hardy's poem but what matters is that he, like Gray, describes a series of totally familiar, "custom'd" scenes which are so much associated with the poet that his personality has become part of them. The landscape is humanised through the memories and associations that inhere in it. Both Gray and Hardy point to the sacredness of habitual action and because they describe themselves in the third person, as they appear to others who observe them, they succeed in giving themselves an objective existence. Both conceive of immortality in secular, social terms, though Gray's melancholy epitaph, his talking headstone, is totally unsatisfactory compared with Hardy's casually voiced: "He was a man who used to notice such things."

There are more such observed things in "Genoa and the Mediterranean":

> Out from a deep-delved way my vision lit
> On housebacks pink, green, ochreous—where a slit
> Shoreward 'twixt row and row revealed the classic blue through it.
>
> And thereacross waved fishwives' high-hung smocks,
> Chrome kerchiefs, scarlet hose, darned underfrocks;
> Often since when my dreams of thee, O Queen, that frippery mocks.

Bailey supplies more facts in his handbook to the poems: the "deep-delved way" is a railway tunnel, nearly two miles long, just before Genoa's Station Piazza Principe. This information may be useful because if you apply it the poem seems to be deliberately organised around the first fleeting impressions of Genoa that flashed on Hardy's eyes as his train sped out into Mediterranean sunshine from a tunnel whose darkness would have made the colours all the more vivid and intense, like a vision after resurrection. Unusually, he describes numerous bright colours—pink, green, ochre, blue, scarlet, chrome—whose brightness might be due to this sudden transition from darkness to light. Bailey treats the poem as a photograph that "presents the Hardy's first impression of Genoa," but doesn't appear to realise that the passage which he quotes from Emma's diary flatly contradicts this: "dull weather, no blue sea." I'm pointing to this because I think it's important that we take seriously Hardy's remark that "the exact truth as to material fact . . . is a student's style." This poem is organised very skilfully around various observed facts but Hardy naturally isn't tied to a literal transcription of the facts which happened to meet his eyes one day in 1887 when the train carrying him and his wife emerged from the last tunnel before Genoa's main station. He has carefully composed the visible scene by leading the eye, as in a painting, through the glaring, alkaline colours that clutter the foreground to the distant chink of cool "classic blue." This is the tourist's glimpse of that "Epic-famed" sea whose classical beauty, he suggests, has been "wronged" by Genoa's dowdy state of undress. Naturally he's being facetious here because he prefers the mundane, backstreet actuality of washing, housebacks and railway sidings to the city's epic fame and marbled beauty. He prefers, in other words, the dingy beauty of human association to a statuesque beauty of aspect.

This preference for scenes which have human associations is reflected in the ugly, banal setting of "In a Waiting-Room":

> On a morning sick as the day of doom
>   With the drizzling gray
>   Of an English May,
> There were few in the railway waiting-room.
> About its walls were framed and varnished
> Pictures of liners, fly-blown, tarnished.
> The table bore a Testament
> For travellers' reading, if suchwise bent.

This is by no means an entirely successful poem: the lines are flaccid, the opening quatrain doesn't manage a combination of the portentous and the banal as "Genoa" does, and the comparison later of the children's sudden appearance to the eastern flame of a "high altar" overstates a deliberate incongruity. These faults are probably due to the way the poem's form vacillates uneasily between a fully fledged monologue spoken by a dramatic character, and one spoken by that surrogate persona present in many of Hardy's poems. Nevertheless it does have some of the strengths and virtues that characterise his best work. Its strength lies in its observation of a drab reality and in the way it extracts beauty from ugliness by infusing it with human associations. The poem has a different meaning for each person in it—it varies with its perceivers. For the bagman the waiting-room was just a place where he could absentmindedly scribble his accounts in the margins of a bible, for the soldier and his wife—they have a "haggard look/Subdued to stone by strong endeavour"—it's the scene of their tragic parting, and for the children the room is beautiful because it contains pictures they see as being "lovely." And it's then that the room becomes beautiful for the speaker. The episode's "smear of tragedy" is transformed by the children and their excited happiness spreads "a glory" through the squalid, gloomy room. Though it's not insisted on, there is a pathetic irony in the different significances the pictures hold for the couple and the children: they are looking forward to seeing the ships and hearing the band play, while the soldier and his wife are not because he will be sailing on one of them, probably to the brassy strains of a military band. The poetry of this scene may vary with its perceivers, but the detached narrator feels that the children give it a value which is more permanent than the fluid relativism of its variable values. The drab room is given a human connection by the emotions of the people who wait in it.

The observing eye, sharp for the stories implicit in things is at work in "A Gentleman's Second-Hand Suit":

> Here it is hanging in the sun
>   By the pawn-shop door,
> A dress-suit—all its revels done
>   Of heretofore.
> Long drilled to the waltzers' swing and sway,
>   As its tokens show:
> What it has seen, what it could say
>   If it did but know!
>
> The sleeve bears still a print of powder
>   Rubbed from her arms
> When she warmed up as the notes swelled louder
>   And livened her charms—
> Or rather theirs, for beauties many
>   Leant there, no doubt,
> Leaving these tell-tale traces when he
>   Spun them about.

"On looking close," Hardy says, the suit seemed rather old-fashioned, and he goes on, inevitably, to ask where the man and the women he danced with now are:

> Some of them may forget him quite
>   Who smudged his sleeve,
> Some think of a wild and whirling night
>   With him, and grieve.

The smudges are like clues to a mystery and he carefully scrutinises them, like a detective trying to piece together the events and experiences behind them. This clearly isn't one of his better poems but it does suggest something of the interested observation and human sympathy he brought to inanimate fact. It's a poem of observation, not vision. And my comparison of its cold scrutiny to a detective training his magnifying glass on a fingerprint is not an idle one for Hardy made it himself. He once sat for Sir William Rothenstein who recalled that he

> remarked on the expression of the eyes in the drawing that I made—he knew the look he said, for he was often taken for a detective. He had a small dark bilberry eye which he cocked at you unexpectedly.

Like a detective, the positivist needs a visible fact, a "print," to work on. What matters is "the wear on a threshold . . . the print of a hand"; indeed, any lump of dead fact that holds a trace of humanity—like the marks of fingers baked on old bricks. Experience can saturate bricks and plaster:

> 'Babes new-brought-forth
>   Obsess my rooms; straight-stretched
> Lank corpses, ere outborne to earth;
> Yea, throng they as when first from the Byss upfetched.
>
> 'Dancers and singers
>   Throb in me now as once;
> Rich-noted throats and gossamered flingers
> Of heels; the learned in love-lore and the dunce.
>
> 'Note here within
>   The bridegroom and the bride,
> Who smile and greet their friends and kin,
> And down my stairs depart for tracks untried.

So says the old house to the brash modern house beside it in "The Two Houses." These are the "shades" which he tells the new house will "print on thee their presences as on me."

The poem's mixture of tender sympathy and eerie wit is characteristic; and so is its insistence that what's dead and gone can still be seen, is still somehow there. This happens again in "Haunting Fingers" where the musical instruments in a museum mutter to each other like the dead in "Friends Beyond," though sadly:

> And they felt past handlers clutch them,
>   Though none was in the room,
> Old players' dead fingers touch them,
>   Shrunk in the tomb.

The harpsichord laments how:

> 'My keys' white shine,
> Now sallow, met a hand
> Even whiter. . . . Tones of hers fell forth with mine
> In sowings of sound so sweet no lover could withstand!'

> And its clavier was filmed with fingers
> Like tapering flames—wan, cold—
> Or the nebulous light that lingers
> In charnel mould.

The objects become phosphorescent—fact is spiritualised and the spiritual becomes a visible object. The dead fingers are like "tapering flames." Hardy is seeking to realise and objectify immortality in a series of observed facts, and it is this kind of immortality which he anticipates in "Afterwards" and tries to discover in "Shelley's Skylark." He insists everywhere on things being visible, and one of the curious features of "To my Father's Violin," "The Two Houses" and "Haunting Fingers" is the shape which the stanzas make on the page—though this is not so very unusual as all his poems are intended to have a distinctive shape. Like George Herbert he tries to ensure that each poem is a unique object with its own special identity.

Each stanza of "To my Father's Violin" seems roughly to imitate the body of a violin, like an early concrete poem:

> In the gallery west the nave,
> But a few yards from his grave,
> Did you, tucked beneath his chin, to his bowing
> Guide the homely harmony
> Of the quire
> Who for long years strenuously—
> Son and sire—
> Caught the strains that at his fingering low or higher
> From your four thin threads and eff-holes came outflowing.

There is a tune in these lines—a smart jolly tune which contrasts with its lugubrious second line and which carries over that line like the rhythm of "Beeny Cliff" bridging the faltering pause at "elsewhere." It is still firmly there at the beginning of the last stanza:

> He must do without you now,
> Stir you no more anyhow
> To yearning concords taught you in your glory.

But as Hardy turns to describe the actual state of the violin the tune begins to falter and share in its disintegration:

> While, your strings a tangled wreck,
>   Once smart drawn,
> Ten worm-wounds in your neck,
>   Purflings wan
> With dust-hoar, here alone I sadly con
> Your present dumbness, shape your olden story.

Looking at the real object seems to destroy his compelling evocation of the sounds his father once drew from it. And when we read each stanza of the poem we both hear this tune and see the shape of a violin roughly before us on the page. He literally does "shape" its story, so that again this is a positivist's poem, a visible and audible fact.

Heaven in these poems is part museum, part junk shop, while in "Voices from Things Growing in a Churchyard" and "Transformations" it's a sunny graveyard where the dead are busily and happily turning into green shoots on the yew tree or "entering this rose." Hardy starts with the familiar and uninspiring idea of pushing up daisies and makes it work. There is nothing of Dylan Thomas's windy, rhetorical assertion that "Though they be mad and dead as nails/Heads of the characters hammer through daisies." Instead he lets the characters speak for themselves and populates a heaven that is actual:

> —I am one Bachelor Bowring, 'Gent,'
>   Sir or Madam;
> In shingled oak my bones were pent;
> Hence more than a hundred years I spent
> In my feat of change from a coffin-thrall
> To a dancer in green as leaves on a wall,
>   All day cheerily,
>   All night eerily!

It is this idea of naturalised immortality that Eliot is partly slighting in "The Dry Salvages" when he says:

> We, content at the last
> If our temporal reversion nourish
> (Not too far from the yew-tree)
> The life of significant soil.

Eliot means that significance is not one of the properties of soil, but Hardy gives distinct human personalities to some of the plants and trees it nourishes and so suggests that it is meaningful. Bowring's gruff certainties and self-importance follow Fanny Hurd's twittering meekness, Thomas Voss has "turned to clusters ruddy of view" and Lady Gertrude is splendid in laurel. Each speaker has a unique voice, a "murmurous accent," as well as surviving naturally and visibly. Again, this positivistic concept of immortality is also social because people who move in society must be seen in order to be. But underneath the robust social comedy of the graveyard there is also a mysteriousness and an ecstatic energy. It's there in the "radiant hum" and dancing freedom of "Voices from Things" and at the end of "Transformations" where

> they feel the sun and rain,
> And the energy again
> That made them what they were!

The physical basis of life gives Hardy no cause for despair in these poems and unlike Eliot he feels no need to reject a non-significant biological materialism, for it enables him both to create character and imply the forces underlying it. There is more than the obvious joke in the fact that Eve Greensleeves, "the handsome mother of two or three illegitimate children," has now been changed into an "innocent withwind," a climbing plant that is also called "virgin's bower." She has been kissed by many men:

> Beneath sun, stars, in blaze, in breeze,
> As now by glowworms and by bees.

This beautifully suggests a feeling of dazzling light, breezes and warmth which also become the expression of her free sexuality. As ever she is eternally virgin and promiscuous. Each of her names has uninsistent reverberations which also help to give a profound sense of female character. She is made to live more deeply than in her social personality as the subject of long-vanished village ribaldry.

Just as he must think of Shelley's lark living on in the "coming hue" of a grape, Hardy tries throughout this poem to realise a number of unique human lives in a series of visible objects and though there is nothing narrow in his response to visibility here, this kind of positivism can be imaginatively limiting, even stultifying. In the end we really face the fact and it's simply and inanimately there, like the battered violin. When the deceptive, illusory and borrowed light of the moon has been shut out—when the pathetic fallacy has been exposed and rejected—then there only remains a "common lamp-lit room" where the eyes and mind are "prisoned." The positivist's facts are just dingy surfaces. For Donald Davie, Hardy's poems never get beyond this "quantifiable reality," a reality that is about as inspiring as a dual carriageway on a grey afternoon (Hardy's equivalent is a railway waiting-room). To speculate about, to try to get inside, the lives of the people who occupy that mundane reality is one way out of this imaginative dead end, but it leads only so far because sooner or later we come back to the worm-eaten violin, the second-hand suit, the meaningless soil. We come back to the realisation that the only afterlife is a secular one in which the dead are remembered, for a while, by the living. But in both "Transformations" and "Voices from Things" there is a quality somewhere around the edges of this eventually constraining positivistic humanism which is liberating and totally imaginative (and just in this instance I'm identifying humanism with social comedy). There is a kind of witty seriousness beyond the comedy of Bachelor Bowring and Lady Gertrude. It's there throughout the poem, though it can be sensed especially in Eve Greensleeves's voice—less so in Lady Gertrude's, for she is more simply social and superficial, and her shining laurels inevitably suggest a certain sterility in her character, a glinting or glistening light on a stagnant darkness. Eve Greensleeves, on the other hand, climbs in many flowers, lacks this artificial veneer and is constantly kissable, while Bachelor Bowring has been so solidly "pent" in such good quality oak that it has taken him over a century to perform his "feat of change" from rigid prisoner to leafy dancer. It seems appropriate that old Squire Audeley Gray, who grew weary of life and "in scorn withdrew," should also be an evergreen like Lady Gertrude for there must always have been a deadness at the centre of his life too—there seems to be a natural morality as well as a natural concept of immortality in the poem.

At the end of "On the Physical Basis of Life," the essay Bailey refers to in his account of this poem, Huxley says that "the errors of systematic materialism may paralyse the energies and destroy the beauty of a life," and the materialism of Hardy's poem is not as systematic as it appears to be— in fact it's profoundly committed to a series of escapes from narrow sepulchres and coffins which, as in "Heiress and Architect," represent the straight lines and rigidities of a limiting system. The "dead humus of buried bodies lives again in plants," but the poem doesn't stop at this idea of the heads of characters bashing through daisies. Fanny Hurd is not just the "daisy shapes" above her grave—she is the wavy movement of the daisies where she once "flit-fluttered like a bird" and she is there in the eerie-cheery, swaying sound of the poem. She is still a meek virgin soul, and that essentially religious word is the right one because the poem's sense of awe at the forces of life and the forces in human character is not that of the "sentimental materialist" as one of Hardy's reviewers called him. An irreducible sense of mystery attaches to each character and voice.

Thomas Hardy: Moments of Vision

GEOFFREY HARVEY

As the growing list of Hardy criticism testifies, his poetic achievement is at last being given the degree of attention which has for so long been accorded almost exclusively to his novels. Donald Davie's *Thomas Hardy and Modern British Poetry* (1973) recognizes Hardy as a major influence on modern English verse and more recently we have had Paul Zietlow's *Moments of Vision: The Poetry of Thomas Hardy* (1974) and Tom Paulin's *Thomas Hardy: The Poetry of Perception* (1975). Together these studies mark the beginning of a revaluation of Hardy's poetic art which is long overdue, and in their concern with the nature of Hardy's poetic imagination and their emphasis on the qualities of compassion and hope in his poetry, Zietlow and Paulin go a long way to redress the balance in Hardy criticism. J. Hillis Miller, for instance, in *Thomas Hardy: Distance and Desire* (1970) regarded Hardy primarily as a passive poet trapped in a mechanistic universe; while Geoffrey Thurley in *The Ironic Harvest: English poetry in the twentieth century* (1974) marshalled an apparently strong case against Hardy. For him, because the existentialist's search for meaning can result only in total self-effacement, Hardy "annihilates . . . metaphysics, mythology, transcendence, rhetoric."[1] Thus, in Thurley's view, Hardy marks the degeneration of English verse from the Romantics' pursuit of transcendence and its accompanying rhetoric of the egotistical sublime and what has been lost in Hardy and subsequent poets, he concludes, is "the *sense of meaningfulness* associated with poetic rhetoric."[2]

Both Tom Paulin and Paul Zietlow take a more positive view. Although Paulin regards Hardy's imagination as "imprison·d in a Humean universe of sense-data" he also recognises that Hardy is "somewhere between a utilitarian empiricism and a romantic idealism" and that "he would prefer [his imagination] to have a transcending freedom, though he knows this is impossible."[3] And Paul Zietlow affirms that Hardy's idealistic impulse leads him to place his faith in human compassion.[4] However, both these views of Hardy are limiting. For these critics, too, Hardy's poetry does not achieve transcendence and his optimism is restricted to fighting a rearguard action against human

Geoffrey Harvey, "Thomas Hardy: Moments of Vision," in *The Romantic Tradition in Modern English Poetry / Rhetoric and Experience* (London: Macmillan, 1986), pp. 47–70. Copyright, Macmillan, 1986; reprinted by permission.

suffering and misery. And as far as the majority of Hardy's poetic output is concerned they are right. But in my view there is a relatively small group of poems, which includes some of Hardy's finest verse, in which his imagination does indeed achieve a transcending freedom, a liberation of the spirit and an abundant "sense of meaningfulness." In them Hardy strives to establish an authentic mode of being predicated on existence itself and on his own capacity to transcend it; but the paradox of his art, at least in those poems which I would argue lie close to the centre of his poetic genius, is that he achieves the finest articulation of his existential statement within the context of the Romantic tradition.

Hardy's achievement, unique I think in modern English poetry, is his attainment of a synthesis of profound disillusion with a vitality and joy that is almost Wordsworthian. It has often been noted that Hardy's poetry shares some features with Wordsworth; he writes in the tradition of Wordsworth's ruralism, displaying the same deep feeling for rustic society and for landscape and, indeed, his suffering, stoical peasantry, wresting significance from their narrow lives, are direct descendants of Wordsworth's Michael. But the affinity between the two poets is, in my view, deeper than this. The major concern of both poets is, in my view, deeper than this. The major concern of both poets is the relation between the human imagination and the natural world, Hardy's belief that poetry should deal with *"the other side of common emotions"*[5] echoes Wordsworth's concern in his Preface to *Lyrical Ballads* with the intensity of emotional experience and with what he called "the fluxes and refluxes of the mind."[6] More significantly, Hardy's intention to make nature's defects the basis of his art by irradiating them with " 'the light that never was' on their surface, but is seen to be latent in them by the spiritual eye"[7] recalls Wordsworth's description of the visionary process in "Tintern Abbey," where the mystical experience is what eye and ear perceive and also what they "half-create." And Hardy amplifies his insistence on the transfiguring power of the imagination:

> The "simply natural" is interesting no longer. . . . The exact truth as to material fact ceases to be of importance in art—it is a student's style—the style of a period when the mind is serene and unawakened to the tragical mysteries of life; when it does not bring anything to the object that coalesces with and translates the qualities that are already there,—half hidden, it may be—and the two united are depicted as the All.[8]

What Hardy strove for, the co-operation between the dead world of fact and the imagination is, indeed, what Coleridge laments the loss of in his "Dejection Ode" when he states that if we wish to know something beyond the inanimate cold world then, "Ah, from the Soul itself must issue forth / A light, a glory, a fair luminous cloud."

Hardy frequently refers to Wordsworth and Coleridge in his prefaces to his poetry and in his personal writings and it is clear that their poetry and poetic theories were of particular significance to him, especially Coleridge's concern with the transfiguring power of the imagination. But the difference between Hardy's poetic experience and that of Coleridge is as important as the parallels. Whereas in Coleridgean terms the imagination, operating under the gentle control of the will, co-operates in a reciprocal way with an active universe in order to create a living relationship between mind and objects, for Hardy the imagination works in a somewhat different way and fulfils an inevitably different function. Unlike Coleridge and Wordsworth, Hardy's imagination is not intuitive because, quite simply, for him there was nothing "out there" in the universe to be intuited. Moreover, in his art the function of the imagination is not, as Coleridge suggests, to bring "the whole soul of man into activity"[9] but rather to bring it into being. Nor can it achieve the vision of some immanent ideal, but strives instead to gain some fundamental sense of meaning grasped and articulated. This is why J. Hillis Miller's suggestion that Hardy regarded the mind as little more than a puppet of the Universal Will is, in my view, too large a generalisation.[10] Although in the poem, "He Wonders About Himself," Hardy admits that "Part is mine of the general Will," like Schopenhauer, his favourite philosopher, Hardy felt that there are moments when the imagination gains its freedom, "actuated by the modicum of free will conjecturally possessed by organic life when the mighty necessitating forces—unconscious or other— that have 'the balancings of the clouds,' happen to be in equilibrium, which may or may not be often."[11] This statement goes a long way to explain the comparative rarity of visionary poems in Hardy's large output of verse, for it is only in this state that the poet is able to create a clearer vision of the world, a state of "pure perception" in Schopenhauer's terms. More importantly, it makes plain that the imagination is liberated in conjunction with the will, not subordinated to it as in Coleridge's view, but rather it seems to co-operate with it in such a fundamental way, in the poems I propose to discuss, that they become a single creative force—which might perhaps best be described as "poetic will." Hardy's moments of transcendence are therefore very different from those of Wordsworth and Coleridge. They are not vague stirrings—"a sense sublime of something far more deeply interfused," as in "Tintern Abbey"—nor an attempt to reach beyond the material world to an ideal state as in "Kubla Khan." Instead they register the achievement of meaning; they assert the joy of being here and now and Hardy constantly seeks to establish poetic structures to capture this.

It is important to insist on the positive quality of the poems I wish to consider because J. Hillis Miller again overstates his case, it seems to me, when he argues the corollary of his remark about Hardy's passivity—that in Hardy "the act of coming to self-awareness does not lead to a recognition of the intrinsic quality of the mind [but] is a revelation about the outside world, a recognition of the mute detachment of external objects. . . ." On the contrary, Hardy's visionary poems are fundamentally a record of self-discovery and a celebration of meaning and value and this is a process in which the obstinate facts of the external world are internalised and transfigured. Indeed, the intrinsic quality of the mind is the overt subject of the title poem of *Moments of Vision*. Working in co-operation with the poetic will, which functions intermittently when the universe is in equilibrium, sometimes in the depths of night or in the moments before death, the imagination, symbolised as a "magic" mirror which is both passive and active, has the power not only to transfigure the outer world but to "[throw] our mind back on us, and our heart, / Until we start." It penetrates the inmost recesses of consciousness "like a dart," making us "such a breast-bare spectacle see / Of you and me. . . ."

This poem displays Hardy's profound sense of the relation between true selfhood and moral identity which is also evident in his reply to the charge of pessimism so often brought against him—that it constituted only " 'questionings' in the exploration of reality" necessary as "the first step towards the soul's betterment."[13] His position is the opposite of, for instance, Dostoevsky's Kirilov in *The Possessed*, who cries, "If God does not exist, everything is allowed." Because, in Hardy, the poet transcends himself not towards God but towards man, the achievement of being brings not only enormous freedom but also responsibility, both to himself and to others. Like Schopenhauer, whom he often quotes as a philosopher of hope, Hardy stresses the central importance of loving-kindness in human relations; he affirms the fundamental human values of love and fellowship. And because it thus overcomes alienation and despair, Hardy's finest poetry also embodies a sense of profound joy.

As Donald Davie has pointed out, there is no clear line of development in Hardy's work.[14] His major visionary poems occur sporadically throughout his career and they do so because the unfettered operation of his poetic will was a rare accident, dependent on his sense of equilibrium in the universe. This feeling permeates "The Darkling Trush," for instance, a poem of the highest imaginative order. Apparently a modern lament for the death of God and of Nature, the poem employs a universalised and visionary landscape to record the end of place and time—"The land's sharp features seemed to be / The Century's corpse outleant," the frost is "spectre-gray," the clouds form a "crypt" and the wind provides a "death-lament"; even the "ancient pulse of germ and birth / was shrunken hard and dry, / And every spirit upon earth / Seemed fervourless as I." This awful nullity, which is developed by the image patterns of the first two stanzas, is mirrored in the consciousness of the poet himself. The century's outleant corpse makes a parallel with the poet who "leant upon a coppice gate" the "weakening eye of day" creates a metaphor for the darkened vision of the poet, while the tangled bine-stems scoring the sky "Like strings of broken lyres" is a further image of poetic sterility. The poet stands in mute contrast to the joyous thrush, the only other inhabitant of this ghastly landscape and to the creative impulse of the bird's "full-hearted" song.

Hardy's central distinction between the poetic sterility of the man for whom the universe is dead and the thrush which experiences "Some blessed Hope, whereof he knew/ And I was unaware," appears to justify Hillis Miller's criticism of Hardy as a detached and passive observer whose poetry displays a fundamental withdrawal from life. But this view does not do justice to the complexity of the poem. Here, as in several of his visionary poems, Hardy inhabits the world of the poem not only as a neutral spectator, but also as an active participant. This duality of experience is embodied in the structure of the poem, which creates a profound connection between the two inhabitants of its desolate world, the nihilistic poet and the optimistic thrush. Of course the thrush has a richly symbolic function; on one level its instinctive song represents the natural world's anticipation of spring and regeneration; it is also a universalised symbol of humanity; but fundamentally, "aged . . . frail, gaunt, and small," like Hardy himself, the thrush functions in the poem as its governing symbol for the continued creative activity of the poetic will, which is still at work below the level of conscious thought and which is free to operate because the temporal frame of the poem crystalises a moment of poise in the universe. Like the poet, who is both observer and agent, the thrust creates his essential self by means of an act of will; he has *"chosen* thus to fling his soul / Upon the growing gloom" (my italics)—a defiant action which images his attempt to transcend the way he has been "thrown" into the world in an existential sense. The thrush's affirmation of the sheer joy of being in the present moment and the accompanying sense of significance is given peculiar force by the poem's terrible context of non-being and by the awful irony of the poetic "persona's" inability to grasp the meaning offered. Nevertheless, its song of ecstatic optimism, an unwitting act of loving-kindness, forges a contact between itself and the poet, creating a sense of his solidarity with all living things, and because the thrush also represents the enduring connection between the poet and his creative imagination the poem is allowed to stand as a courageous celebration of the poetic will and of the possibility for the survival of undeceived joy in a world of dissolution.

Hardy also turns to his own life in order to explore the way in which the achievement of a sense of personal value is contingent on the perfect interrelation of time and place. "The Self-Unseeing" records a moment in his boyhood when he danced in the parlour to the music of his father's violin, while his mother sat by the fireside. Such moments, Hardy stresses, must be seized and utilised because, as he bleakly admits in this poem, the opportunity frequently passes unrecognized. This particular moment was unusually propitious because, as Hardy demonstrates, it was a moment of perfect universal balance. Here time, which in Hardy is always the chief threat to the attainment of joy through self-definition, is disciplined, harmonised and humanized by music and dance. As the insistent repetition of the word "here" suggests, place is of fundamental importance in the process, not only because limited space and the present moment are the only contexts we have to create our integrity, but because for Hardy place contains both past and present and therefore has the almost magical power to suspend time. Place is concretely realised by the "ancient floor" and, paradoxically, by the images of feet walking and dancing, which frame the poem and reinforce the dominant image of stillness, of time annihilated by place. But the potential amount of transcendence is lost because the actions of the man, the woman and the child are involuntary. Listening to the music they enter a hypnotic state of euphoria, which is emphasised by the heavy alliterative effect of the final stanza. The woman muses, rapt, staring into the depths of the fire, the man plays his violin in isolated abstraction, while the child dances "in a dream." Passive and self-regarding, they are firmly linked with the "dead feet" at the opening of the poem, with time outside of place, time the destroyer which they apparently have controlled but which in truth obliterates them. That the moment described is one of sheer escapism rather than fulfilment is evident in Hardy's indulgent description of the cosiness of the scene; the warmth of the fire, the cliché of emotion in the phrase "glowed with a gleam" and the ironic undercurrent that runs through the too emphatic "Blessings emblazoned that day." Ostensibly connected by time, manifested in music and dance, they fail to realise that what connects them fundamentally is place, the "ancient floor" on which they act and which symbolises a deeper and more sacramental relation of human lives. Visionary moments like this, if grasped, offer unparalleled opportunity for people to transcend themselves by unifying acts of love, but in denying what links them they only confirm their human isolation and as Hardy unflinchingly records, the pleasure that they have gained is won at the cost of turning their faces away from a profounder reality.

By contrast, the achievement of genuine human fellowship is presented dramatically in "At the Railway Station, Upway," a poem in which once again Hardy's strange sense of special moments of equilibrium permeating human affairs is strongly in evidence. The station is an area of stasis where time is suspended as people occupy a limbo between trains and where different lives come together and then diverge without achieving any significant connection. The three figures waiting on the platform, the innocent young boy, the police constable and the handcuffed convict, create a universalised image of the human condition, but Hardy is fundamentally concerned to suggest the possibility of its transformation. The child's instinctive pity for the convict and the contrasting complacent indifference of the worldly constable establish perspectives of irony and sympathy which by the poem's conclusion have been transmuted into a unifying mood of common human charity. The boy's spontaneous act of loving-kindness in playing his violin to cheer the criminal creates the grounds for the convict's transcendence of both the boy's pity and the constable's indifference. His strange, apparently ironical singing about freedom is not sheer bravado, but a profound act by which he creates a sense of his own particular momentary value. Hardy employs the apt coinage "grimful glee" to describe the singular mood in which his stern assertion of will paradoxically produces a deeply felt liberating energy. What the moment reveals is the *"other side* of common emotions," the joy that lies beyond despair, the transcendence that can be achieved only through an awareness of tragic experience. What is more, the convict discovers in the same act not only an inner freedom, but a new sense of human responsibility. His song is also a kindly response to the boy's overwhelming need to feel that he has somehow helped the suffering man. And through the song the convict achieves solidarity not only with the boy, imaged in the music which they share, but also with the constable, imaged in their exchange of smiles which negates the corresponding earlier image of the cruel manacles. Subjection has been replaced by fellowship and the poem's dominant tableaux— the boy playing his violin and the handcuffed convict singing of freedom to the constable on the station platform between trains—establishes a complex and powerful symbol of the human will triumphantly wresting significance from the tragic absurdity of daily experience.

Hardy wryly defines his own sense of alienation from the modern world, with its illusory promises of purpose, action and progress, in that splendid visionary poem, "Old Furniture." It is a deeply personal poem in which Hardy, although aware that "the world has no use for one today/ Who eyes things thus—no aim pursuing!" nevertheless courageously asserts the absolute value of his own mode of vision. Indeed, the poem is organised by its many images of perception—"see," "eye may frame," "I see," "Who eyes things thus," "Creeps to my sight"—as Hardy enacts a magical resurrection. Time is brilliantly encapsulated by place and although the past is shown to be progressively and irretrievably past, the poem bears no trace of corrupting nostaglia because the co-operation between place and the eye of vision, which both perceives and half-creates in Wordsworth's phrase, makes the pasts of all the generations simultaneously present. Hardy's juxtaposition of the living candle-flame and the cold mirror which reflects it creates a factual yet visionary image for the simultaneity of the warm hands of the past generations and the shiny, dark solidity of the furniture which they caress. Although the poem's emotion is carefully controlled by Hardy's use of homely language and by the quiet, intimate tone, there is a magical effect created by the imaginative fusion of object and vision. Insensate things come alive at the moment of vision through the co-operation between delicate images of wraithlike movement—hands "dallying," the flickering reflections of the candle-flame, the "foggy finger" moving with "tentative touches," fingers "dancing"—and the static, inert solidity of objects like the clock, "this old viol" and "that box."

For Hardy the neutral objects of the material world are given meaning as they are stamped by people's creative existence and he lovingly recreates in the vision the way people's identities have been captured in the almost sacramental "relics of householdry" around which their daily lives were built. He celebrates their love of domestic warmth (the box for tinder), punctuality and order (the finger putting the clock right) and harmony (the music of the viol), simple acts of human assertion which were once defined by place but which have been apparently obliterated from the surface of things by time. Yet the values which they won from their futile routine are available to the eye of vision and are given in the poem a permanent value outside time. Hardy's identification with the past generations stresses his profound feeling for the continuity of human life, which is evident, for instance in "Heredity" or "In Time of 'the Breaking of Nations,' " but in "Old Furniture" his resurrection of the dead is fundamentally an act of pure loving-kindness and while it emphasises his isolation from the past as well as from the present, it creates at the same time a deeper sense of human solidarity.

Hardy's manipulation of time so that place is allowed to symbolise both past and present also has a liberating effect. It allows human actions to be redefined and revalued. As the generations live again, Hardy gives new meaning to their lives and they in turn bestow on him a surer sense of being. Hardy thus creates his own spiritual values in the face of the awful inexorability of time by a supreme act of poetic will. Indeed, the controlling image of this marvellously delicate poem is that of the poetic will at work, waxing and waning like the viol bow receding and advancing and the fact "glowing forth in fits from the dark" until inevitably it falters and, like the linten cinder, it "goes out stark." But not before there has been an achievement of knowledge, the recognition of human fellowship, the apprehension of beautiful lives, of meaning grasped, with an accompanying spiritual renewal.

Hardy's special, almost primitive sense of place is central to his visionary poems because for him place contains all time and preserves the significance of human actions, which can then be apprehended by the poet in a state of "pure perception." This awareness is the controlling force behind some of the poems which focus on the loss of his wife, Emma. In that moving poem, "At Castle Boterel," for instance, in which Hardy records his visit to a landscape he had once rambled over with Emma, he feels that the very place exudes her presence. The fact of Emma's existence transcends time because the "primaeval rocks" record "that we two passed" and it is this that gives life to the visionary phantom who remains on the slope long after they have both gone. Another of their favourite haunts, the waterfall in "After a Journey," fulfils a similar function and the revelation of Emma's continued existence gives Hardy the courage to assert that "I am just the same as when / Our days were a joy, and our paths through flowers." The best example of this imaginative process, however, is the third poem of this series, "The Phantom Horsewoman," in which Hardy employs a similar technique to that which governs "The Darkling Thrush." He separates the poet, described from the ironic point of view of a detached observer, as a man in a "careworn craze," from his description of the operation of the poetic will itself. As in "Old Furniture," Hardy draws attention to the uniqueness of his imaginative process by setting it apart from the modern world of scepticism and rationalism. What he presents in the first three stanzas is the conventional view of visions as simply illusions manifested to the insane in unlikely places, obsessive fantasies associated with their pasts that often root them to the spot. People like the observer speculate about the crazy man's vision as a "sweet soft scene," a "phantom of his own figuring." This description is coloured by pity because the vision is felt to be purely subjective and to bear only a limited meaning and value. And this is intensified as the stark reality of Hardy's bleak universe is captured in the dominant image of the desolate shore on which the poet stands staring at the empty waves.

But the separation which Hardy makes between the "persona" of the first three stanzas and the vision created by the poetic will in the final stanzas is his means of holding in tension the horror of the empty universe, imaged by the vacant sands and the bewildering sea mist and the achieved joy of the meaning of being there, symbolised by the moment of vision itself. The final stanzas remove the duality of the observer and the poet to allow immediacy of vision, no longer "drawn rose-bright" but hard and clear, as Hardy creates Emma in defiance of the terrible void of her absence. She is outside time and place but she inhabits the place and moment of his vision as she "draws rein and sings to the swing of the tide." Reality and vision are united in the final stanza because Hardy only achieves this moment by facing life squarely. Although Emma is beyond time, the poet himself is not, he is "toil-tried, / He withers daily"; and similarly life and death are held in careful balance in Hardy's description of Emma as a "ghost-girl-rider." Hardy's vision is not offered as a metaphysical reality, as Tom Paulin suggests,[15] nor is he withdrawing from life. In "The Phantom Horsewoman" Hardy captures starkly the horror of a desolate universe and the awful finality of death, but he also bravely affirms that life is neither absurd nor futile if by a positive act of poetic will he can resurrect Emma, if she has a living presence in his being which gives a continued meaning to his life.

In Hardy such moments as these are won by the mind itself, for only the mind can give meaning to reality. Hardy's moments of vision are created out of lived experience and their fundamental commitment to life gives them a universal validity. This wholeness of life, mind and art is perhaps best seen in the final poem that I wish to consider, "During Wind and Rain," in which Hardy draws once more on his memories of Emma, this time of her family home in Cornwall. In some respects it is a puzzling poem on first reading and critics have responded to it in various ways. Basically, the poem is divided into four discrete, beautiful moments of vision which embrace human fellowship and harmony as positive joys, each of which, however, is undercut by a cruel refrain which reminds the reader of the inevitable passing of time and of mortality. A straightforward approach to the meaning of the poem is to see this division as marking a simple structural irony of the kind which operates in *Satires of Circumstance*. The vision of domestic harmony on a winter evening in the first stanza, with its magical co-operation between fact and imagination, is contrasted with the falling leaves. In the second stanza the family's instinct to combat the burgeoning of the natural world in the spring, by clearing the moss in order to make way for human concerns, is contrasted with the threatening spring gales and the malevolent storm birds. The domestication of nature is significant in the third stanza as a context for human fellowship, imaged by the sacramental breakfast under the summer tree, but it, too, finds its destroyer in time which rips the "rotten rose" from the wall. While in the final stanza the family's removal to a "high new house," symbolizing their courageous attempt to re-define their humanity in different places, puts their achievement of a poised, assured selfhood in jeopardy, like their furniture on the lawn exposed to the autumn rain. Time, present in the rhythm of the seasons, co-operates with place and with human lives, yet it also carries a threat, a reminder of the inherent futility of even their noblest actions.

One view of the poem is that Hardy simply offers two distinct perspectives and allows them to stand in silent commentary on each other. Another interpretation regards these moments of vision, incomplete as they are, as having greater vividness, more impact and significance than the negative images of the refrains. But a clue to a more fruitful approach to the meaning of "During Wind and Rain," in my reading of it, is given by its title, which is an echo of Feste's song that concludes *Twelfth Night*, a song which is itself both a profound recognition of the fundamental absurdity of the universe and a beautiful celebration of human life and values. Hardy's poem, I suggest, achieves a similar transcendence. In "During Wind and Rain" the moments of vision are not created in opposition to, or even in ignorance of, the waste and futility of life; nor are those poles of human experience permitted to stand in mute dichotomy; rather the terror of a meaningless universe is incorporated into the poem, not simply as a structural unity, but into each discrete moment of vision, subtly qualifying it and becoming part of its statement. This becomes evident if one pays close attention to Hardy's superb technique. His breaking up of the elaborate symmetry between the four stanzas by his metrical variations in the last line of each stanza suggests how, for the neutral observer, each idyllic moment is dissolved by a harsher reality. Yet the cluster of images conveying the delicate world of the poem also contains within it this ineluctable force of dissolution. The beautiful image in the opening stanza of the candles "mooning each face," both factual and visionary, includes within it the suggestion of decay, for even as they illumine the gathering the candles are burning out, and the moon is itself a powerful traditional symbol of change. Similarly, the springtime vision of the second stanza comprehends the creeping moss which remains an enduring threat to human significance; while in the third stanza the sea, which can be glimpsed by the breakfasting group, is also a potent symbol for the mutability of life and experience. And finally, the furniture left in the open air on the lawn makes a poignant image of human vulnerability and frailty. The moments of vision themselves thus include a strong sense of an indifferent universe, of dissolution as inevitable and of human action as ultimately absurd. But this knowledge, which permeates the places in which they choose to act, is shared by the inhabitants of the world of the poem. The careful symmetry of these stanzas is the formal correlative of the way in which they nevertheless impose order and beauty on the flux of experience. Their awareness of a terrifying nullity at the heart of things is transcended by actions which celebrate love, fellowship and the sheer joy of being, which displays a powerful sense of achieved selfhood, of purpose, adventure and gaiety.

To some extent the current uncertainty about the value of Hardy's poetry derives from the critical tendency to regard his work as exemplifying his "philosophy." But Hardy, like Wordsworth and Coleridge, developed a significant part of his thinking from mature reflection upon his poetic experience. Indeed, this informs both the prefaces to his poetry and his personal writings. And as I have been arguing, a more fruitful method of approaching his work than that of simply applying his ideas to his poetry is to consider how his poetic art illumines his thought. From this point of view, Hardy's well-known discussion of the relation between the Universal Will and the individual will, which is often regarded as the linchpin of his thinking, is not simply an abstract formulation of his view of a deterministic universe, but is also the result of a subjective analysis of his own poetic experience. Read in the context of those poems I have been considering, Hardy's assertion of the possibility of the liberation of the will and his insistence on the transfiguring power of the imagination explain how some of his finest poems came to be written. These moments of vision which, I think, lie at the centre of Hardy's poetic genius, offer a positive response to the modern experience. They rescue life from futility; they assert the significance of human values; they embody a strenuously achieved, undeceived response of profound joy and they reaffirm in a new form the continuing romantic ideal of transcendence.

Notes

1. Geoffrey Thurley, *The Ironic Harvest: English Poetry in the twentieth century* (London: Edward Arnold, 1974), p. 32.

2. Thurley, p. 34.

3. Tom Paulin, *Thomas Hardy: The Poetry of Perception* (London: Macmillan, 1975), p. 36.

4. Paul Zietlow, *Moments of Vision: The Poetry of Thomas Hardy* (Cambridge, Mass.: Harvard University Press, 1974), p. 10.

5. As early as 1868 Hardy had proposed to write a volume of poems on this subject. See Florence Emily Hardy, *The Life of Thomas Hardy* (London: Macmillan, 1962), p. 58.

6. See Wordsworth's Preface to *Lyrical Ballads*, ed. R. L. Brett and A. R. Jones (London: Methuen, 1965), pp. 244–5.

7. *Life*, p. 114.

8. *Life*, p. 185.

9. Coleridge, *Biographia Literaria*, ed. George Watson (London: J. M. Dent, 1956), p. 173.

10. J. Hillis Miller, *Thomas Hardy: Distance and Desire* (Cambridge, Mass.: Harvard Uniersity Press, 1970), p. 22.

11. Hardy, Apology to *Late Lyrics and Earlier* in *Thomas Hardy's Personal Writings*, ed. Harold Orel (London: Macmillan, 1967), p. 53.

12. Hillis Miller, p. 4.

13. *Personal Writings*, p. 52.

14. Donald Davie, *Thomas Hardy and Modern British Poetry* (London: Routledge & Kegan Paul, 1973), p. 28.

15. Paulin, p. 138.

Hardy's Winter Words

WILLIAM H. PRITCHARD

In 1926 Virginia Woolf visited Thomas Hardy at his Max Gate home in Dorchester, and recorded the following impressions in her diary:

> He seemed perfectly aware of everything; in no doubt or hesitation; having made up his mind; and being delivered of all his work, so that he was in no doubt about that either . . . The whole thing—literature, novels, etc.; all seemed to him an amusement, far away too, scarcely to be taken seriously. Yet he had sympathy and pity for those still engaged in it. But what his secret interests and activities are—to what occupation he trotted off when we left him—I do not know.

Although Hardy was eighty-six at the time, the younger writer's observation strikes me less as an insight into the poet at an advanced stage of his life, than as a permanent truth about the extraordinary character of a man for whom "the whole thing"—literature, other people, the great world— seemed far away. But a very likely occupation for him to have trotted off to after Virginia Woolf left, would have been the writing of another poem.

At that time, Hardy had written no novels for thirty years, had written instead an astonishing number of poems; in the long line of English and American poet-novelists—Scott, Emily Brontë, Melville, Meredith, D. H. Lawrence—he assumes a commanding position. But these poems, presented in a single volume, are forbidding. James Gibson's 1976 edition of them runs to 930 pages exclusive of miscellaneous material, and contains 919 individual poems, of which the 117th—located just two places before "The Darkling Thrush"—has, like many others, been overlooked. "Winter in Durnover Field" carries a scenic epigraph which serves to introduce us to a conversation between some inhabitants of that field:

Scene—*A wide stretch of fallow ground recently sown with wheat, and frozen to iron hardness. Three large birds walking about thereon, and wistfully eyeing the surface. Wind keen from north-east; sky a dull grey.*

(Triolet)

Reprinted by permission from *The Hudson Review*, Vol. XXXII, No. 3 (Autumn 1979). Copyright © 1979 by The Hudson Review, Inc.

ROOK: Throughout the field I find no grain;
            The cruel frost encrusts the cornland!

STARLING: Aye: patient pecking now is vain
            Throughout the field, I find . . .

ROOK: No grain!

PIGEON: Nor will be, comrade, till it rain,
            Or genial thawings loose the lorn land
            Throughout the field.

ROOK: I find no grain:
            The cruel frost encrusts the cornland!

It may be noted that although Starling and Pigeon are at no loss for words to express this deplorable situation, are eager to be agreeable or hopeful about the future, it is Rook who has the first and the last words, as well as an interpolation in the middle of the poem—"No grain!" Rook doesn't rationalize or understand his predicament; he exclaims, and his emphasis is negative, on what he *doesn't* find. Nor does he feel the need to be social or thoughtful, ruminative or complex: like Hardy in Virginia Woolf's portrait, he is in no doubt or hesitation, having made up his mind.

Why should any poet write such a poem and how are we to understand the kind of sensibility from which it could spring? How do we take "Winter in Durnover Field"? As yet another illustration of Hardy's pessimism? As a winter bagatelle, barely worth pausing over? Perhaps both, though hardly interesting on such counts. It is at least curious and worth remarking how much attention, of a special sort, Hardy has lavished on his little creation. He informs us that it is a Triolet, and its lines are prefaced by careful stage directions even down to the flat information that the field has "large birds walking about thereon." When we try to visualize the scene it turns into an animated cartoon, though not in color; and it is surely hard to devote much energy to teasing out a deeper or thematic significance—one doesn't want to push those large birds out of the way so as to get at some presumed "meaning."

In his slyly composed *The Later Years of Thomas Hardy*, ostensibly written by his second wife, Florence, but in fact written by Hardy himself, he makes, in a chapter dealing with his return to writing poetry in his fifties, an extended statement or defense of his poetic practice. There is an often-quoted plea for the importance of "cunning irregularity" in poetry, as well as in architecture, the profession of his young manhood. Hardy insists that what critics might mistake for unwitting awkwardness in his poems was in fact contrived and practiced exploitation of the irregular in rhythm. Further evidence is produced to show that he was no mere "apprentice," that he had accumulated many notes on rhythm and meter, and carried out many experiments. He then goes on to emphasize "lastly" what readers have taken to heart even less than the image of him as a craftsman: that he had a "born sense of humour, even a too keen sense occasionally," and that reviewers deficient in that quality were thus at a loss to know how to proceed. He defines this humour as Swiftian rather than Dickensian: "verses of a satirical, dry, caustic, or farcical cast" were the sort he often produced.

Hardy's reputation as an ironist (a collection of his stories is titled *Life's Little Ironies*) adheres mainly to his earlier novel-writing self; while the poetry is praised for possessing a quite opposite effect of deep, if sometimes stumbling and awkward, sincerity. As Donald Davie has pointed out, this is really a way of condescending to him. If Yeats and Eliot and Pound were subtle, allusive, complex, and weighty, Hardy was, well . . . sincere. Anyone who studied poetry in American universities after World War II, in the age of the New Criticism, probably remembers an exciting first encounter with "Sailing to Byzantium" or "Gerontion" or even perhaps with "Mauberley." By contrast, acquaintance with Hardy's poems, if it occurred at all (he was often just omitted from courses, being neither quite Victorian nor quite Modern), was through the more familiarly "poetic" voice of the "The Darkling Thrush," a poem few found too difficult or remote. Certainly no one owned a copy of *Complete Poems*, the volume which any reader of Hardy must learn to live in even though he will never familiarize himself with all of its individual parts. Prolonged immersion in it reveals how persistently interesting and compelling is Hardy's presence.

My way of evoking that presence is to direct attention where it should always be directed when lyric poetry is the subject—to matters of what I call, if confusingly at times, *voice*. When the poet is Yeats one can hardly ignore the voice, or the changing voices, through which his poems speak to us, often speak very loudly to us. With Hardy, voice is dangerously easy to ignore, to the advantage of neither poem nor reader. We should emphasize further the cunning irregularity of his mind, and the "born sense of humour, even a too keen sense occasionally" which the voice displays or expresses. When, in a word I believe was first used about Hardy's poems by R. P. Blackmur, that voice is anonymous its effect is no less powerful, though harder to specify. There is a nice paragraph of characterization in *The Later Years*, devoted to contesting the notion that Hardy was "simple." No, says the biographer, "he had the formal subtlety peculiar to his own generation; there was something deliberately 'ordinary' in his demeanour which was a concealment of extraordinary fires." These fires burn throughout the poetry.

Hardy's official career as a publishing poet stretches from *Wessex Poems* (1898) to *Winter Words* which appeared in 1928, the year of his death. In *The Later Years* we are told that because of the "misrepresentations" he had suffered from being the author of *Tess of the D'Urbervilles* and *Jude the Obscure*, he determined, in 1896, to write no more novels, only poetry. But, he says, these misrepresentations turned out ultimately to be the best thing that could have happened; for they well-nigh compelled him, in his own judgement at any rate, if he wished to retain any shadow of self-respect, to abandon at once a form of literary art he had long intended to abandon at some indefinite time, and resume openly that form of it which had always been more instinctive with him, and which he had just been able to keep alive from his early years, half in secrecy, under the pressure of magazine writing.

His recent biographer, Robert Gittings, suggests that in addition to whatever frustrations Hardy felt about the public reception of *Jude*, or his wife's distaste for the novel's doctrine as she understood it, he was coming to find the writing of novels a physical burden in their sheer weight of words. Gittings also suggests that the "highly personal themes of his secret youth" could express themselves more judiciously in poems than in novels. Hardy had written a number of poems in the 1860s of which the most impressive was "Neutral Tones"; now, writing seriously again, he began to reap what Ezra Pound called "the harvest of having written 20 novels first," and continued to do so for the last thirty-odd years of his life.

During these years in which Hardy became an ever more honored literary giant, so that by the time Virginia Woolf visited him in 1926 it must have been like going to meet a mythical figure, the most significant event—for our purposes here the sole significant event of his later life— was the sudden death in 1912 of his wife Emma, from whom he had been seriously estranged since the 1890s. Although Hardy enjoyed going up to London, staying at the Athenaeum, attending plays and social gatherings, and although he engaged in a number of romantic affiliations with younger women, one of whom was to be his second wife (these affiliations are described by Mr. Gittings with meticulous care and tact), his life became identified with his poetry to an extent only matched among the modern poets by Wallace Stevens. With Yeats or Eliot or Pound, life and poems seem almost equally interesting; with Hardy, particularly with later Hardy, the poet of our concern here, one is interested in the life of the poems.

His career as poet may be divided into three parts, of which the first comprises the work from his first three volumes (*Poems of the Past and Present*, 1901, and *Time's Laughingstocks*, 1909, followed *Wessex Poems*). Some of these poems bear dates from the 1860s and the London addresses where Hardy lived at that time. One group of them flowers out of a visit to Italy and the Continent in the late 1880s; another group, dated 1899, was stimulated by the Boer War; another, larger group is made up of narratives and ballad-like anecdotes in which eternal traits of character are displayed. I pass over these groups without further comment, though they contain many lively and capable performances. But Hardy's most characteristic and finest voice is found in the following shorter poems from these volumes, in order of their appearance in *Complete Poems*: "Neutral Tones," "The Impercipient,"

"At an Inn," "I Look Into My Glass," "Drummer Hodge," "The Souls of the Slain," "Rome: At the Pyramid of Cestius near the Graves of Shelley and Keats," "A Broken Appointment," "Wives in the Sere," "The Last Chrysanthemum," "The Darkling Thrush," "The Self-Unseeing," "The Rejected Member's Wife," "The Farm-Woman's Winter," "Shut Out That Moon," and "On the Departure Platform."

The last of these illustrates Hardy's deepest, most pervasive qualities and also points up the peculiar kind of difficulty there is in writing about his art. It is one of his lesser-known poems, presumably written about the woman who was to become his second wife, though such information is of no help in understanding what makes the poem distinctive:

> We kissed at the barrier; and passing through
> She left me, and moment by moment got
> Smaller and smaller, until to my view
>   She was but a spot;
>
> A wee white spot of muslin fluff
> That down the diminishing platform bore
> Through hustling crowds of gentle and rough
>   To the carriage door.
>
> Under the lamplight's fitful glowers,
> Behind dark groups from far and near,
> Whose interests were apart from ours,
>   She would disappear,
>
> Then show again, till I ceased to see
> That flexible form, that nebulous white;
> And she who was more than my life to me
>   Had vanished quite. . . .

These first four stanzas of the poem tell us what happened, enacting with considerable skill a voice in process of saying how it was that day; and we follow along, participating in the man's "diminishing" perspective, moving from one stanza to the next as "She would disappear, / Then show again. . . ."

The best tribute ever paid to Hardy's poetry was Ezra Pound's in *Guide to Kulchur* (1938) where he made two essential points: "No man can read Hardy's poems collected but that his own life, and forgotten moments of it, will come back to him, a flash here and an hour there. Have you a better test for true poetry?" Whether for "man" here we can read "man or woman" I am not sure, since the perspective of most, though not all, of the poems is a male one. But what clearly animates this particular one is the poet's bringing back to himself a hitherto forgotten moment which he proceeds to rehearse in most delicately careful detail. The final two stanzas ruminate about the experience:

> We have penned new plans since that fair fond day,
> And in season she will appear again—
> Perhaps in the same soft white array—
>   But never as then!
>
> —'And why, young man, must eternally fly
> A joy you'll repeat, if you love her well?'
> —'O friend, nought happens twice thus; why,
>   I cannot tell!'

Hardy may not have found the perfect way to end this lyric—the interpolated question by a "friend" creaks more than a bit—but what comes through most clearly are the exclamatory negatives, particularly the four words "But never as then!" When in Pound's phrase a forgotten moment comes back to the speaker in a Hardy poem, his truest response to it is to insist upon its uniqueness and the impossibility of repeating it. The exclamation mark is a wonderfully expressive device with which to make this insistence, since along with the regret, the pang of loss when the past moment is viewed in memory's landscape, there is also a present exhilaration of not merely recalling the moment but of asserting its forever-lostness: "nought happens twice thus," and so "never as then."

There is an analogy between this exhilaration and the sort which animated Rook (in "Winter in Durnover Field") as he kept announcing that throughout the field he found no grain. Or there is "The Rejected Member's Wife," a poem about a woman whose husband has been defeated in the parliamentary election; thus she will never again stand smiling in her pain, at his side, waving to the crowd that has rejected him. Other people will come along and go through the same delights of triumph and agonies of defeat:

> But she will no more stand
>   In the sunshine there,
> With that wave of her white-gloved hand,
>   And that chestnut hair.

The poem is secure enough to end with just that much said and no more. Donald Davie speaks of Hardy's "playful and mournful serenity"; something like that quality is felt in these reiterated pledges that things will not come back, not ever again be the way they once were.

Pound's other significant point in his tribute to Hardy succinctly locates the difficulty anybody experiences in writing about the poems: "When a writer's matter is stated with such entirety and with such clarity there is no place left for the explaining critic." This remark has particular application to Hardy and is not merely a matter of poet kicking critic out of the way of another poet. Certainly Pound is making use here of terms central to his own way of thinking about what poems should do: they should *present* or state "matter," not write about or describe or strike attitudes toward it. (I am speaking at least of Pound the Imagist, circa 1913.) Yet because of its allusive weight, its diction, the elaborations of its verse structure, there is usually some room or need for the critic of Pound's poetry to do a bit of explaining, even when the poem's "matter" is rather slender. But consider how "The Darkling Thrush" states everything with such clarity as to silence commentary or render it superfluous:

> The land's sharp features seemed to be
>   The Century's corpse outleant,
> His crypt the cloudy canopy,
>   The wind his death-lament.
> The ancient pulse of germ and birth
>   Was shrunken hard and dry,
> And every spirit upon earth
>   Seemed fervourless as I.

It is difficult to believe in the fervourlessness of a central presence here, since the poet goes about his task of charting the landscape then announcing the thrush's song, always with such unerring confidence and accuracy. In other words, the poem's "I" is a relatively conventional one, lacking the rich dramatic interest built up around the first person in a poem by Robert Frost, say, or Robert Lowell. Neither the poem's formal properties nor its display of a speaking "I" seem to demand much in the way of explanatory analysis.

On occasion the "explaining critic" inserts himself into the plot of one of Hardy's poems, as in a little-known gem tucked between "The Darkling Thrush" and "Winter in Durnover Field." For five stanzas "The Last Chrysanthemum" sings with elegance about deprivation:

> Why should this flower delay so long
>   To show its tremulous plumes?
> Now is the time of plaintive robin-song
>   When flowers are in their tombs.
>
> Through the slow summer, when the sun
>   Called to each frond and whorl
> That all he could for flowers was being done,
>   Why did it not uncurl?
>
> It must have felt that fervid call
>   Although it took no heed,

> Waking but now, when leaves like corpses fall,
>   And saps all retrocede.
>
> Too late its beauty, lonely thing,
>   The season's shine is spent,
> Nothing remains for it but shivering
>   In tempests turbulent.
>
> Had it a reason for delay,
>   Dreaming in witlessness
> That for a bloom so delicately gay
>   Winter should stay its stress?

Wordsworth's "The Lesser Celandine" is behind this someplace; and it is not surprising that when Hardy chose to write about a flower he would find one that came too late, had no business being there at all, and was in for a hard season of shivering. This is the flower he can love, just as he can welcome the thrush if it is on its last legs ("Aged," "frail, gaunt and small"), and admire a grainless rook or a rejected member's wife. Yet never does he command a language more "delicately gay" than in this poem's fifth stanza; nor is the question asked a real question. Hardy has stated his matter with such entirety and clarity, has made up the best that can be said for this lonely, lovely chrysanthemum, that anything more is superfluous. So the final stanza of the poem comes as an embarrassing bit of gaucherie:

> —I talk as if the thing were born
>   With sense to work its mind;
> Yet it is but one mask of many worn
>   By the Great Face behind.

Here Pound's explaining critic has intruded, reminding us that he's committed the pathetic fallacy, and saluting—under one of its many names—the Great Face (in other poems it is the Immanent Will or Purblind Doomster). But in truth the poem has already completed itself; its "matter"—the plight of belatedness—has been stated wholly. Nothing Hardy wrote over the ten years following "The Darkling Thrush" requires us to give a radically different account of it, so it is not surprising that critics found more to work on as they observed Yeats's changing style in the new century's first decade, or at the end of it encountered the earliest work of Pound. Hardy, who had turned seventy in 1910, could hardly be expected to provide any further surprises.

With various stirrings of new life visible in the volumes of poetry published in and around the year 1914, one might understandably have overlooked the appearance of yet another by Hardy—his fourth book of poems, *Satires of Circumstances: Lyrics and Reveries with Miscellaneous Pieces*, published in November of that year, after England had entered the great war. We learn from J. O. Bailey's useful handbook on the poetry that the title was supplied by Hardy's publisher (Macmillan) who took it from his title for the last group of poems in the book, "Satires of Circumstance in Fifteen Glimpses." These short poems had been published in a magazine in 1911 and took ironic attitudes toward various human foibles and affectations. Hardy was uneasy about the thus-titled volume since, as he says in *The Later Years*, the fifteen earlier "satires" were "caustically humorous productions which had been issued with a light heart before the war":

> So much shadow, domestic and public, had passed over his head since he had written the satires that he was in no mood now to publish humour or irony, and hence he would readily have suppressed them if they had not already gained such currency from magazine publication that he could not do it.

As if to atone, he assures us that the "Lyrics and Reveries" section of the new volume "contained some of the tenderest and least satirical verse that ever came from his pen."

The domestic shadow which had passed over Hardy's head was the death of his wife in late November of 1912. During the next few months he wrote the remarkable "Poems of 1912–13," a group of eighteen lyrics (three more were added later) in response to that death. Although these are placed after the "Lyrics and Reveries" section of *Satires of Circumstances*, we can safely assume that he thought of them as prime examples of his "tenderest, least satirical verse," and that he worried about how his reputation as professional pessimist and "bitter" portrayer of life's little ironies might deform responses to what were very personal poems. Yet Macmillan's title was really the right one for the volume, and the 1912–13 lyrics are of great interest partly because they are not just tender, do not forego the strengths of his best satirical poetry.

But before taking up these poems and their biographical genesis, two of the most rightly anthologized of Hardy's works deserve attention as fine examples of the "public" poet's satiric strengths. "Channel Firing" and "The Convergence of the Twain" are the second and third poems in the "Lyrics and Reveries" section from *Satires of Circumstances*, but this heading fails to suggest the fabulous quality of each poem and the ambiguous way each reveals Hardy's presence. "Channel Firing" begins quietly and firmly with the voice of a dead man speaking from his coffin in rather four-square fashion:

> That night your great guns, unawares,
> Shook all our coffins as we lay,

> And broke the chancel window-squares,
> We thought it was the Judgment-day
>
> And sat upright. . . .

The man proceeds to relate how God had to reassure these dead people that it was not in fact the Judgment-day but merely the nations preparing for another war (Hardy dates the poem April, 1914), and that since the world was still mad they were not to get their hopes up. At this news the dead subside, one of them, Parson Thirdly, opining that instead of preaching he should have "stuck to pipes and beer." So far it looks to be a satire of circumstance in a familiar Hardyan vein, an exercise turned out with perhaps too much facility. But the final stanza tolls its message:

> Again the guns disturbed the hour,
> Roaring their readiness to avenge,
> As far inland as Stourton Tower,
> And Camelot, and starlit Stonehenge.

One of Hardy's very best critics, John Crowe Ransom, has nicely pointed out how the meter makes us stress the "henge" in Stonehenge. Ransom paraphrases the end of the poem this way: "Our expectations have been defeated, but we still insist on our moral universe; the roar of the guns prevails, but now it assaults the shrines without effect"; and he concludes that "The thing heard upon the air is evil, but the thing seen is the religious monument hung and illuminated beneath the stars."

There is nothing in the poem that forbids this elegantly humanistic way of understanding it; but suppose instead one chose to emphasize, for the sake of discussion, how *far* the roaring of the guns penetrated. As far as Camelot and Stonehenge, a long way back in history and myth; thus one might read the conclusion in a less affirmative way than Ransom does, and might say instead "Look how far back war goes, learn how it will ever be with us, realize how little there is you can do about it." Different emphases are possible since all the poem's voice does is to declare, with rapt attentiveness and rhythmic power, what the guns are doing. But what everyone can agree about, I should think, is the sense of elevation—mainly through its use of romantic names, places and monuments—achieved by the final stanza, and perhaps felt by Hardy as he composed it. It may be that no statements about Man and War and History are as true as the juxtapositions and repetitions given expression here. Somehow the roaring of the guns ends up feeling dignified; and the reader may find himself entertaining some ennobling thoughts about war, rather than musing regretfully on the folly of mankind.

There is a similarly odd deflection from humanistic attitudes in his famous poem about the *Titanic* disaster. Much has been written in admiration of the marmoreal stanzas in which the great sunken ship is described:

> Over the mirrors meant
> To glass the opulent
> The sea-worm crawls—grotesque, slimed, dumb, indifferent

and through which Hardy, in explaining what happened, carefully prepares the coming together of the ship and its mate:

> And as the smart ship grew
> In stature, grace, and hue,
> In shadowy silent distance grew the Iceberg too.

The ending of the poem in which they meet, in which "consummation comes, and jars two hemispheres," is at the least a memorable one. But when we inquire about the reader's cumulative response, I think few would describe it as a sagely grave nodding at the ironical consequence of overwhelming pride and vanity. The "Convergence" is just too much fun to read for such responses seriously to exist; in fact it is but a slight overstatement to compare this poem with another utterance about the *Titanic* sinking, a song whose chorus ends with the ringing declaration "It was sad when the great ship went down" ("Husbands and wives / Little children lost their lives" etc.) to be boomed out with enthusiasm by communal singers who have drunk deep.

By designedly avoiding a personal, thoughtfully elaborated response to War or Disaster; by giving us instead such intricate constructions as "Channel Firing" or "Convergence of the Twain," Hardy appears as an ingenious, highly inventive entertainer, enlivened by the very examples of human folly which in life saddened or horrified him, as when he lost two acquaintances in the *Titanic* disaster. It comes as no surprise then to hear his second wife announce in a letter that her husband is upstairs, "writing an intensely dismal poem with great spirits." These facts may be born in mind when confronting the expressive sadness of "Poems of 1912–13."

In those poems, more than at any other place in his work, we see Hardy writing out of his experience of pain, loss and guilt, to make more dramatic and more "open" utterances than the entertaining and impressively-crafted ones observed thus far. Yet crafted and entertaining they still are. Robert Gittings tells us that in 1891 Emma Hardy had begun the diary which may or may not have been titled "What I Think of My Husband." We shall never know for sure, since upon reading it after her death Hardy committed it to the flames. In 1899 Emma wrote to a woman who had asked her for marital advice, that at age 50 (Hardy was nearly 60) a married man gets restless: "Eastern ideas of matrimony secretly pervade his thoughts and he wearies of the most perfect and suitable wife chosen in his earlier life"—a sentence both touching and comic in its pretense at disinterested worldly wisdom. Whatever Eastern ideas came and went in his head, Hardy formed a number of relationships with other women, and in 1907 met Florence Dugdale, a young Dorset-born girl who was to be his love and his mate after Emma's death.

What we know of Hardy's marriage to Emma in its later years is depressing. Though they lived together at Max Gate, the Dorchester house where Hardy spent the remainder of his life, they saw each other only at dinner and even then, Gittings says, did not speak. Hardy's stays in London were increasingly done on his own. When the Robert Louis Stevensons visited at Max Gate, Mrs. Stevenson afterwards wrote patronizingly of "A pale gentle, frightened little man, that one felt an instinctive tenderness for, with a wife—ugly is no word for it—who said 'Whatever shall we do?' I had never heard a human being say it before." More significantly, it appears that Emma's death might not or need not have been quite so unforeseen as her husband's poems after the event were to claim. She had been visibly suffering from impacted gall-stones, but Hardy managed rather successfully to shut his eyes to her condition. Thus the claim made at the end of "The Going," first of the 1912–13 poems, that "O you could not know / That such swift fleeing / No soul foreseeing— / Not even I—would undo me so" becomes a trifle more problematic if we try to match up the "I" with Hardy the man.

Yet neither embarrassment nor cynical knowingness are helpful attitudes to carry into our reading of these poems; and there is no reason not to affirm, even if it is a difficult and uneasy affirmation, Eliot's separation between the man who suffers and the mind that creates—between the life and the art. One might also note that Emma left behind her another personal manuscript which Hardy also read but did not burn, and which was eventually published—what J. O. Bailey describes as a "childlike but appealing record of Emma's girlhood and youth up to the time of her marriage." The editors of this published manuscript say that reading it "threw Hardy back to that joyful enchanted time, forty years earlier, when they had met and become engaged." Thus the poems originated as much in loving memory as in guilt and bad conscience. At any rate they have been handsomely admired by a number of critics beginning with Middleton Murry in 1921. F. R. Leavis saw them (at least saw "The Voice" and "After a Journey") as standing at the very center of Hardy's distinction as a poet, and called them "a triumph of character." More recent accounts by Douglas Brown and Irving Howe have hailed their imaginative integrity, richness of design, and vocal authenticity. In Brown's words, Hardy succeeds in remaining "most naturally himself when most deeply distressed." If these poems have been praised at the expense of others which don't spring so directly from Hardy's life, they will now—if we accept his biographer's account of that life—have to pay their own way, create their integrity and authenticity wholly by means of their internal shape and gestures, rather than by their correspondence to external fact. And in these terms they most assuredly succeed.

"The Going," first in the sequence and one of the best, begins gently and with sad playfulness, by reproaching the woman for not letting her husband know she was going to die:

> Why did you give no hint that night
> That quickly after the morrow's dawn,
> And calmly, as if indifferent quite,
> You would close your term here, up and be gone
>   Where I could not follow
>   With wing of swallow
> To gain one glimpse of you ever anon!

Now she teases him by seeming to appear "At the end of an alley of bending boughs," and is remembered as the heroine of romance from forty years ago:

> You were she who abode
> By those red-veined rocks far West,
> You were the swan-necked one who rode
> Along the beetling Beeny Crest. . . .

The closing stanzas of "The Going" point up most clearly Hardy's distinctive procedure in these poems:

> Why, then, latterly did we not speak,
> Did we not think of those days long dead,
> And ere your vanishing strive to seek
> That time's renewal? We might have said,
>   'In this bright spring weather
>   We'll visit together
> Those places that once we visited.'
>
>   Well, well! All's past amend,
>   Unchangeable. It must go.
> I seem but a dead man held on end
> To sink down soon. . . . O you could not
>   know
>   That such swift fleeing
>   No soul foreseeing—
> Not even I—would undo me so!

Rhythmically speaking, we note how what they "might have said"—the lines in quotation marks from the penultimate stanza—take on a lilting simplicity which the unsonglike pace of the final verse movingly opposes. Douglas Brown finds the distinction of this, as well as the other elegies, to lie in "*dramatic* vitality" and goes on to make the following interesting remarks:

> . . . the peculiar excellence lies in the disengagement of the self. There may be an "I," named or speaking, for whom this loss has happened; but the grief does not turn inward upon "I, Thomas Hardy" nor ask attention for him.

And he notes that a number of poems in the sequence break off just at the moment when grief threatens to become self-regarding, resulting in an effect that is both human and impersonal, "dramatic" and poised.

I agree that "The Going" is an absolutely distinctive Hardy poem, its first-person presence ("while I / Saw morning harden upon the wall") felt in more vividly particular ways than that of "The Darkling Thrush" or "On the Departure Platform," where the focus is importantly somewhere else. But more can be said in explanation of its dramatic life. The poem is dated December 1912, and either the writing of it helped Hardy clarify his feelings about Emma's death, or they had already been clarified in this letter to Florence Henniker on the 19th of that same December:

> In spite of the differences between us, which it would be affectation to deny, and certain painful delusions she suffered from at times, my life is intensely sad to me now without her. The saddest moments of all are when I go into the garden and to that long straight walk at the top that you know, where she used to walk every evening just before dusk, the cat trotting faithfully behind her and at times when I almost expect to see her as usual coming in from the flower-beds with a little trowel in her hand.

This is admirably direct and fully expressed; it also points up, by contrast, the indirection and strangeness of Hardy even at his presumably most "sincere," as in "The Going." There his impulse toward the dramatic propels the voice into putting questions which are not put in the letter to Mrs. Henniker. The letter-writer expects her to understand what "delusions" Emma suffered from, and knows it would be "affectation" to deny the differences which had separated the Hardys; nonetheless, his life is now "intensely sad" without her.

But "The Going" looks back and questions the relationship in its less than glorious aspect: "Why, then, latterly did we not speak, / Did we not think of those days long dead," as the syntax continues into the next line. But within the first line itself, merely "did not speak," an enormous and unanswerable question compared to the what-might-have-been-saids that follow. The "I" is thus precipitated into the bleakness of the last stanza: "Well, well!"—an exclamatory gesture that can be heard in various ways and refuses to be pinned down to any one of them: "All's past amend," and "It must go"—two desperate gestures at saying eternal commonplaces, the saying of which gives little help; the ellipsis after "soon," words having failed him. . . ; and the final exclamation, passionately negative as so often in Hardy: "O you could not know . . . No soul foreseeing— / Not even I—." In an important way the poem is a satire of circumstance after all, as Hardy's letter is not. To paraphrase: "It's not your fault that you didn't say good-bye to me when you died, though it does seem rather thoughtless of you to have left the world quite so abruptly. I wonder why your illusion suddenly appears before my eyes, deceiving me into thinking you're alive? After all, you *were* the girl of high romance I courted years ago; why when neither of us was speaking much to each other didn't we recall those days?" No wonder the throttled reflections of the last stanza seem the only appropriate way to conclude. One has been instructed in the way this tragic event is also an instance of life's rather large ironies: the irony, the joke, is on the man who's left behind to experience them.

Perhaps the most pleasurable and satisfying effect of reading these poems in sequence is the way they lead up to the great affirmation of "At Castle Boterel." Early in the sequence stands "Rain on a Grave" ("Clouds spout upon her / Their waters amain / In ruthless disdain,—") and "I Found Her Out There" ("I found her out there / On a slope few see / That falls westwardly")—vigorously expert poems of the fancy which aspire to protect the dead woman from the elements, or somehow spirit her away from Dorset to the Cornwall of her true home. This geographical distinction forms the basis for Donald Davie's fine account of what he terms the poems' "Dantesque focus"

> by which "every natural site has the ethical rank of the rational beings who dwell in it"—[precluding] not just the psychological analysis so brilliant in Meredith's *Modern Love*, but also any moral discrimination, and apportioning of blame between the two partners to a marriage that had gone disastrously wrong. Max Gate is simply the landscape of treason; thereabouts he will betray her, she will betray him. North Cornwall is the landscape of loyalty; thereabouts he will be true to her, she will be true to him. The use of landscape is as starkly emblematic as that.

And he goes on to argue, perhaps with some overstatement, that "remorse" and "reproach" are thus excluded from the poems.

As I understand Hardy's temperament the "Dantesque focus" of these poems is indeed crucial, since his poetry does not typically display the complexities either of psychological analysis or of moral discrimination. Once again, in Pound's terms, to be a poet who states his material with "entirety and clarity" precludes the sorts of tentativeness and qualification necessary—at least as our modern understanding has it—for certain kinds of complexity. One might add that Hardy's strongly-rhymed (not always felicitously so) lines and tight formal stanzas, are also difficult to exploit in ways that half-state or insinuate or suggest in "psychological" terms. For example, in the eighth poem of the sequence, "The Haunter," the dead woman speaks for the first time, confiding in us about the man whom she's hovering near but whose words she can't answer. She lets us know, however, that when she was alive, when she *could* answer, he didn't much want to talk:

> When I could let him know
> How I would like to join in his journeys
> Seldom he wished to go.

And eventually she asks us to "Tell him a faithful one is doing / All that love can do / Still that his path may be worth pursuing, / And to bring peace thereto." It sounds noble; but reread and juxtaposed with "The Voice" which follows, it appears that circumstances have their satirical side, since her pledge of faithfulness ("If he but sigh since my loss befell him / Straight to his side I go") is also a pledge not to let him alone.

"The Voice" ("Woman much missed . . .") has been widely admired, is one of Leavis' "great" Hardy poems, yet I doubt that a convincing account can be given of why it is clearly superior to a good many others. Here the man fancies that the woman is calling to him; he can't believe his ears, calls back her "Cornwall" self for inspection once more, then doubts the whole business:

> Or is it only the breeze, in its listlessness
> Travelling across the wet mead to me here,
> You being ever dissolved to wan wistlessness,
> Heard no more again far or near?

and sums up:

> Thus I; faltering forward,
> Leaves around me falling,
> Wind oozing thin through the thorn from norward,
> And the woman calling.

Yes, it is you that I hear; no, it is only the breeze: the final stanza in refusing to choose one over the other (the wind keeps "oozing thin" and the woman "calling") calls a halt to further dramatic development, looks back at itself and names once more the "faltering" hero's situation. It is less a poetry of argued, progressive statement than a talismanic charm which fascinates and enchants by a line such as "Wind oozing thin through the thorn from norward," which is nothing less or more than a tour de force of expression. "The Voice" is not notable for moral or psychological discriminations; its circumstantial satire is of more elemental concern and is felt mainly through the element of sound.

But the two masterpieces from the sequence are "After a Journey" and "At Castle Boterel," poems which register most fully, humanly and particularly, the man's recovery of himself in his saying of the most that can be said about his relationship with the dead woman. No longer "faltering forward," there is a leisured amplitude in both poems into which the reader is led, as her spirit leads the man:

> Yes: I have re-entered your olden haunts at last;
>   Through the years, through the dead scenes I have
>   tracked you;

In "After a Journey" the pursuer's voice is released into speaking with a range of tones, and it can address the "Voiceless ghost" of its first line with a lovely mixture of supplication, teasing reproof, and tender vouchsafing:

> What have you now found to say of our past—
>   Scanned across the dark space wherein I have lacked you?
> Summer gave us sweets, but autumn wrought division?
>   Things were not lastly as firstly well
>   With us twain, you tell?
> But all's closed now, despite Time's derision.
>
> I see what you are doing: you are leading me on
>   To the spots we knew when we haunted here together,
> The waterfall, above which the mist-bow shone
>   At the then fair hour in the then fair weather,
> And the cave just under, with a voice still so hollow
>   That it seems to call out to me from forty years ago,
>   When you were all aglow,
> And not the thin ghost that I now fraily follow!

The truths about how summer was sweet, autumn not so; of how their relationship didn't maintain its glorious beginning—are true but somehow irrelevant. "All's closed now" has no particular referent but is an absolute gesture of conclusion. Yet the next stanza opens up with a great recovery of powers to the wonderful point where, suddenly, the cave calls out as if from forty years ago (that almost monosyllabic line is itself a wonder!) and where the clichés of romance ("When you were all aglow") now feel fresh and alive. It is the life and power of the poetic imagination to call up and call back the past, which "After a Journey" testifies to especially in its last four lines:

> Trust me, I mind not, though Life lours,
>   The bringing me here; nay, brings me here again!
>   I am just the same as when
> Our days were a joy, and our paths through flowers.

Leavis rightly thinks these lines moving and the poem a "triumph of character." One might add though that the assertion of sameness—"I am just the same as when / Our days were a Joy . . ."—is also a loyal simplification of the man's character: we have seen the sense in which he isn't the same, in which "Time's derision" has taken its toll. In this poem, being "just the same" is less a condition than a hard-won assertion. We remind ourselves that Hardy was a poet back then, just as he is now in 1913; that forty-five years previously he had written a poem about love gone wrong called "Neutral Tones." The imagination persists, despite time's derision.

"At Castle Boterel" is the companion poem which though less appreciated than "After a Journey" strikes me as even deeper in its commitment to the imagination's persistence and dominion over Nature. What makes the particular expression so interesting here is the way Hardy's voice manages to discover rather than merely assert a truth—a discovery which happens before our eyes and before his too. In a drizzle the man looks behind him at a "fading byway" and it is suddenly replaced by a forty-years-ago scene of "Myself and a girlish form benighted / In dry March weather." Having climbed the road the couple alight to ease the pony's load, then "it" happens:

> It filled but a minute. But was there ever
>   A time of such quality, since or before,
> In that hill's story? To one mind never,
>   Though it has been climbed, foot-swift, foot-sore,
>   By thousands more.
>
> Primaeval rocks form the road's steep border,
>   And much have they faced there, first and last,
> Of the transitory in Earth's long order;
>   But what they record in colour and cast
>   Is—that we two passed.

There is perhaps no more expressive dash in lyric poetry than the one in that last line, as the voice moves all the way from acknowledging, in grandly spacious ways, how much the rocks have "faced" of transitory Nature ("Earth's long order") to another kind of "facing," as the man looks to see what they have to tell him—which is "that we two passed." As human a moment as can be found in Hardy's poems, the concluding stanzas give it further poignancy:

> And to me, though Time's unflinching rigour,
>   In mindless rote, has ruled from sight
> The substance now, one phantom figure
>   Remains on the slope, as when that night
>   Saw us alight.
>
> I look and see it there, shrinking, shrinking,
>   I look back at it amid the rain
> For the very last time; for my sand is sinking,
>   And I shall traverse old love's domain
>   Never again.

No longer, as in "After a Journey," does he cry out "Nay, bring me here again!" The imaginative expenditure has been such as to render further expeditions unwise or unnecessary, certainly anticlimactic. But for the most unillusioned of modern poets to have said this much, to have recorded as a great fact "that we too passed," is Hardy's triumph over his own penchant for the anonymous, also a fine moment in the poetry of our century.

> Next day she found that her lover,
>   Though asked, had gone elsewhere,
> And that she had possessed him in absence
>   More than if there.
> —from "In the Marquee"

In his useful and incisive book on the poetry, Samuel Hynes observes that it is easier to characterize Hardy's style by saying what it is *not* than what it is—not lyrical, not melodious, nor spare, nor austere. The "Poems of 1912–13" are his most eloquent efforts in the direction of a strongly individual style; "After a Journey" and "At Castle Boterel" prime examples of vigorous and intense dramatic performances. At the end of the latter poem the voice records a shrinking of a "phantom figure" and vows to "traverse old love's domain / Never again." The real Hardy lived to write many more poems, some about his relationship with Emma, but never, in respect to the dead woman, with the fullness of "traversing" seen in the 1912–13 group. Perhaps the crowning irony with regard to those poems is that Florence Dugdale, living at Max Gate though as yet unmarried to Hardy, was deeply distressed by the flood of poems Emma's death had occasioned. While at the same time, the guilt and remorse which so spurred Hardy's creative and elegiac energies were partly in consequence of the attention he had paid Florence over the last five years, at the cost of ignoring—even to her death—his own wife.

Aged seventy-two when he wrote those poems, Hardy was to publish four further volumes which contain some of his finest efforts, as for example "During Wind and Rain," "In Time of the Breaking of Nations," "Midnight on the Great Western," "And There was a Great Calm . . . ," "The Fallow Deer at the Lonely House"—and a number of others. He continued to indulge his inclination to say no, not, nor, and other negative affirmations. An oddly humorous moment occurs late in *Complete Poems* when #918 announces itself as "We Are Getting to the End," a poem about the end of "dreams" and unreal expectations about the world, but also (we may feel) about our heroic struggle to read through the previous 917 poems. Poem 919, "He Resolves to Say No More," contains four stanzas whose last lines reveal the following progression: "Yea, none shall gather what I hide!"; "What I discern I will not say"; "What I have learnt no man shall know"; "And show to no man what I see." In other words, any talk about grimness or pessimism of thought in these two final poems must contend with the quite unmistakeable current of wry playfulness and verbal aggressiveness which informs them and strikes us more interestingly than do the grim thoughts themselves—hardly a new thing for Hardy to be thinking.

"Why should not old men be mad?" Yeats asked in the title of one of his own last poems. Hardy's late volumes in their sanity answer that question, though never of course by entertaining it directly. Occupied with his second wife in writing the two-volume autobiography, living on at Max Gate as a famous personage, he kept as always his own company. Robert Gittings provides an amusing instance of this in the form of an anecdote Florence told about accusing her husband of not having spoken to anyone outside the house for twelve days. "I have spoken to someone," said Hardy triumphantly, "the man who drove the manure cart." Much impressed, Florence asked what he said to the man: "Good morning," was Hardy's reply. There exists also a document titled "The Domestic Life of Thomas Hardy," purportedly written by a "Miss E. E. T." who was his parlour-maid near the end of his life. From her reminiscences one takes away gossip like the following: "Hardy was, in a sense, a negative character whom, one gathers, the staff neither liked nor disliked." We learn that he always spoke "quietly and softly," that he never showed anger, that he sought solitude, played no games, collected nothing. "I think of him as always writing" says "Miss E. E. T."

He was writing mainly about the effects of time as observed and felt in his own life and in the world of nature he became, if anything, increasingly sensitive to and observant of. Yet the real distinction of poems ensuing from this observation lies not in matters of apt imagery or "wise" reflections about life, but in the unearthly detachment with which a voice speaks. Reading through the four volumes from the last ten years of his life, beginning with *Moments of Vision* in 1917, we are struck by the predominance of this toneless voice somewhere from underwater or from beyond the grave, speaking to nobody in particular—though we are permitted to listen—with complete, assured, and impartial authority. Frequently the situation is generalized, pointed even more toward allegory and fable than were the earlier poems. In the concluding words of "Going and Staying," a charming poem published in *Late Lyrics and Earlier* (1922), the lovers look close at Time

> And saw his ghostly arms revolving
> To sweep off woeful things with prime,
> Things sinister with things sublime
> Alike dissolving.

It is this impartiality of change and equality of dissolution, despite season or age, that most grips his imagination. In "The Missed Train" (from *Human Shows, Far Phantasies*, 1925) the man thinks back to the time when he traveled home after visiting his lover, missed the train and had to spend the night in a small inn where all night he dreamed about her, feeling both lonely and consoled by her spirit. The poem concludes

> Thus onetime to me . . .
> Dim wastes of dead years bar away
> Then from now. But such happenings to-day
> Fall to lovers, may be!
>
> Years, years as shoaled seas,
> Truly, stretch now between! Less and less
> Shrink the visions then vast in me.—Yes,
> Then in me: Now in these.

To use language as "dead" as this and make the result very much the opposite, is an achievement. How much it is necessary and how much we are invited to fill in the blank spaces, the ellipsis, the dash, with inexpressible and unsayable yearnings and musings—one cannot specify. But the familiar words are able to assert, simultaneously, how far behind him is his own past, momentarily recovered in a poem, and how this is not just his but "maybe" anyone's past: how it's all different, but always the same in the anonymous community of ultimate things. The last line is perfectly, finally balanced, as in an epitaph, since these are surely the last words.

The late nature poems show another, related kind of anonymity. *Human Shows, Far Phantasies* is filled, not surprisingly, with winter scenes, and "A Light Snow-Fall After Frost," one of Hardy's least-known, most delightful poems has three stanzas presenting, with great subtlety and particularity, the appearance on a country road of two men seen in succession against the backdrop of a snow-fall. What is concluded from these unextraordinary events?

> The snow-feathers so gently swoop that though
>   But half an hour ago
> The road was brown, and now is starkly white,
> A watcher would have failed defining quite
>   When it transformed it so.

Not even the observer-poet, but just "a watcher" who "would have failed" if he had tried to do what nobody in fact has tried to do. To praise a line like the concluding one, with its single "it" doing the work of transformation—whenever it happened—on another "it," is to recognize Hardy's strange distinction as a poet. There is no one who writes in quite this way, nor is less likely to be eagerly imitated.

Even when the poem's "I" bears affiliations with the eighty-some year old man who wrote it, the presence is disengaged, almost spectral. Consider a poem from *Human Shows* with the promising Hardyan title "Nobody Comes":

> Tree-leaves labour up and down
>   And through them the fainting light
>   Succumbs to the crawl of night.
>   Outside in the road the telegraph wire
>   To the town from the darkening land
> Intones to travellers like a spectral lyre
>   Swept by a spectral hand.
>
> A car comes up, with lamps full-glare,
>   That flash upon a tree:
>   It has nothing to do with me,
> And whangs along in a world of its own,
>   Leaving a blacker air;
> And mute by the gate I stand again alone,
>   And nobody pulls up there.

We might remark that if somebody had pulled up there Hardy wouldn't have written a poem about it. Here is "The Darkling Thrush" twenty-four years later, without even the consolations a man might feel in at least imagining a thrush to be aware of some "blessed hope" he himself is not. In this late poem everything is depoetized: even the heightening at the end of the first stanza consequent upon the repetition of "spectral," and the anapestic lilt, give way to the passing car, so remote an intruder it may as well be characterized with a word Hardy uses only once in the *Complete*

Poems—"whangs." In his handbook Bailey softens the poem by suggesting that the man must be feeling "expectation, disappointment, and loneliness" after the car passes. But who is to say? Who can penetrate that "blacker air" or dare to ascribe a tone (sadness? wistful regret? stoic fortitude?) to "And nobody pulls up there"? "A watcher would have failed defining quite / When it transformed it so," and so must the watcher as reader fail to define quite—in the sense of an understanding, sympathetic comprehension—the feelings (if they can be said to be feelings) of this man alone. In "The Darkling Thrush" he was "unaware"; he is now "mute." It is hard to resist summoning up once more the voice of Rook: "Throughout the field I find no grain."

Hardy had hoped to publish his last volume on his 88th birthday but fell some months short of it, dying peacefully in January of 1928. In his introduction to *Winter Words* he tells us that it is probably his "last appearance on the literary stage" and that it would be "idle" to pretend he is excited about publishing these poems; still "the pieces themselves have been prepared with reasonable care, if not quite with the zest of a young man new to print." This lively tone also holds us at arm's length, lest we should be too zestful in applying fierce standards of excellence to the volume. Although Harold Bloom has claimed that it shows a sudden and dramatic recovery of Hardy's poetic powers, a look at the volume or volumes published prior to it reveals to me no heightening or diminishment of poetic quality in the final one.

When the poems in *Winter Words* deal most directly with other people they tend to be sensationally morbid in Hardy's blackly humorous way. In the dialogue "Her Second Husband Hears Her Story," a wife relates how she sewed up her drunken first husband in bed, so as to be safe from any possible amorous offerings. The husband consequently dies of a stroke, though whether that too was in her intent she will not say. " 'Well, it's a cool queer tale!' " says second husband gamely, perhaps taking thought for his own future. In "Henley Regatta" a young woman is first presented weeping that she will be unable to go to the Regatta because it is raining; years later, and another Regatta Day, she is "a Regatta quite her own":

> Inanely
> She laughs in the asylum as she floats
> Within a water-tub, which she calls 'Henley,'
> Her little paper boats.

And "The Mongrel" is a quite unbearable piece about how a man betrays his dog by tossing him to his death in the harbour so as to avoid paying the dog tax. There are no complications of feelings in these poems; they are strikingly effective, cruel exercises in "pessimism," and they mock their author's prose attempts to show that he was always above such things.

At the other extreme, but issuing from the same sensibility, are the "elemental" poems Hardy wrote all his life but never with quite the simplicity of statement he managed in old age. "Throwing a Tree," once thought to have been the last poem he wrote, does no more than lay down, in alternately rhymed anapests, the cutting down of a tree in the New Forest, concluding this way:

> . . . Reached the end of its long
> staying powers
> The tree crashes downward; it shakes all its
> neighbours throughout,
> And two hundred years' steady growth has been ended in less
> than two hours.

And what do you think of that? the poem seems to be content with saying. There is no statement, no "wisdom" into which the reader can move comfortably; nor does the poem's surface attempt to charm or engage us. That is part of what Hardy's final simplicity entails.

At his best in these last poems he does without self-consciousness what the young Hemingway was making his career out of doing at the same time (*A Farewell to Arms* and *Winter Words* were published but a year apart!). "An Unkindly May" is by any standards a slight poem; yet another thing Hardy's late work does is make us think twice about what is "slight" and how we can tell for sure. It is merely a poem of a few lines about bad weather in May—pigeons, rooks, vultures, flowers, and sheep all getting soaked. But it is framed, at beginning and end, by a couplet about a shepherd: beginning, "A shepherd stands by a gate in a white smock-frock, / He holds the gate ajar, intently counting his flock," and ending "That shepherd still stands in that white smock-frock, / Unnoting all things save the counting his flock." The wording, which could so easily have been cute, charming or clever, resolutely refuses to be any of them, and the shepherd remains.

Let us end where we began, with birds, and with the poet at his most impersonal, most elemental in his concerns:

> The thrushes sing as the sun is going,
> And the finches whistle in ones and pairs,
> And as it gets dark loud nightingales
> In bushes
> Pipe, as they can when April wears,
> As if all Time were theirs.

> These are brand-new birds of twelve-months' growing,
> Which a year ago, or less than twain,
> No finches were, nor nightingales,
>   Nor thrushes,
> But only particles of grain,
>   And earth, and air, and rain.

Here one notices the artful, subtle rhyme-pattern and appreciates how entire was Hardy's commitment to rhyme; yet we read the poems scarcely noticing the rhyming cement that holds them together in a central way. And as the "as if" moment of the first stanza is trumped once more by the deeply-stressed negatives of the second, ending up with an "only"—"only particles"—that leaves us to do what we will with the miracle of life and its evanescence, we can echo and extend Pound's comment on Hardy's poetry: "Now *there* is a clarity. There is the harvest of having written 20 novels first." "Proud Songsters," poem #816 in the *Complete Poems,* is the harvest of having written roughly 815 poems first.

On Hardy's Badnesses

SAMUEL HYNES

During the twenty years that Monroe Beardsley and I were colleagues, we collaborated on a number of projects, from a joint letter to the *Times Literary Supplement* to a book-length study of our college's policies. But there was one joint venture that we never managed to complete, though we talked about it a good deal. It was to be an essay on Poetic Badness, and we only got as far as some elaborate graphs (though Beardsley, being more energetic than I am, did, of course, write his fine lecture on bad poetry in *The Possibility of Criticism*). My remarks here might best be regarded as my tardy contribution to our abandoned project, one more speech in the long dialogue with Monroe Beardsley from which I have learned so much.

My subject is related to Beardsley's "Bad Poetry" lecture but is different. He dealt—as no doubt an aesthetician should—with the general theory of badness; and he used as his examples poems of such extreme ineptitude that some critics might hesitate to call them poems at all—works, for example, by Julia Moore, "The Sweet Singer of Michigan," and contributions to the *Poetry Anthology*, one of those vanity collections in which all the contributors are also subscribers. Whereas I mean to consider only one poet—and that one widely regarded as the greatest English poet of this century.

When you discuss the badness of a major poet, you are taking up a tender subject, as I know from experience. Twenty years ago I wrote a book on Hardy's poetry in which I rather stressed the fact (which seemed to me obvious) that not all of Hardy's poems are excellent. I have been scolded ever since for my lack of positive critical thinking, and by some of the weightiest of Hardy's admirers—by Philip Larkin, for instance, who "trumpeted" (his word) "the assurance that one reader at least would not wish Hardy's *Collected Poems* a single page shorter, and regards it as many times over the best body of poetic work this century so far has to show."[1] And the most recent survey of Hardy criticism is still complaining of my "unwillingness to endorse Hardy's greatness."[2] Still, I am unrepentant. I do not doubt that Hardy was a great poet, but I also think that he was peculiarly

Samuel Hynes, "On Hardy's Badnesses," in *Essays on Aesthetics / Perspectives on the Work of Monroe C. Beardsley*, ed., John Fisher (Philadelphia: Temple University Press, 1983), pp. 247–257. Copyright © Samuel Hynes, 1983. Reprinted by permission.

72

prone to write bad poems, and I see nothing irreverent or wrong in saying so: surely it is never the function of a critic simply to endorse greatness. "If way to the Better there be," Hardy wrote in a poem, "it exacts a full look at the Worst"; in his case, at least, that seems a reasonable position from which to begin a critical examination of his work.

A full look at the worst will not take us far, though, until we develop some ways of deciding which poems *are* the worst. On this basic question Hardy himself will be of no use at all, since he seems to have been entirely lacking in self-criticism. The *Collected Poems* show this lack very clearly: the book contains virtually every poem Hardy ever wrote, and there were no exclusions from later editions, no sober second thoughts. Apparently Hardy liked everything he wrote and kept it all (another evidence of that is the way, in his later years, he would dig up early poems and include them in his new collections). But more than that, Hardy seemed peculiarly unable to recognize what the unique, excellent, Hardy-ish qualities in his poems were. He did not often comment on his own works, but the judgments he did make were exceptionally fallible, and such poetic principles as one can abstract from his critical remarks are, when applied to Hardy's poems in general, usually wrong.

Consider, as examples, the following self-judgments. First, a remark on "When I Set Out for Lyonnesse": the poem, Hardy said in a letter, "showed something of the song-ecstasy that a lyric should have."[3] I am not entirely certain what "song-ecstasy" is, but Hardy must have meant the qualities of musicalness and strong feeling that have traditionally been associated with the word "lyric"; it is the sort of remark that you might find in any turn-of-the-century review of current poetry. Applied to "Lyonnesse," Hardy's remark does have a certain vague appropriateness, but he seems also to suggest that these are necessary conditions of lyric poetry. If that is true, then either most of Hardy's poems are not lyrics, or they are unsuccessful ones. But this is a point that Hardy evidently did not perceive, since he went on calling groups of his poems "Love Lyrics," "Lyrics and Reveries," and "Late Lyrics." That is, he seemed to go on believing that "song-ecstasy" defined a category to which most of his short poems belonged. And that is simply not the case.

Another example of his judgment comes from a letter to a friend, written in 1901 shortly after the publication of Hardy's first book of poems, *Wessex Poems*: "As you have been re-reading my books I shall ask you when I see you what you think of my opinion that 'Her Death and After' and 'The Dance at the Phoenix' . . . are two as good stories as I have ever told?"[4] Here Hardy is judging two of his poems simply as narratives; and, indeed, the two poems do have some of the characteristics of Hardy's short stories. But not many critics would argue that Hardy was an important, or even a very good, short-story writer, and it might well be argued that the qualities that these poems share with the prose stories are in fact weaknesses. This may seem paradoxical—after all, we are talking about a man who was a great novelist as well as a great poet—but it is nevertheless true: he was not good at short narrative, whether in prose or in verse; and he was if anything rather worse at versified narrative, simply because the verse form offered him opportunities for additional kinds of badness.

What these two self-judgments have in common is a conventional sense of what a poet is: he is a singer, and he is a storyteller. Much of Hardy's poetic energy went into performing these conventional roles, as a glance at *Collected Poems* will show; without the songs and the stories, it would be quite a slender—but marvelous—book. And he was also a conventional poet in other ways: he wrote many occasional poems—poems on the deaths of Queen Victoria, Swinburne, and Meredith, and war poems for both the Boer War and the First World War. He also wrote what one can only call "poetic" poems: poems that seem to exist mainly to show the poet's technical virtuosity (and which Hardy later labeled "Sapphics" and "Onomatopoeic" when critics overlooked his demonstrated skills). In all these instances, Hardy was behaving like a *poet*, as his generation understood the role (that, I take it, is what "conventional" means): this Hardy was not only the contemporary of Alfred Austin and William Watson; he was their fellow.

"What we really object to in a so-called 'bad' literary work," Beardsley wrote, "is a peculiarly incongruous combination of oversimplification and disorganization that is fatal to the integrity of the work."[5] I would argue that this sort of fatality occurs in Hardy's poems most commonly when he is conventionally and self-consciously being "the poet": in his narratives, in his public poems, and in his virtuoso pieces. This is not the common view of Hardy's poetic limitations; that view, indeed, takes the opposite position, that Hardy was worst when he was *least* conventionally poetic. Richard Ellmann, for example, writing recently in the *New York Times Book Review*, chides a critic for approving lines of Hardy's verse "that blend cliché and ineptitude." "The problem is crucial in Hardy," Ellmann continues: "He claimed to have been awkward to avoid being mellifluous, but other means of avoidance were possible. Awkwardness is in him sometimes a kind of inverted narcissism—see how unbeautiful I am!—and a serious impediment to articulation."[6] But it seems to me that Ellmann is here describing not Hardy's badness, but the central properties of his excellence: that the "narcissism" (which I would call "inwardness" or simply "privacy") creates the essential Hardy relation to reality, and that the "awkwardness," if it is an impediment to articulation, is a necessary impediment, and creates the essential Hardy relation to language.

We have here a provisional theory of Hardy's badness: let us test these propositions by looking at some bad poems. First, "My Cicely," a narrative that Hardy fancied enough to recommend as a poem for performance, stressing especially the sound effects. In the poem the speaker, who has thought his West Country sweetheart dead, learns that she is alive (it was someone else of the same name who died) and rides from London to Exeter to be reunited with her. He finds, however, that she has married beneath her and has become a barmaid; so he rides back to London and persuades himself that it really was his love who died. So much for the plot; here are a couple of stanzas to demonstrate the verse form:

> "Alive?"—And I leapt in my wonder,
>   Was faint of my joyance,
> And grasses and grove shone in garments
>   Of glory to me.

> "She lives, in a plenteous well-being,
>   Today as aforehand;
> The dead bore the name—though a rare one—
>   The name that bore she."

A reader with an attentive ear will notice that these two stanzas rhyme (so do the twenty-nine that follow, all on the same -*ee* sound), and that they are written in an elaborate and unusual meter: clearly "My Cicely" is one of Hardy's virtuoso pieces, as well as a narrative.

But what, exactly, is *bad* about "My Cicely"? Well, first of all it is a clear example of what Beardsley calls the disproportion of insensibility.[7] The speaker rejects his beloved because life has made her older and, to his mind, coarse; and this is a crude and inadequate response to the situation. At the end he acknowledges that some people think him odd for pretending that the living woman is the dead one, but the poem itself confirms his rejection:

> Frail-witted, illuded they call me;
>   I may be. Far better
> To dream than to own the debasement
>   Of sweet Cicely.

But it is not far better, and the poem, by saying so, reveals a fundamental lack of humanity. This is essentially a moral judgment of the poem, though Beardsley has tried to make it an aesthetic one by calling it "disproportion." Not being a philosopher, I do not share Beardsley's concern for philosophical tidiness, and I would prefer to keep the moral questions in moral terms: indeed, it seems to me necessary to keep in mind that one kind of poetical badness is *moral* badness.

But if "My Cicely" is a morally flawed poem, it is also bad in strictly aesthetic terms. One might employ a number of other Beardsley terms to give names to some of its most striking aesthetic weaknesses: "privative," "disruptive," "reductive," "too muchness," "too littleness"—the poem is guilty of all of these. It lacks metrical variety and interest, for instance; Hardy was proud of the way he had made the meters imitate the action of a galloping horse, but if you stop to think of it, galloping is a pretty monotonous rhythm, and that is what the poem has. It contains details that work against unity (the scenic and historical particulars along the route, for example, which Hardy thought enough of to illustrate in the first edition). It is oversimplified in its treatment of a complex human relationship. It contains too much geography, and too little feeling.

All of these failings would be flaws in any poem, but there is one other element in "My Cicely" that is a peculiarly Hardyan weakness: the poem enacts an *action*—the journey down, the meeting, the return—and Hardy simply could not do actions in poems. It was not a matter of being unable to control narrative movement in verse, but something more complex: an inability to find actions that would adequately express his sense of the world, an inability to make his actions symbolic. Why Hardy, whose novels move so powerfully and symbolically, should have been unable to do this in his verse I am not sure: it may have to do with the fact that he wrote virtually all of his poems after he had ended his novel-writing career; or that they are the poems of late-middle and old age (a time of retrospection and meditation, not of action); or that his philosophic understanding of the human situation had changed. But whatever the reason, the fact is clear: he could no longer shape causal, sequential actions into poems without reduction and distortion.

It would be easy to compile a substantial list of Hardy's narrative poems to support this conclusion: "Her Death and After," "The Dance at the Phoenix," "The Supplanter," "The Rash Bride," "The Vampirine Fair," "The Re-enactment," "The Satin Shoes," "The Turnip-Hoer," "The Bird-Catcher's Boy," "Burning the Holly"—examples leap to the mind. And they come from every one of Hardy's eight volumes of verse, for he never stopped writing narratives, and he never stopped writing bad ones.

On the other hand, it is extremely hard to find examples of really *good* narrative poems. Even those few excellent occasional poems in which you might reasonably expect action—poems like "The Convergence of the Twain," which is, after all, about the sinking of the *Titanic*, and the few good war poems (" 'And There Was a Great Calm,' " or "In Time of 'The Breaking of Nations' ")—are in fact meditative and static. The only exceptions to this general judgment are a few of his ballad-tragedies ("The Tramp-woman's Tragedy," "A Sunday Morning Tragedy"), where Hardy was sufficiently supported by a tradition to succeed.

Narrative verse, then—the poet-as-storyteller—is one kind of Hardy badness. Aggressive lyricism—the poet-as-singer—is another. The easiest way to explain what I mean by this category is simply to quote a few striking examples:

I've never gone to Donaghadee,
That vague far townlet by the sea;
In Donaghadee I shall never be:
Then why do I sing of Donaghadee,
That I know not in a faint degree?

Once engrossing Bridge of Lodi,
    Is thy claim to glory gone?
Must I pipe a palinody,
    Or be silent thereupon?

When up aloft
I fly and fly,
I see in pools
The shining sky,
And a happy bird
And I, am I![8]

These are all examples of sound effects that are awkward or monotonous or mechanical—effects that seem unmediated by Hardy's great poetic intelligence. Not that he was not an extraordinarily skillful metrist—he was: there are more than 700 different verse forms among his 900-odd poems, and most of them are handled with great finesse. But sometimes one feels a disjunction between the ostensible subject of the poem and the particular lyrical virtuosities that Hardy has hit upon (why *that* cadence, *that* rhyme-scheme for a poem about not going to Donaghadee?), and this disjunction is likely to be most apparent where the musical effects are most insistent. It often seems as though Hardy, having arbitrarily committed himself to an elaborate formal pattern, is determined to complete it, at whatever cost to other, more important elements in the poem: he is ostentatiously, publicly *being a poet* by striving for conventionally poetic effects that are contrary to his true gift.

I suggested, in commenting on Richard Ellmann's remarks, what I thought the true nature of that gift was: that it was a mode of inward discourse, an impeded, unmellifluous articulation of private feelings. The good poems are made of the two constituents of private experience: sense data and consciousness itself. Hardy was an acute and precise observer of the physical world, and especially of small-scale nature—insects, drops of water on a gate, a leaf falling—no doubt because the world he *saw* was all the reality that he was sure of. He took the recording of the actual as a central poetic act and would defend even a trivial poem with the argument that it had actually happened (as he did with "In the Days of Crinoline").[9] The great examples of this faith in the confirming authority of actuality are the poems concerned with the death of his first wife and his recollections of their life together—the "Poems of 1912–13" and related later poems. "I myself (naturally I suppose) like those best which are literally true" he wrote to a friend just after *Moments of Vision* was published, though he added that these poems "perhaps are quite unattractive to readers, and may have little literary merit."[10] But clearly, for this kind of private poetic act, attractiveness and literary merit were not considerations that troubled him.

One way to describe Hardy's best poems is to say that they are all spoken with a private voice. The teller of the tales is a storyteller; the voice of the poetical lyrics is a singer: in both cases a sort of public role is assumed. And so is an audience: telling and singing imply persons spoken or sung *to*. But the good, private Hardy poems address no one, except the self. And this is true even when Hardy is speaking in a voice not his own: when he speaks from a woman's point of view, for example, as he does in the fine "Bereft." In the universe of these poems, there are the particulars of nature, and there is a self, but there is nothing and no one else.

Often the essential poem seems to have pre-existed in actuality, a kind of *objet trouvée*, and Hardy's creative act has simply been the recording of it. He told his friend Edmund Gosse, for example, that the scene of "Autumn in King's Hintock Park" as he actually witnessed it was a poem, though he might not have gotten it down properly on paper, and he went on to describe exactly where it had taken place. In telling Gosse all this, Hardy was not simply identifying his source: clearly he believed that a poem's roots in actuality somehow sustained it.

But though the poems are rooted in the actual, they do not readily reveal its meaning: there are, as Ellmann observed, impediments. These reveal themselves in the articulation of the subject, but the causes are deeper than style. The best poems have a hovering mysteriousness about them. No doubt this is in part a consequence of the private nature of the discourse. Insofar as Hardy is expressing private feelings, he is naturally (given his nature and his time) reticent; insofar as he is addressing himself, he does not need to be explicit, since a mere glancing allusion to an occasion of suffering or loss will recover the whole experience: remembered pain, as any adult knows, is responsive to the slightest reference. But the mysteriousness is more than simply personal; it is in Hardy's world, which withholds the satisfactions of order and meaning—the impediment, that is, is *out there*. In Hardy's world, feelings exist, but they exist independently of meaning; the subjects of his poems are those feelings, including most prominently the feeling of the absence of meaning.

One further thing needs to be said about the good poems: they are not actions. They occur after the event—most often after an experience of loss—and what they are concerned with is not the experience itself (they are not narratives), but the states of mind that follow from, and endure, loss. I could offer many examples but will content myself with one minor one, not much noticed by Hardy's critics, but entirely characteristic.

The Division

Rain on the windows, creaking doors,
　　With blasts that besom the green,
And I am here, and you are there,
　　And a hundred miles between!

O were it but the weather, Dear,
　　O were it but the miles
That summed up all our severance,
　　There might be room for smiles.

But that thwart thing betwixt us twain,
　　Which nothing cleaves or clears,
Is more than distance, Dear, or rain,
　　And longer than the years!

"The Division" is a modest, minor poem, but it contains the elements of Hardy's best work—for example, the 1912–13 elegies. It says, as elegies do say, that loss is one condition of existence, and the impossibility of doing anything about it is another. And that is *all* it says. It has nothing to say about the questions that might reasonably occur to one, given the situation: What caused the division? What can be done about it? That is, it is not concerned with action, with the place of the poem's situation in a narrative line. Nor is it concerned with consolation: it simply expresses the feelings appropriate to irrecoverable loss, as a condition of human existence.

　"The Division" is not a particularly awkward poem, but it is nevertheless an "impeded" one. It says very little, it is not vividly metaphorical, and its language seems strained without being "poetic"—as though the poet had to make do with a small and randomly selected vocabulary, not especially appropriate to the occasion. It has, you might say, a slightly strangulated quality: it is working as hard at *not* saying things as most poems do at being eloquent. In all of these ways, it is a representative *good* Hardy poem.

　And how do the good poems relate to Hardy's *bad* poems? I can think of a number of possible theories of the relationship. You might say that in the world of poetry, as in the world of morals, badness is a corruption of goodness, and that Hardy's bad poems simply show a misuse of his gifts. Or you might say that goodness is a transformation of badness—that Hardy managed somehow to raise what were essentially the wrong principles to excellence. Neither of these in fact seems to me to describe Hardy's case. It comes nearer the mark to say that in his work badness is an absence of goodness, a *departure* from his true gifts. Certainly it is true that the essential properties of privacy, mystery, and impeded articulation are lacking in the really bad poems, though you could put this the other way round, too, and say that the properties of storytelling and song are missing from the good poems.

The point, clearly, is that Hardy was two poets. One believed that poetry is an imitation of poetry, that it takes public and conventional forms, that it is, in short, *literature*. When Hardy wrote in this mode, when he consciously attached himself to the literary high culture of his time and became the Last Victorian, he was a bad poet: not just relatively unsuccessful, but awful. The other poet took poetry to be an ordinary but private activity, like meditation, or day-dreaming, or despair. This poet had no audience, and no immediate precursors: he wrote in an English tradition, but I think largely unconsciously, drawing on folk poetry and hymnology and the Bible, and on the natural world, as other English poets had done before him, but not for literary ends, not to be a *poet*. His great precursors were anon., Hodge, and God.

The poems of the public, literary Hardy are mostly bad poems. They withhold nothing: indeed, they often give us more information, and a fuller interpretation of themselves, than we want ("My Cicely" is a dire example). The poems of the private Hardy, the good poems, tell us almost nothing: like life, they frustrate our desire for explanation. The bad poems have plots; the good ones (like "The Division") suggest nonexistent plots, but withhold them. There is a difference of reference, then, a different sense of "aboutness" in good and in bad poems. The aboutness of the bad poems is likely to be a story, or sometimes poetry itself; the good poems are about states too vague, or too impeded, to be paraphrased.

To say all these rude and negative things about Hardy's bad poems is not to say—as Larkin seemed to fear—that one wishes all the bad ones destroyed. Far from it: Hardy would not be Hardy without his bad side; it explains much about him and his ambitions, and by contrast it illuminates the private consciousness out of which the good poems came. Hardy was right: a full look at the Worst *is* necessary. He did not mean that phrase as a critical principle, but it will do for his case.

Notes

1. Philip Larkin, "Wanted: Good Hardy Critic," *Critical Quarterly* 8 (1966): 179.

2. Richard H. Taylor, "Thomas Hardy: A Reader's Guide," in *Thomas Hardy: The Writer and His Background*, ed. Norman Page (London, 1980), p. 255.

3. Viola Meynell, ed., *Friends of a Lifetime: Letters to Sydney Carlyle Cockerell* (London, 1940), p. 285.

4. W. M. Parker, "Hardy's Letters to Sir George Douglas," *English* 14 (1963): 221.

5. Monroe C. Beardsley, *The Possibility of Criticism* (Detroit, 1970), p. 110.

6. Richard Ellmann, "The Story of Modern Poetry," *New York Times Book Review* (27 April 1980), p. 34.

7. Beardsley, *The Possibility of Criticism*, p. 102.

8. The poems quoted are "Donaghadee," "The Bridge of Lodi," and "The Robin."

9. C. Day-Lewis, "The Lyrical Poetry of Thomas Hardy," *Proceedings of the British Academy* 37 (1953): 163.

10. Letter to Florence Henniker, dated 7 February 1918; in Evelyn Hardy and F. B. Pinion, eds., *One Rare Fair Woman* (London, 1972), p. 179.

HARDY AND OTHER POETS

♦

The Influence of Shelley

FRANK B. PINION

It is no exaggeration to say that Shelley's influence on Hardy's thought and basic outlook was greater than that of any other writer. Philosophical views which scholars commonly ascribe to later writers such as Schopenhauer and von Hartmann had become convictions for Hardy in the mid-1860s when he read Shelley with enthusiastic assiduity in London. In his poetry he found an exhilarating freedom and intellectual intrepidity, a scientific view of the universe consistent with Darwinism, and principles for social reform which were to make him sympathetic to much in the writings of Comte and later philosophers. Shelley's ideas helped enormously to free Hardy from the shackles of convention.

He was enraptured by Shelley's lyricism, and in his later years described him as "our most marvellous lyrist." Some of Shelley's imagery was appropriated by Hardy's creative imagination, but his influence on Hardy's poetic style was negligible compared with that of Browning's dramatic and lyrical use of speech idiom in verse. Not surprisingly, when Hardy was on holiday in central Italy in 1887, Shelley and Browning, though so different "in their writings, their mentality, and their lives," mingled in his thoughts "almost to the exclusion of other English poets equally, or nearly so, associated with Italy, with whose works he was just as well acquainted."

Nothing concerning Shelley was too insignificant for Hardy's interest. He told his secretary Miss O'Rourke that he was the poet whom above all others he wished to have met, and many Shelleyan quotations and allusions are to be found in his works. Even before he left Dorset for London in 1862, Hardy had been impressed by Walter Bagehot's essay on Shelley in his *Estimates* of 1858 (afterwards entitled *Literary Studies*). Much later, his romantic interest in the poet was renewed and extended by Edward Dowden's *Life of Shelley* (1886). From Geneva in June 1897 he informed Mrs Henniker that he "thought of going this afternoon to try to find the cottage in which Shelley and Mary lived, a little way below Byron's 'Campagne Diodate' (*vide*

Frank B. Pinion, "The Influence of Shelley," *Thomas Hardy: Art and Thought*, Chapter Thirteen (London: Macmillan, 1977), pp. 148–157. Copyright © Macmillan, England, 1977. Reprinted by permission. A few minor revisions have been made by the author and incorporated in this reprinting of the original essay.

Dowden's *Shelley*)." His own *Life* shows how he loved to think that, when he and his mother travelled in his boyhood to her sister's at Hatfield, they had stayed in the room at the Cross Keys, Clerkenwell, which was occupied by Shelley when he met Mary Godwin there at week-ends. They were married at St Mildred's, Bread Street, to which Hardy took his friend Sir George Douglas in 1899 to see their signatures in the register; he had been there before, he adds parenthetically. In the story "An Imaginative Woman" he compares a poet's scribbling on the wallpaper to Shelley's manuscript scraps; in the Apology to *Late Lyrics and Earlier* he refers to his love of sailing paper boats. His visit to the graves of Shelley and Keats in Rome inspired one poem, and the knowledge that Shelley composed "To a Skylark" at Leghorn led him to write "Shelley's Skylark" when he was near Leghorn in March 1887.

Hardy's poem is on a more pedestrian level, but it recalls the "ecstatic heights in thought and rhyme" of Shelley's poem. Believing with St John that "the truth shall make you free," Hardy recognized in Shelley a fellow-spirit. The implications of "To a Skylark" had been revealed in *Prometheus Unbound*: the freedom of man would come with enlightenment and love. The bird is

> Like a Poet hidden
>   In the light of thought,
> Singing hymns unbidden,
>   Till the world is wrought
> To sympathy with hopes and fears it heeded not.

If only the Poet of Liberty, as Hardy called him in *Jude*, had the joy and inspiration of the skylark, the world would listen to his message. Thinking of the "poet" as a man of vision (writer, artist, or legislator), Shelley wrote:

> The most unfailing herald, companion, and follower of the awakening of a great people to work a beneficial change in opinion or institution, is poetry. . . . Poets are the unacknowledged legislators of the world.

"If you mean to make the world listen to you, you must say now what they will all be thinking and saying five and twenty years hence: and if you do that you must offend your conventional friends," Hardy advised his author-friend Mrs Henniker in 1893.[1]

In London Hardy's Shelleyan fervour helped to kindle his political and revolutionary zeal. In 1865 he listened to a political speech from J. S. Mill, whose treatise *On Liberty* he knew "almost by heart." The following year he was intoxicated by the word-magic and passionate revolt of Swinburne's poetry. By the end of 1867 he had completed the first draft of *The Poor Man and the Lady*; it was a sweeping dramatic satire of the squirearchy and nobility, London society, the vulgarity of the middle class, modern Christianity, church-restoration, and political and domestic morals in general, the author's views, in fact, being obviously those of a young man with a passion for reforming the world— those of many a young man before and after him; the tendency of the writing being socialistic, not to say revolutionary.

Yet it was Shelley's (and Swinburne's) fearless attack on the blind or tyrannical Power to whom responsibility was attributed for the cruelty of Nature and the plight of man which made the greatest and most lasting impact on Hardy. In *The Revolt of Islam* winter represents the hardships suffered by man which Shelley believed could be removed or alleviated by revolution and enlightenment. From the euphoric vision of this poem—best summed up in the closing lines of "Ode to the West Wind":

> Be through my lips to unawakened earth
> The trumpet of a prophecy! O, Wind,
> If Winter comes, can Spring be far behind?

—comes the wintry imagery in Hardy which connotes man's trials, setbacks, and tribulations. "Crass Casualty" or "the Frost's decree" can be mitigated by science and enlightenment, by co-operation and "loving-kindness," but there is much in it which is subject to natural law and seemingly inevitable.

In the face of adversity, Shelley counsels "Gentleness, Virtue, Wisdom, and Endurance":

> To suffer woes which Hope thinks infinite;
> To forgive wrongs darker than death or night;
>   To defy Power, which seems omnipotent;
> To love, and bear; to hope till Hope creates
> From its own wreck the thing it contemplates;
>   Neither to change, nor falter, nor repent;
> This, like thy glory, Titan, is to be
> Good, great and joyous, beautiful and free;
> This is alone Life, Joy, Empire, and Victory.[2]

For Hardy the essence of this is synonymous with the spirit of Christian "charity" (which involves long-suffering); he embodies it in Tess, not absolutely but humanly, as far as circumstances and probability allow. More dramatically *Prometheus Unbound* exemplifies the power of love in the salvation of mankind. Influenced also by Comte's stress on altruism to the same end, Hardy says in "A Plaint to Man" that a brighter future depends

> On the human heart's resource alone,
> In brotherhood bonded close and graced
> With loving-kindness . . .

In this way the will of mankind, by being part of the "general"[3] or Immanent Will, could, Hardy dared to hope at the end of *The Dynasts*, do something to make "the Cause of Things" conscious of suffering in a Darwinian and irrational world.

There can be little doubt that Hardy was influenced by the form as well as the spirit of *Prometheus Unbound*. Its chorus of spirits "From the depths of the sky and the ends of the earth" suggested the aerial spirits of *The Dynasts*, though Hardy gave them roles more distinct and diversified in accordance with his own modes of thought and feeling. One of Shelley's choruses presents the "Gentle guides and guardians . . . of heaven-oppressed mortality," and in them Hardy's Spirit of the Pities may be seen. More often they appear as the flower of man's intelligence, like the Chorus at the end of Part First of *The Dynasts*. They come

> from the mind
> Of human kind
> Which was late so dusk, and obscene, and blind,

representing man's highest Thought, Wisdom, Art, and Science. Hardy's Shade of the suffering Earth has its obvious original in Shelley's lyrical drama, and the Fore Scene of *The Dynasts* echoes a Shelleyan note when the Chorus of Pities sings to aerial music:

> We would establish those of kindlier build,
> In fair Compassions skilled . . .
> Those, too, who love the true, the excellent,
> And make their daily moves a melody.

In *Prometheus Unbound*, and elsewhere in Shelley, music and musical imagery reflect happiness and the ideal; and it is in accordance with this that Hardy's Spirit of the Pities avers:

> Things mechanized
> By coils and pivots set to foreframed codes
> Would, in a thorough-sphered melodic rule,
> And governance of sweet consistency,
> Be cessed no pain.

The chorus and semi-choruses of *Hellas*, Shelley's second lyrical drama on the subject of human liberation, also affected the form of *The Dynasts*. Perhaps its final expression of uncertain hope weighed with Hardy when he chose to end his epic drama more hopefully than history (or the Spirit of the Years) warranted.

Important though *The Revolt of Islam* and *Prometheus Unbound* are in the development of Hardy's thought, it is doubtful if either affected him quite as much as *Queen Mab* and its extensive notes, completed by Shelley at the age of twenty, and the repository of most of his philosophical and revolutionary thought. Here, like Hardy's "Cause of Things," Nature is represented as neutral or amoral, loveless and hateless. She is referred to as the "mother," as happens frequently in Hardy's poetry, and more significantly (on the score of influence) in his first published novel, *Desperate Remedies*. As in *Tess of the d'Urbervilles*, one of the images illustrating the ruthlessness of Nature in Shelley's poem is the "ceaseless frost" of the Polar regions (viii, 58–69).

Among the notes to *Queen Mab* which Hardy must have read with approval, the following are of special importance:

1. On the plurality of worlds and the immensity of the universe, which make it inconceivable that the Spirit pervading "this infinite machine" (cf. *The Dynasts*) "begat a son upon the body of a Jewish woman" (cf. "Panthera"); "or is angered at the consequences of that necessity" (natural law throughout the universe), "which is a synonym of itself."

2. Necessity as "an immense and uninterrupted chain of causes and effects, no one of which could occupy any other place than it does occupy, or act in any other place than it does act." "Motive is to voluntary action in the human mind what cause is to effect in the material universe. The word liberty, as applied to mind, is analogous to the word chance as applied to matter: they spring from an ignorance of the certainty of the conjunction of antecedents and consequents."

   Although the general evidence confirms Hardy's belief in a "modicum of free will,"[4] Shelley's statement admirably elucidates what Hardy implies when he says that we are "bond-servants to Chance" or subject to the "whimsical god . . . known as blind Circumstance." "Circumstance" includes personal as well as external factors; motivation depends on character, and character (to some extent) on heredity (cf. Hardy's poem "The Pedigree").

3. On marriage. Shelley's views seem more relevant to Hardy than those of Milton in *The Doctrine and Discipline of Divorce*:

   i. "Love withers under constraint: its very essence is liberty: it is compatible neither with obedience, jealousy, nor fear; it is there most pure, perfect, and unlimited, where its votaries live in confidence, equality, and unreserve." Hardy's familiarity with this passage was due primarily to Bagehot's essay on Shelley.[5] Similar views may be seen in his poems "The Ivy-Wife" and "At a Hasty Wedding." Pre-eminently they are voiced by Sue Bridehead, who is afraid that the "iron contract" of marriage will extinguish tenderness, and abhors the thought of being "licensed to be loved on the premises." Hardy found its best expression in the words of Thomas Campbell:

> Can you keep the bee from ranging
> Or the ring-dove's neck from changing?
> No! nor fetter'd Love from dying
> In the knot there's no untying.

ii. "A husband and wife ought to continue so long united as they love each other: any law which should bind them to cohabitation for one moment after the decay of their affection would be a most intolerable tyranny, and the most unworthy of toleration." This applies to the marriage of Grace Melbury and Fitzpiers, and much more explicitly to that of Phillotson and Sue Bridehead.

iii. "Has a woman obeyed the impulse of unerring nature;—society declares war against her . . .; theirs is the right of persecution, hers the duty of endurance." Hardy's sympathy with this view is clear in "The Christening."

His association of the iris or rainbow image with love and hope was reinforced by Shelley. In *Prometheus Unbound* (I. 708–722) the rainbow arch suggests love and self-sacrifice, after storm and disaster at sea; in *Hellas* (43) Shelley refers to Hope's "iris of delight." Two related images in "Epipsychidion" also find their place in Hardy. The first is proverbial:

> This truth is that deep well, whence sages draw
> The unenvied light of hope.

Phillotson had often drawn from it, but to the boy Jude it appeared "from his present position" (both literal and allegorical) like "a long circular perspective ending in a shining disk." In the next lines (186–9) Shelley describes this world as a "garden ravaged" or "wilderness." It is a favourite image with Hardy, harking back to Eden, and to Hamlet's

> How weary, stale, flat, and unprofitable
> Seem to me all the uses of this world!
> Fie on't! Ah, fie! 'tis an unweeded garden,
> That grows to seed; things rank and gross in nature
> Possess it merely.

It is seen at Talbothays when Tess, her young life blighted, is drawn to Angel. Through the mediation of Swinburne it finds a place in *Desperate Remedies* and, in association with the onset of winter, following the lead of Shelley in "The Sensitive Plant," it leaves a trail of significant images in

Hardy's novels and poetry. [When Cytherea's helplessness in the circumstances that compelled her marriage struck her, she stood with Manston in
a meadow by "the fragment of a hedge—all that remained of a 'wet old
garden'— . . . It was overgrown, and choked with mandrakes, and she
could almost fancy she heard their shrieks." In *Far from the Madding Crowd*
when Bathsheba discovers Troy's treachery she leaves home and wakes up
by a swamp dotted with fungi and rotting tree-stumps; with the red and
yellow leaves in her lap Hardy reminds us of Shelley's "Ode to the West
Wind." Late autumn and winter draw on apace, and soon she is left to
ponder "what a gift life used to be." Eustacia Vye attempts her escape from
Egdon Heath on a night of funeral gloom when she is full of a sense of the
injustice of her lot. It is November, and she stumbles over "twisted furze-
roots, tufts of rushes, or oozing lumps of fleshy fungi, which at this season
lay scattered about the heath like the rotten liver and lungs of some colossal
animal." In the woods, when all goes ill for Grace Melbury, the scene is
more Darwinian, but fallen leaves, bright fungi, and rotting stumps confront
her. These passages suggest that Hardy had adopted Shelley's imagery, and
was in danger of resorting to it almost automatically.]

Three of his last four novels suggest that Hardy came to realize the
hazards of Shelleyanism in practice. However much one may agree in principle with Shelley on love and marriage, one can never forget the tragic death
of the wife Harriet whom he deserted. Imagine a sensualist romantically
exalted by the Platonics of "Epipsychidion," and led on by the Vision or the
Idea into philandering and infidelities, and you have someone like Fitzpiers.
Basically, but less ideally, he is moulded on the theme of "Alastor or the
Spirit of Solitude." Like the youth of Shelley's poem, he is "conversant with
speculations of the sublimest and most perfect natures"; and "the vision in
which he embodies his own imaginations unites all of wonderful, or wise,
or beautiful, which the poet, the philosopher, or the lover could depicture."[6]
Fitzpiers in his solitude at Hintock reads widely, his mind passing "in a
grand solar sweep through the zodiac of the intellectual heaven" in the course
of a year. He is unpractical, a dabbler in science and medicine; and he has
no roots in the country. In such circumstances, Hardy writes:

> A young man may dream of an ideal friend . . . but some humour of the
> blood will probably lead him to think rather of an ideal mistress, and at
> length the rustle of a woman's dress, the sound of her voice, or the transit of
> her form across the field of his vision, will enkindle his soul with a flame that
> blinds his eyes.

The self-centred seclusion of Shelley's idealist brings its "alastor" or retribution. When he seeks to find the veiled maid of his vision, a companion
of similar intelligence to his own, "a prototype of his conception," he is
disappointed and dies an early death. Unlike the youth of "Alastor," Fitzpiers

is a man of corrupted feelings, a dilettante humbug who knows all the
virtues of Schleiermacher, tries to flatter Grace by saying that she practises
all of them unconsciously, but is incapable of observing any of them himself.
In accordance with the idealism of "Epipsychidion," he pursues the shadow
of the idol of his thought (the "prototype of his conception") from woman
to woman, and adopts an irresponsible, Shelleyan attitude towards marriage:

> I never was attached to that great sect,
> Whose doctrine is, that each one should select
> Out of the crowd a mistress or a friend,
> And all the rest, though fair and wise, commend
> To cold oblivion, though it is in the code
> Of modern morals, and the beaten road
> Which those poor slaves with weary footsteps tread,
> By the broad highway of the world, and so
> With one chained friend, perhaps a jealous foe,
> The dreariest and the longest journey go.

In Shelleyan theory "nothing exists but as it is perceived."[7] "Human
love is a subjective thing," so that it is very much a matter of chance on
whom the "rainbow iris" is projected, Fitzpiers tells Giles Winterborne,
after quoting a verse on his Vision from *The Revolt of Islam* (II. xxiii): "She
moved upon this earth a shape of brightness. . . ." Grace Melbury first
appears to him as a vision, her image being reflected in a mirror as he
momentarily wakes. Later he wonders whether he has seen this "lovely form"
in a dream, or whether he could have been awake. "I fancied in my vision
that you stood there," he tells her when she returns; "I thought, what a
lovely creature! The design is for once carried out. Nature has at last recovered
her lost union with the Idea!" Despite his rainbow iris theory, he is "enchanted enough" to "fancy" that the Idea or Platonic ideal had found its
"objective substance" in her when he goes to the Hintock wood on Midsummer Eve, ironically to end the night on a haycock with Suke Damson. After
his marriage to Grace, the Idea takes this Tannhäuser to Felice Charmond,
and he murmurs lines from "Epipsychidion" as he goes:

> . . . towards the lodestar of my one desire,
> I flitted, like a dizzy moth, whose flight
> Is as dead leaf's in the owlet light.

The search for the Idea in one woman after another is presented both
tragically and sarcastically in *The Woodlanders*; in the lighter fantasy of *The
Well-Beloved* it is viewed for the most part in a comic light. The form the
story took owed much to "the remark of a sculptor that he had often pursued
a beautiful ear, nose, chin, etc., about London in omnibuses and on foot."[8]

The sculptor Jocelyn Pierston is neither selfish nor sensual like Fitzpiers. He is a victim of the Vision, the "migratory, elusive idealization he called his Love" having "flitted from human shell to human shell an indefinite number of times" before taking up its abode in the first Avice when he is a young man of twenty. "A young man of forty," and still a "young man" at sixty, he falls in love with her daughter, and then her grand-daughter. The *reductio ad absurdum* comes when, deciding to confide in the latter, he tells her his past, and she asks whether he had been in love with her great-grandmother. Jocelyn suddenly becomes old; the Vision of the Well-Beloved and his artistic sense abandon him, never to return. After a marriage of convenience, he turns to utilitarian occupations for the benefit of the local community. Hardy described the novel as a tragi-comedy; Edmund Gosse, as "The Tragedy of a Nympholept." The title-page quotation "One shape of many names" comes from *The Revolt of Islam* (I. xxvii), where it refers to "the Spirit of evil"; and Pierston maintains that he is under a "curse" or "doom" as long as he is lured on by the "Jill-o'-the-wisp" Idea. Nevertheless, Hardy does not seem to have taken the story very seriously in human terms. His most positive statement suggests a rather allegorical significance: "There is, of course, underlying the fantasy followed by the visionary artist the truth that all men are pursuing a shadow, the Unattainable, and I venture to hope that this may redeem the tragi-comedy from the charge of frivolity."[9]

The inadequacy of the Shelleyan lover is presented in Angel Clare. Whether his name alludes to Arnold's description of Shelley as "a beautiful and ineffectual angel, beating in the void his luminous wings in vain" is doubtful, but his love for Tess is "imaginative and ethereal" rather than real. "She was no longer the milkmaid, but a visionary essence. . . . He called her Artemis, Demeter . . ."; and he regards her as the embodiment of "rustic innocence." As soon as he finds the "vision" of her "mocked by appearances," he is overcome by an antipathy which "warps" his soul. His love had been "ethereal to a fault, imaginative to impracticability. With these natures, corporeal presence is sometimes less appealing than corporeal absence; the latter creating an ideal presence that conveniently drops the defects of the real." Similarly Jocelyn Pierston finds that he loves the first Avice when she is "dead and inaccessible as he had never loved her in life." The most apposite criticism of Angel Clare from Hardy is implied in his note of 28 November 1891, when he may well have had the subject of *The Well-Beloved* in mind:

> It is the incompleteness that is loved, when love is sterling and true. This is what differentiates the real one from the imaginary, the practicable from the impossible, the Love who returns the kiss from the Vision that melts away. A man sees the Diana or the Venus in his Beloved, but what he loves is the difference.

Yet, whatever reservations Hardy formed on some of Shelley's principles and imaginative flights, he never ceased to admire his poetry and spirit. He had a tendency to think in terms of Shelley's imagery. It is noticeable in his earliest fiction and in his last (for the influence of 'When the lamp is shattered' on "Neutral Tones," see my book *Hardy the Writer,* 1990, pp. 278–81). *"Cold reason"* comes back to *"mock"* Tess after she has answered some of her friends with superiority, on her return from The Slopes; when Angel turns against her, his propensities are as *"dead leaves* upon the tyrannous *wind* of his imaginative ascendency." To Pierston, when he is subject to his "gigantic fantasies," the sight of the new *moon,* "representing one who, by her so-called *inconstancy,* acted up to his own idea of a migratory Well-Beloved, made him feel as if his wraith in a changed sex had suddenly looked over the horizon at him."

Nowhere is Hardy's imagining in Shelleyan terms more important than in *Jude the Obscure,* and the reason is not far to seek. Hardy had become a victim of the Vision; he had met and fallen, imaginatively at least, in love with Mrs Henniker. They were, he felt, kindred spirits. He discovers that they have been reading "Epipsychidion" at the same time, and is certain it must have happened by "mutual influence." He then regrets that she "who is pre-eminently the child of the Shelleyan tradition" has "allowed herself to be enfeebled to a belief in ritualistic ecclesiasticism," and tells her that he must "trust to imagination only for an enfranchised woman." This imaginary woman he depicted in Sue Bridehead; she is the "prototype of his conception." Her ideas on convention and the First Cause are Hardy's, and she shocks Jude when he is training to become a curate. Her ideas on marriage are Shelley's, as has been noted. In the end, disaster gets the better of her reason, and she becomes a slave to "ritualistic ecclesiasticism." When Jude falls in love with her, he feels it is a cruel chance that "the one affined soul he had ever met was lost to him, through his marriage." Sue is "nearer to him than any other woman he had ever met, and he could scarcely believe that time, creed, or absence would ever divide him from her." That is how, at first, Hardy, unhappily married, felt towards Mrs Henniker. He thinks of her in terms recalling Shelley's worship of his "Seraph of Heaven." When he tells her that she is of that "ethereal intangible sort which letters cannot convey," the creative influence of "Epipsychidion" is evident:

> She met me, Stranger, upon life's rough way,
>   . . . An antelope,
> In the suspended impulse of its lightness,
> Were less aetherially light; the brightness
> Of her divinest presence trembles through
> Her limbs . . .

Hardy's imaginative idealization of Florence Henniker[10] is transferred to Jude, and the following passage (III. ix) could be autobiographical in almost every respect:

> Looking at his loved one as she appeared to him now, in his tender thought the sweetest and most disinterested comrade that he had ever had, living largely in vivid imaginings, so ethereal a creature that her spirit could be seen trembling through her limbs, he felt heartily ashamed of his earthliness . . . There was something rude and immoral in thrusting these recent facts of his life upon the mind of one who, to him, was so uncarnate as to seem at times impossible as a human wife to any average man.

In comparison, the quoting of "Epipsychidion" by Sue with reference to herself (IV. v) is factitious; but the conception of her here and elsewhere as an "aerial being" is typical of Hardy's heightened imagining under the influence of Shelley's poetry, and not inappropriate to Fitzpiers or Pierston.

Notes

1. *The Collected Letters of Thomas Hardy, Vol. II, 1893–1901* (Oxford: Clarendon Press, 1982), p. 33.
2. *Prometheus Unbound*, IV. 562, 570–78.
3. See the poem "He Wonders About Himself."
4. The question of free will or "liberty, as applied to mind" seems insoluble. Necessity for Shelley is the scientific principle of cause-effect. He states that if man were omniscient and could see all cause-effects ("the conjunction of antecedents and consequents"), he would not think in terms of chance. Hardy would have agreed with this, and he sometimes uses the terms "Law," "Necessity," and "necessitation" in ways which seem to approximate Shelley's absolutism. Natural law includes heredity, but man, when not swayed by prejudices and passions, is capable of reflecting and making rational decisions, and it is in this sense that Hardy refers to man's "modicum of free will." If he had not believed in its existence, he could not have held out hope of human progress. The Apology to *Late Lyrics and Earlier* (1922) contains his most important passages on this question, and it was written later than his less qualified statements on the Rule of Necessity (see F. E. Hardy, *The Life of Thomas Hardy*, London and New York, 1962, 337, and H. Orel, *Thomas Hardy's Personal Writings*, Lawrence, Kans., 1966, and London, 1967, 145–6).
5. See Walter Bagehot, *Literary Studies*, Vol. I (London, 1902), p. 252.
6. From the Preface to "Alastor."
7. Hardy had read this more than once in Bagehot's essay on Shelley, op. cit., p. 270.
8. Evelyn Hardy and F. B. Pinion (eds.), *One Rare Fair Woman, Thomas Hardy's Letters to Florence Henniker, 1893–1922*, London and Coral Gables, Fla., 1972, 66.
9. *Life*, 286.
10. Hardy wanted to name the heroine of *Jude* after Florence Henniker (cf. ORFW. 31), and did, rather surreptitiously (III. vii, iv. ii).

"Dover Beach," Hardy's Version

JAMES PERSOON

The Thomas Hardy who was once praised by critics for his keen observations of nature is being replaced by the Thomas Hardy whose keen eye was often reading a book. On a mission to place himself in a poetic tradition, this new Thomas Hardy writes poems imitative of Milton, Keats, Shelley, and Wordsworth in an attempt to show himself at the end of a line of investigation. In his echoes and borrowings from his poetic forefathers he invariably "completes" earlier poems, often reversing them entirely, to reflect the new truths closing out the old beliefs and old poems of a previous age. This thesis has been argued in several articles on Hardy and gives a new interpretation to his oft-quoted admonition to Robert Graves that all we can do is to write on the old themes, in the old forms (Casagrande, Giordano, Grundy, Persoon). Hardy's comment to Graves—disingenuous to the extent that he changed the old themes—at the same time reminds us of the care he took in studying those themes as a source for his poetry.

Hardy's arguments were never with straw men: he took on the greatest of those whom he thought were behind the times, especially if they lived in his own time. Browning and Tennyson are often targets, sometimes in the same poem, as when in "A Sign-Seeker" Hardy argues with both "Cleon" and *In Memoriam*. But there is an obvious name missing from this short list of eminent Victorian poets whom Hardy felt it necessary to correct: where is Matthew Arnold?

Arnold may have escaped in part because Hardy approved of his attempt to modernize religion by preserving its poetry but purging its literalisms. Hardy first met Arnold at a London dinner in February 1880 and, as his literary notebooks show, began reading widely Arnold's essays during the next several years, snapping up works as soon as they appeared; a passage copied from "Pagan and Mediaeval Religious Sentiment" on "the modern spirit" became central to his next novel, *A Laodicean* (Millgate 208–9, 246). In his extensive "Apology to Late Lyrics and Earlier" Hardy echoes Arnoldian ideas in apparent agreement. But the Hardy who summed up Browning's character as "smug Christian optimism worthy of a dissenting grocer" could

James Persoon, " 'Dover Beach,' Hardy's Version," *Victorian Newsletter*, No. 74 (Fall, 1988), pp. 27–30. Copyright © *Victorian Newsletter*, 1988. Reprinted by permission.

be equally dismissive of Arnold: in a notebook entry for October 7, 1888, commenting on *Literature and Dogma*, Hardy writes "When dogma has to be balanced on its feet by such hair-splitting as the late Mr. M. Arnold's it must be in a very bad way" (*Life* 224). Clearly Arnold's poems do not escape parody or reversal simply because of a general sympathy of ideas. Where, then, is Hardy's poetic response to Arnold?

Hardy read widely but idiosyncratically. In his responses to Milton and Tennyson he took on their best known work, correcting the theology of *Paradise Lost* and finding the comfort of *In Memoriam* too easily won from too little evidence. In the case of Browning, however, the poem Hardy referred to most, quoting from it in seven separate works, "The Statue and the Bust," has never been of central importance to anyone but Hardy. By far the most widely read poem of Arnold's today is "Dover Beach," though that was not so during his own or Hardy's lifetime. Hardy, however, nicely anticipating modern preferences, in his own copies of Arnold's poetry made "Dover Beach" one of only two poems annotated in any way. Significantly, the other annotation, on "Tristram and Iseult," he used in his play *The Queen of Cornwall*. An additional reason to look to "Dover Beach," besides modern interest in the poem and the fact of Hardy's annotation, is that its topic guarantees Hardy's interest—religious belief. A poem like "The Statue and the Bust," with its theme of wasted chances and lost love also guaranteed Hardy's interest. But where Browning's theme invited quoting, Arnold's would invite correction.

If one looks for verbal echoes to "Dover Beach," they are hard to find, leading one to accept Carl Weber's conclusion that Arnold is quoted for his ideas, not his poetic phrasing (Weber 245). "Darkling" is the single word to have been seized on to link "Dover Beach" to Hardy. The link is of course to the commonly anthologized "The Darkling Thrush," and a case has been made that the mood of the two is very close (Paulin 151). If one looks at the ideas of "Dover Beach," an argument can be made for a poem which looks and sounds very little like Arnold's but does indeed echo its theme— "A Cathedral Facade at Midnight," in which the creeping moonlight in a church seems to signal "the ancient faith's rejection / Under the sure, unhasting, steady stress / Of Reason's movement" (Bailey 504).

Rather than search for verbal echoes or similar ideas between "Dover Beach" and any Hardy poem, I would like first to construct a likely way for Hardy to have read the poem as a way into understanding how he might have answered it with a poem of his own. We have no first-hand account of Hardy's response to "Dover Beach," but we do know that during a trip to Belgium with his wife Emma he carried a copy of Arnold's poetry (still extant in the Dorset County Museum) in which he marked next to the title "Dover Beach" his and Emma's initials and the date, "September—1896."

This was characteristic of Hardy, to visit sites associated with people whom he admired. The celebratory trip to Italy with Emma nine years earlier had turned into a pilgrimage for Hardy, each day's itinerary determined by where Keats and Shelley, Gibbon and Napoleon had gone before him. At this time Hardy had written relatively little poetry, but he used the inspiration of this trip to compose eleven "Poems of Pilgrimage," including "Rome: At the Pyramid of Cestius near the Graves of Shelley and Keats" and "Lausanne: In Gibbon's Old Garden: 11–12 p.m." It was almost as if by sitting in Gibbon's garden or standing by Shelley's grave or in the field where Shelley saw his skylark that Hardy could absorb some lingering ambience of the earlier writer to help him on his poetic pilgrimage. The value of human association over any formal aspect of beauty was a principle that Hardy had articulated early on for himself and set forth most completely in the essay "Memories of Church Restoration." Given the primacy for Hardy of a thing's human associations, extending to association of place and even to time (attempting to be in Gibbon's garden during the exact hour when the earlier man had finished his greatest work), it becomes obvious that it was no accident that he happened to have a copy of "Dover Beach" with him before the Channel crossing to Belgium. No Dover poem, however, was composed at this time.

Michael Millgate suggests (378) that it is tempting to see a reconciliation in the Hardys' deteriorating marriage as they read together "Ah, love, let us be true / To one another," though Hardy's placing of the annotation next to the title rather than by these lines dampens this speculation. Regardless of the state of his marriage, it would have been surprising if Hardy had affirmed Arnold's lines, for one of his most consistent themes is the miscarriage of love. In hundreds of poems from the earliest such as the "She To Him" sonnets of 1867 through a poem like "A Question of Marriage" in 1928, Hardy habitually questioned the loyalty of love. One of the few exceptions (out of nearly 1000 poems) is "A Jog-Trot Pair," in which two of the common people "plainest, barest" are "happier than the cleverest, smartest, rarest." Outside of this happy pair the only other loyal Hardy couples are separated, by death or by an impediment such as marriage to another. That is, the loyalty is one-sided or involves yet another disloyalty. We may surmise, then, on the basis of Hardy's own treatment of love as a common and consistent source of loss, how he might have read Arnold's plea to his love to stand true as a comfort against loss.

There is a second attitude toward "Ah, love, let us be true / To one another" that Hardy may have taken. Throughout his life Hardy adopted the posture of the watcher. A frequent comment of visitors to Max Gate was how unimpressive Hardy was and how unremarkable the conversation, yet how attentive and alert the eyes. Hardy himself was aware of the power of his gaze; he sat once for Sir William Rothenstein, who recalled that Hardy "remarked on the expression of the eyes in the drawing that I made—he knew the look he said, for he was often taken for a detective" (Paulin 101). Hardy's stance as passive observer in the poems has frequently been observed.

In addition, Hardy was in the habit of not just watching from within a scene but apparently of so distancing himself from a scene that he felt himself watching from outside it (*Early Life* 275):

> For my part, if there is any way of getting a melancholy satisfaction out of life it lies in dying, so to speak, before one is out of the flesh; by which I mean putting on the manners of ghosts, wandering in their haunts, and taking their views of surrounding things. . . . Hence even when I enter into a room to pay a simple morning call I have unconsciously the habit of regarding the scene as if I were a spectre not solid enough to influence my environment.

This out-of-body perspective became central to his concept for his great verse-drama *The Dynasts*, which has been described by John Wain (xi) as so perfectly anticipating the cinema that any director wishing to turn it into film "would have nothing to do except follow Hardy's instructions" in the many stage directions. The most characteristically cinematic devices of *The Dynasts* are the panoramic views and long-distance, wide-angle shots of the whole terrain. But Hardy goes beyond the normal panoramas of cinema epics, pulling the camera's eye ever farther and farther back until the effect is truly cosmic and we are watching the action from the point of view of the Spirit Choruses. From this lofty vantage point men do not appear to be men nor armies but rather become "a brain-like network of currents and ejections, twitching, interpenetrating, entangling, and thrusting hither and thither" (*Dynasts* 118). All this is to say that while Hardy cared intimately for domestic scenes and the small detail and used them frequently in his works, he habitually tried on another broader perspective we might call cosmic. For Hardy, cosmic perspective was not meant to imply solely a universal vision applicable across the ages and across the boundaries of country, race, and sex; it was much more literally the view from high up.

The essential facts I have so far suggested are Hardy's wide reading and use of that reading as data for his poetry; evidence that "Dover Beach" was a significant poem for Hardy; his characteristically ironic stance toward the loyalty of lovers; his "cinematic technique," used most extensively in *The Dynasts*, written in the first decade of this century. One further element needs mentioning. When the First World War dashed the meliorist spirit of the age (and of *The Dynasts*), the innocence of that pre-war era seemed gone, never again possible. The armies of "Dover Beach" could never again be merely metaphorical.

During the war Hardy published 17 poems in a last section of *Moments of Vision* (1917) called "Poems of War and Patriotism." Some indeed were exhortations to patriotism, such as "A Call to National Service," which begins "Up and be doing, all who have a hand / To lift." But Hardy was no blind patriot and won, for example, Siegfried Sassoon's praise as the man he admired more than anybody living (Fussell 7, 91). What Hardy had created before the war in *Satires of Circumstance* (1909) Paul Fussell argues (6), was "a vision, an action, and a tone superbly suitable for rendering an event constituting an immense and unprecedented Satire of Circumstance." Fussell further argues (69) that a poem in that pre-war volume, "The Discovery," is "a condensed redaction of Arnold's 'Dover Beach,' but with certain adjustments in the idea of the modern since Arnold's day." Where Arnold's ignorant armies are guessed at, Hardy's are palpable in the simile of the cannonades:

> I wandered to a crude coast
> Like a ghost;
> Upon the hills I saw fires—
> Funeral pyres
> Seemingly—and heard breaking
> Waves like distant cannonades that set the land shaking.

I would suggest another war poem as representing how Hardy might have read "Dover Beach" now over a half century after its appearance during Hardy's young manhood. In November 1919 Hardy published "Going and Staying":

> I
>
> The moving sun-shapes on the spray,
> The sparkles where the brook was flowing,
> Pink faces, plightings, moonlit May,
> These were the things we wished would stay;
>   But they were going.
>
> II
>
> Seasons of blankness as of snow,
> The silent bleed of a world decaying,
> The moan of multitudes in woe,
> These were the things we wished would go;
>   But they were staying.

Characteristically, final place and permanence are given to those things we wished would go. The contrast between before and after, the turn from then to now, is characteristic Hardyean irony and was adopted by other younger war poets as a device to mark the catastrophic and fundamental change in their world wrought by the war.

In 1922 Hardy added a third stanza:

III

> Then we looked closelier at Time
> And saw his ghostly arms revolving
> To sweep off woeful things with prime,
> Things sinister with things sublime
>   Alike dissolving.

This stanza has the effect of mitigating the bleak end-of-the-war mood of the first two stanzas. Several interpretations for the image of time have been offered: Hardy could be referring to the hands of some ghostly clock, or imaging an anthropomorphized broom, or echoing Shakespeare's phrase "the whirligig of time" (Bailey 441) or perhaps calling up from folklore the story of Amlet's salt mill (Jason 263). "Dover Beach" gives us another way to interpret this stanza.

In "Dover Beach" Arnold pictures a world controlled by ignorant and violent forces:

> And we are here as on a darkling plain
> Swept with confused alarms of struggle and flight,
> Where ignorant armies clash by night.

Where Arnold writes of metaphoric armies on a plain, Hardy alludes to the real armies still on the plains of France in the very month the poem was published. Arnold's ignorance and violence also appear in Hardy's poem, but modulated by a note of detachment in Hardy's Time, which is both unaware and powerful—unaware of the distinctions between "things sinister" and "things sublime" (those are human distinctions) but powerful enough to dissolve all alike.

Arnold's phrasing before his climactic lines—

> for the world, which seems
> To lie before us like a land of dreams,
> So various, so beautiful, so new,
> Hath really neither joy, nor love, nor light,
> Nor certitude, nor peace, nor help for pain—

is itself an echoing of the language Milton gives to Satan upon beholding his hell and realizing that paradise is lost (Bidney 87). In Arnold's poem, our world has become like that hell by the withdrawal of the Sea of Faith; the beautiful gives way to the loss of the final lines. And in Hardy's poem, the opening stanza with its images of variety, beauty, newness, light, and love gives way to a second stanza showing the effects of armies at war.

In broad terms, Hardy has chosen Arnold's theme: how to behave in an ignorant and violent world. Hardy's answer counterpoints Arnold's, and the image that embodies that answer is built out of Arnold's famous lines. In his third stanza Hardy takes literally Arnold's image of the darkling plain swept with confusion and asks who is doing the sweeping. Hardy transfers Arnold's image to the sphere of the forces responsible for human woe in order to complete from a cosmic perspective his Arnoldian theme. Thus the tone of human closeness in "Ah, love, let us be true / To one another!" can be distanced, as befits a post-war unbelief in faith and in a substitute for faith.

In "Going and Staying" Hardy agrees with Arnold's assessment of the world's condition. But where Arnold looks for some human comfort to face a world swept with confusion, Hardy gives us a robotic Time with a broom. Arnold's armies and love (Hardy's bleeding multitudes and May plightings) are reduced to motes for a dustpan, and then further reduced out of existence, "alike dissolving." In this way Hardy has retold "Dover Beach" freed from the human perspective. In place of the passionate image of ignorant armies by night, he has offered us in his last line an indistinct and disintegrating vision, even its rhythm trailing into nothingness.

This vision is of a world quite different from Arnold's in the 1850's and 60s. Arnold mourned the loss of faith but could yet seek comfort in human tenderness. Hardy peels all that away, but in its place leaves the curious comfort that results from the withdrawal of faith. God may seem to have withdrawn from the world but another deity has remained. In *The Dynasts* Hardy calls this deity such names as the World-Soul, the Eternal Urger, the Immanent Will, or just It. One of the images Hardy there gives to It—"That / Which . . . works . . . / Like some sublime fermenting vat" (Part First, Act VI, Scene iii)—may well lie behind the second image of Time as a force capable not only of sweeping but also of dissolving. In the great solution of his last stanza, that vat in and out of which things sinister and things sublime alike dissolve, Hardy has stripped us of our ability to distinguish between faith and love on the one hand and war and pain on the other. We are not left to end on the note of Arnold's night or Hardy's second stanza of woe. In their place we have the slow camera dissolve taking us higher and higher until we live among personified cosmic forces, immune to the twitches that go on below. This is a very different poem, finally, from "Dover Beach," documenting how very different the 1860s were from the 1920s. Thomas Hardy, of course, wrote and read through both times. He was uniquely positioned as a translator and completer of the earlier time for the post-war generation now ready to recognize in him the poet whom the Victorians had not seen.

Works Cited

Bailey, J. O. *The Poetry of Thomas Hardy: A Handbook and Commentary.* Chapel Hill: U of North Carolina P, 1970.

Bidney, Martin. "Of the Devil's Party: Undetected Words of Satan in Arnold's 'Dover Beach.' " *Victorian Poetry* 20 (1982): 85–89.

Casagrande, Peter J. "Hardy's Wordsworth: A Record and a Commentary." *English Literature in Transition* 20 (1977): 210–37.

Fussell, Paul. *The Great War and Modern Memory*. New York: Oxford UP. 1975.

Giordano, Frank R., Jr. "Allegory and Allusion in Hardy's 'Heiress and Architect.' " *Colby Library Quarterly* 2 (1981): 99–111.

Grundy, Joan. "Hardy and Milton." *Thomas Hardy Annual* 3 (1985): 3–14.

Hardy, Thomas. *The Complete Poems of Thomas Hardy*. Ed. James Gibson. London: Macmillan, 1976.

———. *The Dynasts*. Intro. by John Wain. New York: St. Martin's Press, 1965.

———. *The Early Life of Thomas Hardy*. London: Macmillan, 1928.

———. *The Life and Work of Thomas Hardy*. Ed. Michael Millgate. Athens: U of Georgia P, 1985.

Jason, Philip K. "A Possible Allusion in Thomas Hardy's 'Going and Staying.' " *Victorian Poetry* 14 (1976): 261–63.

Millgate, Michael. *Thomas Hardy: A Biography*. New York: Random House, 1982.

Paulin, Tom. *Thomas Hardy: The Poetry of Perception*. Totowa NJ: Rowman and Littlefield, 1975.

Persoon, James. "Once More To 'The Darkling Thrush': Hardy's Reversals of Milton." *CEA Critic* 4/1 (1986): 76–86.

Weber, Carl. *Hardy of Wessex*. New York: Columbia UP, 1940.

A CLOSER LOOK
AT SPECIFIC TEXTS

◆

Ballads and Narratives

PAUL ZIETLOW

In his country songs Hardy presents, with redeeming sympathy, ordinary people caught in the common, fundamental complexities of life. To the extent that these characters are worth studying as exemplars of the human condition, and that their lives occasionally achieve joyful fulfillment, the poems in which they appear sound a strong, positive note. To see Hardy's country people at their most particular and complex, however, one must turn to his narratives and ballads, where he achieves the fullest realization of his vision of country life.

OLD ILLUSIONS AND NEW

Hardy's ballad "The Dead Quire" (*CP*, pp. 240–243) begins:

> Beside the Mead of Memories,
> Where Church-way mounts to Moaning Hill
> The sad man sighed his phantasies:
>   He seems to sigh them still.

The sad man describes a Christmas Eve past, when youths of Mellstock, carousing at an inn, proposed blasphemous toasts:

> "Now 'tis Christmas morn;
> Here's to our women old and young,
>   And to John Barleycorn!"

They collapsed into a drunken sleep, in which their ancestors from the "Mellstock quire of former years" seemed to them to rise from their graves, singing, as the sad man continued, "words of prayer and praise / As they

Reprinted by permission of the publishers from *Moments of Vision: The Poetry of Thomas Hardy* by Paul Zietlow, Cambridge, Mass.: Harvard University Press, Copyright © 1974 by the President and Fellows of Harvard College.

had used to sing." The youths awakened and went home chastened: "'Twas said that of them all, not one / Sat in a tavern more." The poem ends with the sad man drifting away to the "Mead of Memories." Three degrees of religious perspective are presented here: the piety of the ancient Mellstock choir, the repentance of the fallen youths who experience the miracle, and the wistful melancholy of the tale-teller, who presumably is sad because the conditions for piety and repentance no longer exist ("Church-way mounts to Moaning Hill"). In effect, Hardy depicts the stages in the religious history of a culture. He himself occupies a fourth degree of perspective, for the denizen of the "Mead of Memories" is not Hardy, but the old man. Hardy himself stands in a neutral, distant position, from which the story, told by another, appears to be an interesting "phantasy," worth preserving in a more skeptical age.

"The Dead Quire" is typical of Hardy's ballads and story poems in that the narrator usually appears as a distant observer, either retelling a traditional tale that is current in the society, or recording a factually based story associated with real places and people in the rural Wessex of the past. He seems to be the objective preserver and guardian of the memory of a folk. Hardy's titles reflect this stance. The frequent use of the words "Tale" or "Ballad" suggests a debt to tradition; the time of the action is often the distant or not-so-distant past; and often a Wessex setting is clearly specified: "The Sacrilege: A Ballad-Tragedy (Circa 182–)," "The Supplanter: A Tale," "A Sound in the Night (Woodsford Castle: 17—)," "No Bell-Ringing: A Ballad of Durnover," "At Shag's Heath, 1685 (Traditional)." As a story-teller, Hardy thus remains morally and philosophically neutral. Purportedly the events were shaped by history and tradition, not him. He merely records them in these poems, without comment on their meaning and without using them as occasions for meditation; he experiences no flashes of personal insight. Taken as a group, the narratives imply that any story with a clear shape, an interesting twist, a tantalizing element of mystery, or an instructive lesson is worth the telling. Because it actually happened, or because it represents an imagined response to realities, any story not invented by the author helps to preserve and clarify the history of the society in which it occurred, to sanctify the place where it happened, and to exemplify significant qualities of life.

The logic of his role as historian explains in part why Hardy, the agnostic and iconoclast, wrote narratives describing the intervention of the supernatural in human life. He preserves the memory of a time when the old illusions of truth were current, when, if miracles did not actually occur, at least people believed they did. "The Paphian Ball" and "No Bell-Ringing" describe Christmas and New Year's Eve miracles. "The Lost Pyx: A Mediaeval Legend" (*CP*, pp. 158–160) offers a tale explaining the meaning of a Wessex landmark, the Cross-and-Hand, a mysterious and ancient pillar standing, Hardy reveals in a footnote to the poem, "on a lonely table-land above the

Vale of Blackmore." In the first stanza, Hardy characteristically establishes his role as the recorder of a tale originated by others in the past:

> Some say the spot is banned: that the pillar
> Cross-and-Hand
> Attests to a deed of hell;
> But of else than of bale is the mystic tale
> That ancient Vale-folk tell.

According to the story, a priest, aroused from sleep in a violent storm, refused to make a difficult journey to administer last rites to a dying man. After he fell back to sleep, "a Visage seemed / To frown from Heaven at him." He awakened in a fright and set off "through the dark immense," only to discover that the Pyx containing the consecrated wafer of the Eucharist had disappeared: "I've lost . . . the Body of Christ Himself!" He started back toward home, groping in the darkness until a ray of light from heaven guided him to the Pyx:

> unharmed 'mid the circling rows
> Of Blackmore's hairy throng,
> Whereof were oxen, sheep, and does,
> And hares from the brakes among;
>
> And badgers grey, and conies keen,
> And squirrels of the tree,
> And many a member seldom seen
> Of Nature's family.

The priest marked the scene of the miracle with a pillar. This poem preserves an old illusion of truth in a style approaching the mannered delicacy of Pre-Raphaelite medievalism. The inversions ("badgers grey, and conies keen") and the archaic syntax ("Whereof were oxen," "brakes among") support the effect of remote quaintness. In his footnote Hardy points out that *Tess of the d'Urbervilles* records a different tradition as to the origin of the pillar—the tradition alluded to in the poem that it "Attests to a deed of hell." Faithful to his role as tale-teller, Hardy tells both of these disparate stories to enrich and embellish the meaning of the landscape.

In a larger sense, however, Hardy as tale-teller is not at all neutral. The phrase "old illusion" echoes a term Hardy uses in his essay *The Science of Fiction* (1891), in which he attacks Zola and the school of literary naturalism for falsely assuming that art can be "complete copyism." The essay expresses Hardy's conviction that all artists select and shape facts in ways which reveal their own values and peculiar visions; that no artist can be a neutral recorder; that art presents an illusion of truth, not truth itself. The literary naturalists, in Hardy's view, make the mistake of ignoring "the need for the exercise of the Daedalian faculty for selection and cunning manipulation." This faculty is affected not only by the personal values and idiosyncrasies of the writer, but also by the current ideas of the period in which he lives: "with our widened knowledge of the universe and its forces, and man's position therein, narrative, to be artistically convincing, must adjust itself to the new alignment . . . Nothing but the illusion of truth can permanently please, and when the old illusions begin to be penetrated, a more natural magic has to be supplied."[1]

Poems like "The Lost Pyx" present "old illusions" of the truth. Their reliance on supernatural events appeals merely to an antiquarian interest in the past and to a nostalgic longing for the certainty of old forms of belief. The magic they depend on has been discredited by the "widened knowledge" of a skeptical age. In contrast, the majority of Hardy's ballads and narratives employ the "more natural magic" of intuitive deduction. He creates illusions, but they seem to be true because he imagines them in terms of relationships that the modern age accepts as real, based, for example, on psychological motivation or on naturalistic cause and effect. The more deeply and fully he imagines, however, the more complex and disturbing become his illusions of truth. Often motivations are obscure, and cause and effect are disproportionate. Actuality, as he conceives it, is as mysterious as supernatural miracle. Hardy defines the new magic in *The Science of Fiction*, where he celebrates the writer's power to penetrate "the superficial" and to expose "the intrinsic." The writer's mode of imaginative inference is akin to the scientific method; his powers are natural and human: "What cannot be discerned by eye and ear, what may be apprehended only by the mental tactility that comes from a sympathetic appreciativeness of life in all of its manifestations, this is the gift which renders its possessor a more accurate delineator of human nature than many other with twice his powers and means of external observation, but without that sympathy. To see in half and quarter views the whole picture, to catch from a few bars the whole tune, is the intuitive power that supplies the would-be storywriter with the scientific bases for his pursuit."[2] In Hardy's finest ballads and narratives his "sympathetic appreciativeness of life in all of its manifestations" enables him to "see in half and quarter views the whole picture," and to conjure up the mysterious, bewildering complexity at the heart of things—a vision that has the illusion of truth.

The contrasts between "On Martock Moor" and "A Trampwoman's Tragedy," two ballads similar in many ways, point up the idiosyncratic propensities of Hardy's narrative imagination and the modern twist he gave to the ballad. "On Martock Moor" (*CP*, pp. 777–778) shows his skill in imitating features of the traditional form:

I
My deep-dyed husband trusts me,
He feels his mastery sure,

Although I leave his evening hearth
To walk upon the moor.

II
—I had what wealth I needed,
And of gay gowns a score,
And yet I left my husband's house
To muse upon the moor.

III
O how I loved a dear one
Who, save in soul, was poor!
O how I loved the man who met
Me nightly on the moor.

IV
I'd feather-beds and couches,
And carpets for the floor,
Yet brighter to me was at eves,
The bareness of the moor.

V
There was a dogging figure,
There was a hiss of "Whore!"
There was a flounce at Weir-water
One night upon the moor. . . .

VI
Yet do I haunt there, knowing
By rote each rill's low pour,
But only a fitful phantom now
Meets me upon the moor.

The characters are common ballad figures: the prosperous husband, the poor lover, the unfaithful wife. The action is characterized by the simplicity and violence of traditional ballads: a tryst, discovery by the husband, the death of the lover. The morality of the poem is the primitive, masculine ethic of retribution: the wife's penalty for infidelity is to be called "Whore"; the lover pays with his life. As in many traditional ballads, the ethic reflects the inevitabilities of human emotion rather than an objective moral system. Love demands fulfillment, but with equal force, trust and generosity demand fidelity. The husband's humiliation at his wife's betrayal, on the one hand, and her love for another man, on the other, are both fully valid human facts, and to the extent that her love requires consummation, his humiliation requires revenge. The logic here is merciless, divisive, and tragic, but it goes unquestioned. The characters are victims neither of one another nor of schematized social and moral values, but of the realities of human action and emotion. Yet there is no wailing against the human condition. Nor is there any hint of either romanticism or puritanism, for the husband is no more presented as a villainous oppressor than the wife is pictured as a wayward sinner. Cause and effect are in proportion, and the characters are responsible for what they cause. There is an objective, tragic purity in the presentation of situation and action, a quality common to traditional ballads.

This quality is embodied in the stylistic features of the poem—in the controlled rhythms, the austerity of language, the balance and symmetry, the economy of exposition, and the stabilizing repetition of the word "moor" at the end of each stanza. The first four stanzas set up the dichotomy: the trust, comfort, prosperity, and security of husband, hearth, and home, as opposed to the wife's love, expressed in the outburst of stanza three, for the poor man on the barren moor. The fifth stanza, in a way typical of the traditional ballad, focuses on the key moment, describing it in terms of a few selected facts, things heard and seen rather than emotions felt: the "dogging figure," the "hiss of 'Whore,' " the "flounce at Weir-water." This is the moment of terrifying discovery and violent death, yet the method of description, by leaving the terror and violence to the imagination of the reader, makes an important contribution to the effect of objective, tragic purity created by the poem as a whole. Likewise the last stanza conveys the wife's passion and longing only indirectly. The word "haunt" turns her into a ghost; though living, she is no more alive in her emotional life than is the "phantom" lover, and the reference to her knowledge of the moor recalls the intensity and frequency of their meetings in life. Balance and symmetry also characterize the prosody and alliteration. Lines tend to be defined not only by syllable number, meter, end-stopping, and rhyme, but also by alliterative groupings:

> —I had *w*hat *w*ealth I needed,
> And of *g*ay *g*owns a score,
> And yet I left my *h*usband's *h*ouse
> To *m*use upon the *m*oor.

The variations in the position of the alliterating groups illustrate Hardy's control:

> I'd *f*eather-*b*eds and *c*ouches,
> And *c*arpets *f*or the *f*loor,
> Yet *b*righter to me was at eves,
> The *b*areness of the moor.

In this poem Hardy demonstrates his mastery of the techniques necessary to achieve in narrative verse the effects of control, economy, balance, distance, and objectivity.

Hardy dates "On Martock Moor" 1899, the general period of *Wessex Poems* and narratives like "San Sebastian" and "The Dance at the Phoenix," yet the poem did not first appear until 1925 in *Human Shows*. Both *Poems of the Past and the Present* (1902) and the next volume, *Time's Laughingstocks* (1909), include many narratives involving a wide variety of themes and techniques. It seems strange that Hardy withheld from publication a poem as skillful as "On Martock Moor" when he published other narratives and ballads from the same period. A comparison of "On Martock Moor" with the poems written at the same general time but which Hardy chose for immediate publication suggests a probable answer. Hardy's narratives seldom create the effect of objective, tragic purity produced by "On Martock Moor." Seldom does the logic of emotion and action go unquestioned. Rarely is the structure of situation characterized by simplicity, spareness, and inevitability. Nor does the use of language usually reflect control, restraint, and emotional distance. In his other narratives motives are obscure and ambiguous, situations complicated and ironic, the language diverse, mannered, tortured, highly textured. Instead of a clear vision of the elements leading inevitably to tragedy, Hardy usually reveals a complex, agonizing awareness that tragedy is not inevitable—a consciousness of the fragility of circumstance and motive. A characteristic ending is a leading figure's sense of guilt for his part in the tragedy, rather than the muted acceptance found at the end of "On Martock Moor." That is, in his narratives Hardy reveals an "idiosyncratic mode of regard" despite the neutrality of his narrators. Although he seems to have developed a full mastery over traditional ballad techniques and effects, he preferred to reveal a personal, untraditional vision. He may well have withheld "On Martock Moor" from publication because it fell short of what he wanted in his ballads.

"A Trampwoman's Tragedy" (*CP*, pp. 182–185) provides a fitting contrast, for it was a ballad that Hardy himself much admired. Referring to the year 1902, the biographer of the *Life* stated: "In April . . . he was writing 'A Trampwoman's Tragedy'—a ballad based on some local story of an event more or less resembling the incidents embodied, which took place between 1820 and 1830. Hardy considered this, upon the whole, his most successful poem."[3] In the poem the trampwoman describes her life with an unnamed "fancy-man" and their two companions, Mother Lee and "jeering John." At the climax, the trampwoman flirts with John, her jealous lover kills him and is hanged for the murder, and the trampwoman bears a stillborn baby. At the conclusion she meets with the phantom of her fancy-man, professes her love for him, and lives out her career "Haunting the Western Moor." The similarities with "On Martock Moor" are obvious: the setting, the love triangle, the violent death, the bereft woman haunting the site of her love.

In contrast to the abstraction of "On Martock Moor," the trampwoman describes her wanderings with her fancy-man in terms of concrete physical toil:

> The sun-blaze burning on our backs,
> Our shoulders sticking to our packs,
> By fosseway, fields, and turnpike tracks
>   We skirted sad Sedge-Moor.

What unites the two lovers is their shared struggle, their movement together across the landscape despite obstacles and hardships. The poetry particularizes their efforts by naming places and employing action verbs. The effect is a sense of energy, texture, physicality, and exuberant triumph.

> For months we had padded side by side,
>   Ay, side by side
> Through the Great Forest, Blackmoor wide,
>   And where the Parret ran.
> We'd faced the gusts on Mendip ridge,
> Had crossed the Yeo unhelped by bridge,
> Been stung by every Marshwood midge,
>   I and my fancy-man.

The next stanza names the "Lone inns we loved, my man and I": "King's Stag," "Windwhistle," "The Horse," and "The Hut." The description creates the impression of a concrete landscape, known and loved, harsh but beautiful, dotted with places of human refuge. The goal of the particular journey of the poem, attained at sundown, is a favorite inn near Poldon top, a place of unusual beauty: "I doubt if finer sight there be / Within this royal realm." But it is here, in this longed-for place, that the tragedy occurs. For a second time the trampwoman teases her lover, whereupon he commits the murder:

> Then up he sprung, and with his knife—
>   And with his knife
> He let out jeering Johnny's life,
>   Yes; there, at set of sun.
> The slant ray through the window nigh
> Gilded John's blood and glazing eye,
> Ere scarcely Mother Lee and I
>   Knew that the deed was done.

The violence is described with considerable immediacy: the speed of the killer's spring, the blood, the glazed eye, the irony of the sunlight. The events proceeding from the murder are also described forthrightly in blunt, even crude language: "at Ivel-chester jail / My Love, my sweetheart swung," or "On his death-day I gave my groan / And dropt his dead-born child." Absent is the refining, distancing tact of "On Martock Moor," the economy of exposition that leaves the violence and terror to the reader's imagination.

"A Trampwoman's Tragedy" vividly depicts the moments of violence and terror, transforming the woman who had been touched by the beauty of a natural scene into the equivalent of a beast—she "drops" her dead offspring alone on the barren moor.

Despite superficial similarities in the endings, "A Trampwoman's Tragedy" concludes on a note quite different from that of "On Martock Moor." The wife in the latter poem is in a state of memory and desire, not guilt. She has fulfilled her passion and paid the consequences. The trampwoman, in contrast, meets the ghost of her lover not to commune with him, but to make amends. The ghost asks:

> "Ah, tell me this!
> Was the child mine, or was it his?
> Speak, that I rest may find!"

> O doubt not but I told him then,
>   I told him then,
> That I had kept me from all men
>   Since we joined lips and swore.
> Whereat he smiled, and thinned away.

She tells him when it is too late, then wanders "alone . . . Haunting the Western Moor." She is isolated by her guilt, with memories not of consummated passion but of what might have been. The question arises as to whether she is guilty, and if so, of what. In the answer lies the main difference between "A Trampwoman's Tragedy" and "On Martock Moor."

The trampwoman is both guilty and not guilty. The poem evokes two conflicting perspectives from which to judge its action, and the final effect is ambivalence. From one point of view there is a clear line of responsibility for the tragedy. The brutality of the language is justified by the brutality of the characters, particularly of the trampwoman, whose yielding to a cruel impulse touches off a transformation of beauty into ugliness; she brutalizes her own world. Tramps lead free, unstable lives on the moors, remote from civilizing conventions and humanizing responsibilities. They wander unfettered by place or social structure. In a sense they are outlaws: theirs is the world of "Blue Jimmy," who "stole right many a steed." The fancy-man, who has also been a thief, carries a knife and knows how to use it. Relations are shifting, the couple having traveled together only for months, not years, and death is ever-present. Mother Lee, for example, dies mysteriously before the fancy-man hangs. In such an unstable world the trampwoman's and fancy-man's love is something of a triumph, an instance of fidelity under circumstances where infidelity to person, place, occupation, and conventional social structures is the norm. But the trampwoman betrays the achievement. She allows herself to become a wanderer at heart, a tramp in the sense of "trollop," as well as being a wanderer across the landscape: "I teased my fancy-man in play / And wanton idleness." Although play and wanton idleness are hallmarks of the behavior of irresponsible wanderers, up to this point the lives of the trampwoman and her lover had been characterized by serious struggle and "care" for one another. Almost as an act of will, the trampwoman ignores the effects of her playfulness: "I would not bend my glances on / My lover's dark distress." At the inn she impulsively continues the game, despite the ominous tone in her lover's voice:

> Then in a voice I had never heard,
>   I had never heard,
> My only Love to me: "One word,
>   My lady, if you please!
> Whose is the child you are like to bear?—
> *His?* After all my months o' care?"
> God knows 'twas not! But, O despair!
>   I nodded—still to tease.

The tease is brutal beyond endurance, given their brief history of love and fidelity. In an unstable, lawless world, ever on the brink of death and violence, close to the harshness of nature as well as its beauty, the fancy-man's act of ultimate vengeance seems to follow an inevitable logic of cruelty, developing from the trampwoman's first idle wantonness. It is a logic leading to death, on the one hand, and to isolation and guilt on the other—the fates, respectively, of the fancy-man and the trampwoman.

From another point of view the trampwoman, though she causes the tragedy, is not responsible for it. The disparity between what she had actually done and its result is senselessly out of proportion. No matter how cruelly vain or possessive the impulse to which she surrendered, it does not warrant the consequences. A few thoughtless words and gestures result in three lost lives, and a fourth person condemned to a lonely, guilt-stricken death-in-life. The wife in "On Martock Moor" commits her acts of passion and pays the price without guilt or remorse. The trampwoman makes a heedless mistake, and the result is total catastrophe. She is guilty of a careless yielding to impulse and a failure of perception. she failed to understand that hers was not a situation for play, because of the depth of her lover's feelings and his capacity for jealousy. These are serious errors, meriting correction, but her object lesson is the destruction of her world. What she learns becomes for her no longer worth knowing. Ironically, the means of her instruction destroy the conditions under which her new knowledge could have any value. "A Young Man's Epigram on Existence" (*CP*, p. 281), the last poem in *Time's Laughingstocks*, where "A Trampwoman's Tragedy" also appears, makes explicit the same ironic point:

A senseless school, where we must give
Our lives that we may learn to live!
A dolt is he who memorizes
Lessons that leave no time for prizes.

The logic of "A Trampwoman's Tragedy" thus leads to a grotesque disparity between error and consequences. The poem calls into question the notions of guilt and responsibility and the relation between them in such a way as to make final judgment impossible. And whatever the solution to the moral ambiguities, the facts of death and suffering remain. By showing human beings to the unstable wanderers across a barren land, victims of the uncertainties of both the external world and their own psyches, Hardy infuses into the traditional form of the ballad the modern anguish of rootlessness, precariousness, and complexity. "The Trampwoman's Tragedy" is an excellent example of his attempt to devise a new kind of illusion of truth.

MORAL COMPLICATIONS

In Hardy's narratives and ballads, therefore, despite his pose as the recorder and disseminator of known tales, he exercises the "Daedalian faculty for selection and cunning manipulation." This is not to say that he creates his stories out of whole cloth, for usually, as in the case of "A Trampwoman's Tragedy," there is some historical basis for them.[4] Generally they grow out of hints Hardy actually received from local traditions and the artifacts of the countryside. His imagination, stimulated by these half and quarter views, creates a whole picture, at the center of which is a moral conflict. The sorts of conflict involved tend to be reducible to balanced, simple terms, like love versus duty, husband versus lover, family versus country—the kinds of conflict found in traditional ballads. But there are always complications.

"The Mock Wife" (CP, pp. 723–725) is a useful poem for illustrating the way in which Hardy's poetic imagination worked with historical materials, for he also wrote a full prose account of the incident, based on careful research he had done. The differences between the prose and the poem are instructive. In *Maumbury Ring* (1908), an essay summarizing the history of the Roman earthworks on the outskirts of Dorchester, he describes in detail the case of Mary Channing, who was convicted of poisoning her husband, a grocer, and was executed in the Ring in 1705. Hardy focuses sympathetically on the girl, a "thoughtless, pleasure-loving creature" only eighteen years old, who had been compelled against her wishes to marry a man of her parents' choice. He leaves little doubt that he feels her to have been innocent of the charges brought against her. Having examined the record of the trial "more than once," he reports "no distinct evidence" that she committed the crime, but "much to suggest that she did not. Nor is any motive discoverable for such an act. She was allowed to have her former lover or lovers about her by her indulgent and weak-minded husband, who permitted her to go her own ways, give parties, and supplied her with plenty of money." Hardy shows little sympathy here for the husband. Mary Channing was nevertheless convicted and executed. Hardy describes her skill in conducting her own defense, emphasizes her pregnancy (the execution being delayed until she had given birth to her baby), and dwells on the wasting sickness from which she suffered after the birth. He goes into some detail in his account of the execution: "this girl not yet 19, now reduced to a skeleton by the long fever, and already more dead than alive" is taken by cart to Maumbury Ring, and, before "many thousands" of eager spectators, strangled, apparently not to death but to insensitivity, and then burned to ashes. Hardy concludes, "Was man ever 'slaughtered by his fellow man' during the Roman or barbarian use of this place of games or of sacrifice in circumstances of greater atrocity?"[5] Hardy's view of the historical event is clear: Channing was a fool; his wife, a lively, pleasure-loving girl, was most likely innocent of the crime; and the execution constituted a cruel atrocity.

"The Mock Wife," Hardy's poetic description of the same event, is spoken by a modern man looking back over two centuries to 1705. The poem begins, "It's a dark drama, this," but then continues on a different tack from the prose account: "and yet I know the house, and date; / That is to say, the where and when John Channing met his fate." The setting of the central action of the poem is thus Channing's house. Hardy does not mention the Ring, let alone exploit the ironic potentialities of its pagan and Roman history. Although Mary Channing's possible innocence is referred to three times, and the brutality of the execution is noted, the issue at the center of the poem is the pathos of the husband, not the tragedy of the wife. It is as if Hardy, musing over the case and sympathetically imagining its wider implications, came to see something that "cannot be discerned by eye and ear" in the historical record—namely, that Channing's plight was a source of poetic interest.

The circumstances of Channing's death form the subject of the poem. He does not know that his wife has been accused of poisoning him, and because of his real affection for her, as shown by his earlier indulgence, he wants her to be at his bedside. When he asks to see his wife once again, it poses a problem to the friends gathered around the deathbed, who know that she is already in jail charged with the crime. It is this problem that is at the heart of the poem:

> "Guilty she may not be," they said; "so why should we
>   torture him
> In these his last few minutes of life? Yet how indulge
>   his whim?"

And as he begged there piteously for what could not
  be done,
And the murder-charge had flown about the town
  to every one,
The friends around him in their trouble thought of a
  hasty plan,
And straightway set about it. Let denounce them all
  who can.

The fact of Mary Channing's possible innocence is presented not as the moral crux of the poem but as an element in the quandary of the bedside friends. Since she may, after all, be innocent, it would seem all the more reasonable not to disillusion her dying husband. The friends solve the problem by persuading a "buxom woman not unlike his prisoned wife" to impersonate her:

Well, the friendly neighbour did it; and he kissed her;
  held her fast
Kissed her again and yet again. "I—knew she'd—come
  at last!—
Where have you been?—Ah, kept away!—
  I'm sorry—overtried—
God bless you!" And he loosed her, fell back tiredly,
  and died.

With double irony his dying words are a blessing on the imposter of the wife accused of murdering him, in a situation that recalls the story of the deceived Isaac blessing Jacob instead of Esau. The poem goes on to describe Mary "strangled and burnt to dust" before ten thousand onlookers, "as was the verdict then / On women truly judged, or false, of doing to death their men." Although the possibility of Mary's innocence and the harshness of her execution are here implied, no mention is made of her youth, her pregnancy, or her illness. The concluding stanza returns attention to the quandary of the friends:

Some of them said as they watched her burn: "I am glad
  he never knew,
Since a few hold her as innocent—think such she could
  not do!
Glad, too, that (as they tell) he thought she kissed him
  ere he died."
And they seemed to make no question that the cheat
  was justified.

In Hardy's prose description of the case he makes a clear moral judgment, which implicitly indicts the spectators at the execution. In the poem, the situation is more complicated. On one hand, Hardy is ironically exposing the callousness of the burghers who, as they watch a woman burn, attend to a matter of trivial moral scruples instead of the cruelty and possible injustice of the woman's death. Yet the parallel with the Isaac and Jacob story makes their concern for Channing's plight seem more significant. There was a real moral issue at stake in the friends' quandary, which they dealt with sympathetically. The last line seems absolutely straight: in the complex moral situation surrounding Channing's death, all agree that Channing's happiness was worth what would otherwise have been a cruel deception, just as Esau's selling of his birthright justifies the cruel deception of Isaac. This poem is altogether typical of Hardy's ballads: he chooses what appears to be a clear-cut moral situation as his general subject—in this case the execution of a woman who is probably innocent—and then complicates the issue by imagining attendant circumstances—in this case the circumstances of the husband's death. The reader could condemn the friends for their indifference to Mary's brutal death, or praise them for their sympathetic, flexible response to John's plight. Hardy's treatment of the case in the poem leaves one with a perplexing sense of uncertainty.

Frequently in his ballads and narratives Hardy imagines historical events in terms of individual moral crises. He shows that history results from the particular actio..s of ordinary people faced with the necessity of making a choice under stress. The relationship between an ordinary husband and wife, for example, may play a crucial part in a grand historical drama. The effect is not to reduce history to trivialities; Hardy's intention is not to show that a kingdom was lost for want of a nail. Instead, Hardy views the past as a complex fabric woven of the interlocking destinies of individual human beings, each of whom merits attention. Indeed, it would be a simplistic view of history to remember only the grand significance of an event and to forget the human complexity of attendant circumstances. The betrayal and death of a duke are worth recording; but so is the tragedy of an ordinary life. Although such common tragedies seldom appear in the records, Hardy's poetry shows that a poet, working on the basis of fragmentary hints, can reconstruct the whole picture. He can serve the past as effectively as the historian by affirming imaginatively its human complexity.

In "At Shag's Heath: 1685 (Traditional)" (*CP*, pp. 712–714) the subject is the death of the Duke of Monmouth, but Hardy's focus is on the plight of the woman who betrayed him to his executioners. Newly married, she has been told by her husband that any man making friendly advances "means ill to thee." A handsome stranger, who comes to her door to inquire "but the way to go," seems to confirm the husband's warning by stealing a kiss; fleeing, he asks her to "keep faith!" When the pursuing soldiers tell her that the unknown man claimed to be "King Monmouth," she assumes that he is a deceiver and betrays his hiding place. His words to her before he is carried off to his death convince her that "he was no hind":

"I wish all weal might thee attend
But this is what th'st done to me,
O heartless woman, held my friend!"

The tale is complicated by the way that Hardy merges the wife's guilt
and her disillusionment with her husband. She has betrayed her rightful
ruler, a handsome man who meant her only good, because of her husband's
jealousy: "he'd spoke lies in jealous-wise!" Monmouth admired her beauty
and kissed her, but he had no intention to violate and betray her. The
relation between appearance and reality is more complex, the wife learns,
than her husband has taught her: "As truth I took what was not true." The
poem ends with the wife, haunted by the bloody ghost of Monmouth,
resolving to drown herself:

When comes the waterman, he'll say,
"Who's done her thuswise?"—'Twill be, yea,
Sweet, slain King Monmouth—he!

Ironically, it is the husband's jealousy that makes Monmouth the destroyer
of his wife. Hardy's sources for the poem were local legends, standard histories, and tales handed down through his mother's family, some of whose
members, according to family tradition, had been involved in the Monmouth
rebellion.[6] Characteristically Hardy chooses to work with the traditional
theme of the guilty betrayer, developing it in this instance from a wife's
disillusionment with her husband, to her introduction to the complexities
of reality, her fatal, well-intentioned mistake, and finally her oppressive,
destructive guilt. In Hardy's tale, however, the guilty betrayer is innocent.

Although the poem entitled "The Alarm (Traditional): In Memory of
One of the Writer's Family Who Was a Volunteer During the War with
Napoleon" (CP, pp. 30–34) has a happy ending, it also portrays a moment
important in the historical traditions of Wessex in terms of the moral crisis
of a specific individual. A young soldier on his way to the coast stops "In
a ferny byway / Near the great South-Wessex Highway" to reassure his
pregnant wife that Napoleon is "not like to land!" Marching on alone, he
sees the signal fires announcing the impending invasion—the notorious false
alarm that plays a part in The Trumpet Major and The Dynasts. The soldier
is caught in a moral dilemma: should he return to his wife, or should he
join the battle? Besides his fear for his wife's safety, he is concerned about
her confidence in him:

"Else, my denying
He'd come, she'll read as lying—
Think the Barrow-Beacon must have met my eyes—
That my words were not unwareness, but deceit of her,

>   while vying
>   In deeds that jeopardize."

He sees a bird tangled in undergrowth and decides, before releasing it, that he will take the direction of its flight as a divine sign. The bird flies toward the coast; the soldier marches on, discovers that the alarm was false, and returns home to sing a Te Deum with his wife and friends: "We praise Thee, Lord, discerning / That Thou hast helped in this!" The Lord has helped save the young man as well as the nation. "At Shag's Heath" ends in tragedy; "The Alarm," in an affirmation of divine providence. Hardy's stance is neutral as to the religious and philosophical questions. His values, the shaping and selective processes of his imagination, are evident in what the poems share, their particularization of historical moments in terms of the moral crises in the lives of specific individuals. Both poems merge national history with issues of personal fidelity.

"The Inscription (A Tale)" (*CP*, pp. 641–644), a story allegedly passed down to the narrator by "talebearers," presents a curiously tainted and obscured conflict of fidelities. The object on which Hardy bases his narrative is one of the several tomb inscriptions known to him that included the names of both husband and wife, but the date of death of only the husband; in the poem he refers specifically to a real inscription in Yetminster Church (here called "Estminster") near Dorchester. As Hardy imagines it, the husband died young, leaving his wife still "fair as any the eye might scan." The widow has her name inscribed on the tomb with her husband's, thus "Forgoing Heaven's bliss if ever with spouse should she / Again have lain." She falls in love again, but refuses to marry her new lover, who reproaches her "that one yet undeceased / Should bury her future." After her priest advises her not to marry, she is torn between her new lover and her fear of damnation. Her lover, growing cool, gives her "till Midsummer morn to make her mind clear," but the burden of decision is too much for her. On the fateful day she is found in the church, "facing the brass there, else seeing none, / But feeling the words with her finger, gibbering in fits." The conflict is clear—fidelity to a sacred vow versus love for a man—and from the point of view of Hardy the modernist, whose works include frequent attacks on marriage conventions, judgment is easy; the widow would seem to be the victim of an oppressive ecclesiastical institution.

But the situation is more complicated, for there are hints of impulsiveness and of a tendency toward self-dramatization in the widow which contribute to obscuring the conflict. These qualities are implicit in her act of including her name on her husband's tomb inscription. On impulse, she publicly displays her fidelity. Certainly Hardy makes clear that she is concerned with public opinion, for her fear of social scorn, he reveals, is as important to her as her fear of damnation:

> Moreover she thought of the laughter, the shrug, the jibe
> That would rise at her back in the nave when she
> should pass
> As another's avowed by the words she had chosen to
> inscribe
> On the changeless brass.

She lacks the full courage that her love should provide her.

The priest is aware of the worldly dangers in her situation; for him, "more perceptions moved than one." Hints of what his perceptions might be appear in the description of how the widow fell in love with her new suitor:

> And her heart was stirred with a lightning love to its pith
> For a newcomer who, while less in years, was one
> Full eager and able to make her his own forthwith,
> Restrained of none.

That her "lightning love" might be a dangerous impulse is supported by her suitor's being a newcomer, younger than she, and himself impulsive. The priest, in making his recommendation, seems to be responding as much to his judgment of their shared "impulse of passionate need" as to the sanctity of the widow's vow. It could be a fatal mistake for her to marry an eager lover younger than herself. The priest's objection to the marriage seems to be his way of protecting her from what he sees as a threat. In short, he is not merely a dogmatic oppressor, for he shows awareness that the integrity implied by faithfulness to a vow can be a protection against too-impulsive action. But the results suggest that the priest, despite his apparent decency, gave the wrong advice. His voice makes up as important a part as the young lover's insistency in the forces that drive the widow to madness. In the poem Hardy transforms a melodramatic conflict between faith and love into a study of the bewildering precariousness and complexity of choice.

An even more complicated narrative is "The Noble Lady's Tale (*circa* 1790)" (*CP*, pp. 272–277), most of which is told by the lady herself. Like "The Inscription," it records an entirely imagined incident, but the situation is based on a real marriage between an actor and a lady who lived in the parish of Stinsford in the late eighteenth and early nineteenth centuries. As a boy, Hardy often saw their memorial plaque in Stinsford Church (referred to in the poem as the "yellowing marble" in "Mellstock Quire"), and the disparities in their social stations provoked his curiosity. The poem shows that he brooded not only over the lady's willingness to marry beneath her, which is the salient fact of the story from the conventional point of view, but also over the actor's willingness to abandon his profession for her. In the poem the actor, although he had promised her to leave the stage, is troubled by a wish to perform once more. He confesses his desire to his anxious wife, and she repays his honesty by releasing him from his promise despite her apprehensions:

> "I thought, 'Some wild stage-woman,
>   Honour-wrecked . . .'
> But no: it was inhuman
>   To suspect."

Although there appears to be full confidence, "faith and frankness," between the actor and the lady, both are aware of some nameless threat: "He feared it . . . I, also, / Feared it still more." Ironically, the lady's impulse to suspect is quite natural.

In the event that follows, the threat assumes a psychological reality that ruins the lives of the couple. When the actor returns to his wife, he reports bitterly that he failed in London because he saw her concealed in the audience and lost faith in her trust:

> " '*Faith—frankness.* Ah! Heaven save such!'
>   Murmured he,
> 'They are wedded wealth! *I* gave such
>   Liberally,
> But you, Dear, not. For you suspected me.' "

She protests that she has remained faithfully at home and did not attend the performance. Yet to his dying day he insists on blaming his failure on her, deciding that even if she was not there, the apparition was her wraith "projected . . . Thither, by [her] tense brain at home aggrieved." Neither character sees the possibility that the wraith was a projection of his own guilt, or of his unconscious awareness of her fundamental lack of trust in him.

The major irony is that the professed confidence of the two lovers in one another, their willingness to confess all, turned out to mask deep-seated, unconfessed fears and insecurities. Whether a manifestation of the wife's anxiety or the husband's guilt, a phantom arose from the psychological depths to blight their lives. Their hope for salvation lay in a full confession of their fears and suspicions, but instead, they destroyed their relationship by professing faith. The poem dramatizes how difficult it is to know when to suppress threatening impulses, and when to give them expression. The final stanza reveals the narrator's sympathetic inability to pass conclusive judgment:

> Riddle death-sealed for ever,
>   Let it rest! . . .
> One's heart could blame her never
>   If one guessed
> That go she did. She knew her actor best.

Ironically, she did not know her actor well enough.

Both "The Noble Lady's Tale" and "The Dead Quire" are associated with the history of Hardy's boyhood parish church at Stinsford. By extension, both poems deal with mystery—one with the mystery of a Christian miracle, the other with the more natural mystery of human psychology. Thus, they record the old illusions and the new. Along with Hardy's other ballads and narratives, they also constitute an imaginative history of the Wessex countryside, preserving the memory of a society comprised of sympathetic, imaginative, complex human beings, whose sufferings merit compassionate attention.

THE BURDEN OF GUILT

In the ballads and narratives based on historical materials, Hardy portrays characters who attempt to exert their moral imagination flexibly in the face of complex circumstances, such as the burghers whose deceptions allow a man a happy death, the volunteer who attempts to reconcile duty to country with fidelity to wife, the priest who aims at protecting the vulnerable widow, and the noble lady who tries to put down her fears and indulge a passionate wish of her husband. All of these characters have the qualities that Hardy celebrates in *The Science of Fiction*. In that they attempt humane action based on partial perceptions sympathetically received, they have what the artist must have: "the mental tactility that comes from a sympathetic appreciativeness of life in all of its manifestations."

It is significant that all of these people are from the country, for country people, in Hardy's view, are more fully endowed with imaginative sympathy—more fully human—than city dwellers. This view helps explain Hardy's preoccupation with Wessex as a subject for poetry. As Hardy contends in the biography, children raised in the country are "imaginative, dreamy, and credulous of vague mysteries . . . [because] 'The Unknown comes within so short a radius from themselves by comparison with the city-bred.' " Of the so-called "barbarism" of the peasants, which equates persons with things and founds wide generalizations on slender analogies, Hardy comments: "This 'barbaric idea which confuses persons and things' is, by the way, also common to the highest imaginative genius—that of the poet."[7]

This passage is dated 18 December 1890, while *The Science of Fiction* appeared
in 1891. It seems safe to say that Hardy writes about the countryside partly
because he finds there people who most fully exercise the power to deal with
the mysterious "Unknowns" of life through imaginative sympathy.

Although this power usually has tragic consequences, it occasionally
enables Hardy's characters to break out of the web of circumstances by
making unconventional, unpredictable choices; sometimes they succeed in
ignoring social norms and defying the logic of their selfish inclinations in
order to create more humane and realistic personal standards of conduct. In
"A Wife and Another" (*CP*, pp. 246–248), for example, the wife tells
another woman, whom she suspects of a romantic involvement with her
husband, that he is returning early from the war. Sensing intuitively that
the woman has also received a letter, the wife steals it and discovers a plan
for a secret tryst the night before her husband's return to her. She goes to
the meeting place with plans to break up the affair, but, struck by the
disclosure that her rival is to have a child, she has a change of heart:

> Then, as it were, within me
>   Something snapped,
> As if my soul had largened:
>   Conscience-capped,
> I saw myself the snarer—them the trapped.

Feeling herself the victim, she discovers that she is actually the victimizer.
She releases her husband from his bonds to her and returns home, sad but
confident: "I held I had not stirred God wrothfully." Her ability to sympa-
thize with the lives of others liberates her from the web of circumstance and
removes her to a higher realm of consciousness and morality.

"Her Late Husband (King's Hintock, 182–)" (*CP*, pp. 151–152) also
portrays a woman who recognizes her rival's claim to her husband as greater
than her own. She makes arrangements for him to be buried next to his
mistress, "After whose death he seemed to ail, / Though none considered
why," while providing for her own burial in her family plot. She regards
her act as conforming to a higher morality than social convention, and
imagines that on Christmas, when angels walk, they will say:

> " 'O strange interment! Civilized lands
>   Afford few types thereof;
> Here is a man who takes his rest
>   Beside his very Love,
> Beside the one who was his wife
>   In our sight up above!' "

Again, the nonconforming choice is a successful act of liberation.

"The Burghers (17—)" (*CP*, pp. 20–22), in contrast, presents the more complex case of a man whose moral scrupulosity leads him to question even his humane actions. Knowing of his wife's plans for an elopement, he schemes, with the encouragement of a friend, to surprise the lovers and kill the seducer. When the event occurs, the wife looks quickly at her lover— "Never upon me," says the husband, "Had she thrown look of love so thoroughsped!"—and then attempts to shield him from her husband's blow. "Blanked by such love," the husband pardons them and insists that his wife take with her money and all her possessions. The wife overcomes her scruples at accepting the generosity of a husband she is abandoning and takes the gifts. The poem concludes with an analysis of the complexities and ambiguities in the husband's act:

> " 'Fool,' some will say," I thought.—"But who is wise,
> Save God alone, to weigh my reasons why?"
> —"Hast thou struck home?" came with the boughs'
>   night-sighs.
> It was my friend. "I have struck well. They fly,
> But carry wounds that none can cicatrize."
> —"Not mortal?" said he. "Lingering—worse," said I.

On the surface it seems that the husband's impulse is generous and humane, yet he realizes the potential of his action to feed the lovers' guilt and thus leave worse than mortal wounds. Only God can "weigh" his motive; not even he is sure of the significance of what he has done. His act of liberation has put the lovers eternally in his debt and opened a new realm of possible guilt for himself. His higher morality may be a form of more subtle enslavement.

In Hardy's ballads and narratives the characters usually fail. They calculate humanely and sympathetically, but inaccurately; events deceive; the power of the imagination is inadequate to the circumstances. Yet what is most painful is not their failure but the self-torture resulting from the sort of moral scrupulosity found in the husband in "The Burghers." Despite the relatively small and inconclusive part played by the characters in the concatenation of events leading to death and suffering, again and again they take upon themselves the full burden of guilt. They imaginatively confuse cause with responsibility. This is the most painful irony of all—that the characters, having attempted a moral action according to their best lights, torture themselves with anguished self-reproach. It is this overwhelming guilt, only partially justified, which is Hardy's most compelling theme in his ballads and narratives of the Wessex countryside.

"A Sunday Morning Tragedy (*circa* 186–)" (*CP*, pp. 188–191), for example, is told by a woman in whom crushing circumstances arouse passionate energies of self-reproach. Her daughter has been made pregnant by a man who refuses to marry her, despite the urgings of the mother.

> I plodded to her sweetheart's door
> In Pydel Vale, alas for me:
> I pleaded with him, pleaded sore,
> To save her from her misery.

To induce abortion, the mother gives the girl an herb purchased from an old shepherd, and the result is fatal. As the girl lies on her deathbed on a Sunday morning, neighbors come to chide the family for the secrecy of her impending marriage; surprisingly, the banns were announced in church that day: " 'Ha-ha! Such well-kept news!' laughed they." The lover comes and whispers to the mother that her arguments have changed his mind: "I've felt for her, and righted all." But all is wrong. The mother goes to her daughter's bedside, and her scream draws everyone else:

> There she [the daughter] lay—silent, breathless, dead,
> Stone dead she lay—wronged, sinless she!
> Ghost-white the cheeks once rosy-red.

The circumstances causing the tragedy are shown to be complex and powerful. The young man avoids marriage because he plans to emigrate, presumably to get a job and not merely to escape a moral responsibility: " 'Poverty's worse than shame,' he said." Whether or not his motives are exclusively self-serving, in the final event he shows himself to be susceptible to a moral plea: "I've felt for her." The mother is aware of the tragic absurdities of living in a world where birth can be a curse, as indicated in her observation on the old shepherd's justification of the herb:

> "'Tis meant to balk ill-motherings"—
> (Ill-motherings! Why should they be?)—
> "If not, would God have sent such things?"
> So spoke the shepherd unto me.

The shepherd's logic is weak—that an indication of God's providence is the existence of herbs that will kill unborn children. The mother's view seems closer to the realities: her daughter's predicament is an indication of the perplexing grimness of the human situation. Yet the most touching feature of the tale is the mother's guilt. The refrain "Alas for me!" (not for the daughter) rings again and again, and the poem ends with a self-curse: "My punishment I cannot bear, / But pray God *not* to pity me." One can understand her feeling of guilt, for she unsuccessfully risked her daughter's life in order to avoid scandal. Yet, from an objective point of view, the ultimate responsibility was not hers. She was trapped by external complexities—the lovers' passion, the man's poverty, the "providential" existence of abortifacients, the weight of social pressures, her concern for her daughter's future—

all of which led to her well-intentioned act. Yet she assumes the burden of responsibility. Throughout she believes in the "innocency" of her daughter, who in her view died "wronged, sinless"; but she cannot forgive herself, even though she is a victim of the same circumstances.

"Her Death and After" (*CP*, pp. 34–38) provides an even more painful example of the tragically scrupulous moral imagination at work, for it describes the guilt of a man whose well-intentioned actions are successful. He is called to the deathbed of a woman dying in childbirth, who had refused his suit and married another man. The woman realizes now the mistake of her marriage and fears that her husband, a man of cruel impulses, will mistreat her child, who was born lame. On her deathbed she repents her fidelity to traditional morality:

> "As a wife I was true. But, such my unease
> That, could I insert a deed back in Time,
> I'd make her yours, to secure your care;
>   And the scandal bear,
>   And the penalty for the crime!"

Her fears are realized: the husband remarries, and he and his new wife mistreat the child. The speaker continues to visit the wife's tomb, and one evening he encounters the husband in "the Cirque of the Gladiators," Dorchester's Roman Ring, "Whose Pagan echoes mock the chime / Of our Christian time." In that morally ambivalent place, the speaker makes a strange, unconventional choice. The husband demands that he stop visiting the wife's grave:

> "There's decency even in death, I assume;
> Preserve it, sir, and keep away;
> For the mother of my first-born you
>   Show mind undue!"

On a desperate impulse, the speaker claims that the child is his—"God pardon—or pardon not—the lie"—and offers to care for it. If necessary, he is even willing to fight a duel. The husband then sends him the child, whom the speaker raises and loves—but not without feelings of guilt:

> And I gave the child my love,
> And the child loved me, and estranged us none.
> But compunctions loomed; for I'd harmed the dead
>   By what I said
>   For the good of the living one.
>
> —Yet though, God wot, I am sinner enough,
> And unworthy the woman who drew me so,

> Perhaps this wrong for her darling's good
> She forgives, or would,
> If only she could know!

There is no question in the reader's mind but that the man is a saint, not a sinner; that he is more worthy of the woman's love, not less; that his action merits forgiveness, not condemnation; and that he should feel moral satisfaction, not guilt. But the poignancy of the poem results from his inability to feel free and confident in his action and to accept the girl's love without "compunctions." He has fulfilled the wishes of the woman he loved, risked his life to save another human being from suffering, and found the consolation of loving companionship. Yet he feels guilty for telling a lie that impugns the good name of a dead person, even though the woman herself confessed on her deathbed that she would willingly endure scandal to save her child.

The ending is typical. Again and again Hardy's narratives conclude on a note of guilt. The characters submit to circumstances and feel guilty; they attempt to act according to conventional moral principles and feel guilty; they act courageously and boldly to liberate themselves from conventions and circumstances, and the result is guilt. Guilt drives the wife in "At Shag's Heath" to suicide. Guilt causes the protagonists in "San Sebastian" (*CP*, pp. 17–19) and "A Sunday Morning Tragedy" to bring down curses on their own heads. Guilt makes a wandering outcast of the trampwoman. Thoughts of her guilt obsess the mind of Jenny as she dies at the end of "The Dance at the Phoenix" (*CP*, pp. 38–42). In "The Peasant's Confession" (*CP*, pp. 26–30) a man expresses his guilt for subverting Napoleon's chances at Waterloo in order to prevent the battle from taking place on his own land. "The Sacrilege" (*CP*, pp. 375–379), describing a man's vengeance on a predatory woman who led his brother to his death, ends with the vision of her hair floating in the water and the sound of her dying scream haunting him "Until his judgment-time." "The Caricature" (*CP*, pp. 728–729) concludes with a man driven insane by his guilt for a trivial but cruel act. "The Flirt's Tragedy" (*CP*, pp. 195–198), another tale of love and infidelity, ends with the guilt of a wronged man who failed in his attempts to repair the excesses of his vengeance:

> But pass by, and leave unregarded
> A Cain to his suffering,
> For vengeance too dark on the woman
> Whose lover he slew.

In poetically recording the history of the Wessex countryside, Hardy tells tales of people trapped by their errors, their uncertainty as to proper moral values, their failure of perception, their inability to foresee consequences and to predict the effects of change and chance. But the most interesting theme is the tragic scrupulosity of the moral imagination. Hardy delineates the limitations of his characters' responsibility for their conditions, makes allowances for their good intentions, and forgives them for their mistakes—that is, he brings into play his own sympathetic imagination. But the characters themselves see only their errors, their failures, their moments of temporary malice. Too often they take full responsibility for circumstances that are partially outside their control, and act as unforgiving judges of their own lives. For them, the imaginative sympathy is a burden; their high and flexible sense of morality, their aspirations for the better, their desires to be expansively human bring them grief. In Hardy's verse narratives the characters' afflictions come from chance and circumstance and bitter ironies of situation, but no external forces punish them as unremittingly as their own consciences.

Notes

1. *Personal Writings*, pp. 136, 134–135.
2. *Personal Writings*, p. 137.
3. *Life*, pp. 311–312.
4. Whatever information is available concerning the historical background for any of Hardy's poems is to be found in J. O. Bailey, *The Poetry of Thomas Hardy: A Handbook and Commentary* (Chapel Hill: University of North Carolina Press, 1970).
5. *Personal Writings*, pp. 229–230.
6. Bailey, *The Poetry of Thomas Hardy*, pp. 526–528.
7. *Life*, pp. 202, 230.

Disembodied Voices in Hardy's Shorter Poems

VERN B. LENTZ

Thomas Hardy was fond of a particular kind of poem: the poem in which the words of authority are spoken by a spirit or ghost. Typically, these poems present a problem, and a spirit or ghost speaks words which offer a solution. By rough count, 46 of Hardy's more than 900 poems employ such a disembodied voice. This seems odd, for Hardy was a rationalist and empiricist who did not rely on the supernatural as an answer to any problem. But there they are: 46 poems in which the words of authority are spoken by a disembodied voice. This seems more like Yeats than the agnostic and Darwinian Hardy. What distinguishes this device in Hardy is not that a spirit simply speaks but that its words are authoritative. When Hardy wanted to give speech a special standing he would, frequently, put that speech in the mouth of a spirit; in a Hardy poem ghosts *know* more than mortal humans. Seldom in Hardy's poetry—there are exceptions—does a disembodied voice speak words that are playful, mistaken, or reflective of merely "personal" limitations. Frequently these voices play a didactic role. When Hardy wanted to offer advice or deliver a message he had a spirit deliver that message; when Hardy felt awkward about intruding a comment he apparently felt it was less awkward to have a spirit speak. In one way, these disembodied voices are similar to a moralizing and intrusive narrator in fiction: they offer generalized commentary from an omniscient position. Despite his fondness for ghosts and spirits in poetry, however, Hardy never uses them in fiction. Perhaps this says something about Hardy's notion of the difference between prose and verse: poetry allowed him to be as imaginative and inventive as he chose; prose fiction bound him to the reality of the empiricists.

The best explanation for this rationalist's use of the supernatural lies in H. L. Weatherby's observation that there are "two Hardys" (162): the agnostic, alienated modern Hardy and the Hardy of traditional vision. The first Hardy is "the London and Max Gate Hardy" and the second is "the man who walked to Higher Bockhampton every Sunday and listened to his

Vern B. Lentz, "Disembodied Voices in Hardy's Shorter Poems," *Colby Library Quarterly*, Vol. XXIII, No. 2 (June, 1987), pp. 57–65. Copyright © *Colby Library Quarterly*, 1987. Reprinted by permission.

mother's stories" (163). This second Hardy is quite at ease with spirits and ghosts and naturally expects that humans will hear voices from a supernatural source. In this traditional vision the ghostly voices will have more than human authority. Weatherby argues convincingly that "Hardy is John Keble and D. H. Lawrence by turns and never recognizes (or acknowledges) the contradiction: both facets of his character seem to have intensified with age" (166).

Hardy was fascinated by ghosts in yet another way: he liked to imagine himself as a spectre. This manner of regarding himself is seen in a curious passage from his autobiography, *The Life and Works of Thomas Hardy*:

> For my part, if there is any way of getting a melancholy satisfaction out of life it lies in dying, so to speak, before one is out of the flesh; by which I mean putting on the manners of ghosts, wandering in their haunts, and taking their views of surrounding things. To think of life as passing away is a sadness; to think of it as past is at least tolerable. Hence even when I enter into a room to pay a simple morning call I have unconsciously the habit of regarding the scene as if I were a spectre not solid enough to influence my environment; only fit to behold and say, as another spectre said: "Peace be unto you!"
>
> (218)

To consider himself in this way gave not only satisfaction but a god-like perspective from which to comment on the affairs of men and women; in his poems Hardy frequently assumes this perspective and speaks with the voice of a spirit when he wishes to make a generalizing remark. And when spectral aloofness was his dominant mood Hardy could remove himself as far from life as it was possible to go: into the voice of a bodiless intelligence.

Hardy's poems contain a mix of distinct voices that Hardy assumed, voices that converse with each other. Hardy is chameleon-like in his assumption of discrete voices, no one of which is the sole voice of "the poet." One of these voices is the disembodied voice of the ghost, or, more accurately, various individual spirits populate the poems and generalize on human affairs. Paul Zietlow and Frederick W. Shilstone have explained with precision and comprehensiveness how separate voices interact, i.e., converse, with each other through the whole of Hardy's canon. Zietlow elucidates Hardy's aesthetic and indicates that the poems represent an interplay of various voices and recognizes how Hardy's poetic sensibility manifests itself in a variety of identities:

> The poet's commitment, then, is not a sustained interpretation of life, but to moments of experience and to the accurate recording of them. . . . As the speaker in a poem, his identity is defined by the nature of the impression and its means of conveyance, and may bear little relationship to any "real," historical identity: he writes "dramatic monologues by different characters."

This theory justifies the more playful or fanciful flights of the imagination that often occur in Hardy's poetry. But the theory also sanctions deeply serious modes, because a full response to the unique moment brings the poet's self into temporary focus. For a moment, the poet achieves a clear, fixed identity, crystallized from the surging, contradictory being of his consciousness. . . . At such a moment one becomes a reality—not the totality of what one could be, but a single aspect of that potential . . .

(Zietlow, 57)

Shilstone stresses the way in which these voices talk to each other. His argument is that Hardy became increasingly uncomfortable with the ironic stance to which his fiction had forced him by the time of *Jude the Obscure*. The irony of Hardy's fictional narrators became so sardonic and aloof from human concerns, Shilstone writes, that this narrative voice was devoid of sympathy and compassion, hardened by tragedy into an unfeeling remoteness from life. Such remoteness, and the irony that comes from it, indeed represents one aspect of Hardy's character. Another aspect of Hardy's mind, however, insisted on compassion and what Hardy called "loving-kindness" (2:319). Hardy's desire to separate himself from life manifested itself in irony; his "loving-kindness" manifested itself in a desire to identify himself with the lives and sufferings of fellow humans. In the poetry Hardy's complex character takes the form of separate voices, the speakers of various poems. Hardy was able to move rapidly away from a too cruel irony in one poem to the voice of a different human character in another poem. The disembodied voices represent—except in the "Poems of 1912–13"—the cold and ironic aspect of their creator. But Hardy was not always comfortable with this side of himself and, by placing the irony in the voices of ghosts and spirits, detaches himself from the cruelty of that irony by locating its voice elsewhere. All of these various disembodied voices stand outside the flow of time and natural process and offer ironic comment on mortals who are trapped within "the cell of Time" (1:326). The irony is a product of the timeless perspective of the spirits on the temporal concerns of humans. Recognizing this, it is important to acknowledge, firstly, that Hardy's irony appears in voices other than disembodied ones, and, secondly, that in the poems Hardy employs other voices than those of the ironist.

A basic principle of Hardy's art was his aesthetics of disjunction. The disjunctions of the poems using a disembodied voice involve the juxtaposition of the voices of the living with the voices of the dead, the physical with the spiritual, and, most importantly, the temporal with the timeless. Hardy was quite willing to distort reality as a means of achieving a poetic effect. The disjunctive mode is one in which distortion or disunity of form is a calculated technique designed to convey a truth about the human condition. In his autobiography Hardy discusses this disjunctive mode at several points. In an entry headed "Reflections on Art" he writes that "Art is a disproportioning—(i.e., distorting, throwing out of proportion)—of realities, to show more clearly the features that matter in those realities." And elsewhere, in discussing "the constructional part" of his writing, he says that "the adjustment of things unusual to things eternal and universal" is "the key to the art" (239, 268). Even at those times when the voices of the living seem to converse most naturally and easily with the voices of the dead Hardy is aware that he brings together two presences which are basically dissimilar. Morton Dauwen Zabel noticed these " 'startling touches of weirdness' " in discussing the way in which discordance is central to all of Hardy's poetry and fiction. Hardy was both the modern empiricist and the poet of traditional vision: because of these contradictory facets of his own sensibility it was easy for him to bring together in his verse the living and the spectral to establish an ironic perspective.

Another principle of Hardy's aesthetic underlies his fondness for disembodied voices. In the "Apology" to *Late Lyrics and Earlier* he writes that "the real function of poetry [is] the *application* of ideas to life [in Matthew Arnold's familiar phrase]" (2:320, emphasis mine). That Hardy repeats Arnold's rather mechanical term "application" to describe the way in which poetic ideas bear upon life is significant. In this formulation "ideas" come from the world of the spirits and are "applied" to "life"—the world of mortal humans. The two elements are brought together by the poet and they don't quite fit; a dissimilarity is present that may grate upon the reader. As in the aesthetics of disjunction a discordance exists, a sense of the poet fusing together two realities which are unlike in kind.

The first, in the order of publication, of Hardy's poems using a spectral voice is "A Christmas Ghost-Story" (1:121), one of the poems that Hardy wrote on the occasion of the Boer War. The poem sets a pattern for Hardy's other poems employing a ghostly voice as it begins with a description of ordinary, particularized reality which is then juxtaposed with the voice of a "phantom" who makes a generalizing comment. This poem has a significant place in the group of poems which Hardy titled "War Poems" for it sums up all the rest. The words of the phantom are authoritative; undoubtedly the ghost speaks for Hardy. This disembodied voice is the one voice amongst all those in the "War Poems" that is most clearly the poet's. One other poem in the group does employ a disembodied voice: in "The Souls of the Slain" (1:124) a "senior soul-flame" addresses other ghosts and makes a statement on personal immortality. This poem also begins with a concrete description of the actual world—Hardy even employs a footnote to identify the exact place—after which "A dim-discerned train / Of sprites without mould" appears, speaks, and thus sets the stage for the authoritative words of their leader.

In "Lausanne: In Gibbon's Old Garden" (1:138) Hardy writes of a place he visited and imagines the ghost of Gibbon speaking. Again, the setting is specific and the words of the spectre make a generalizing comment. The juxtaposition is that of the past with the present as well as the solid, physical world with the world of Gibbon's spirit. Hardy was also willing to use disembodied voices for humorous effect; both "The Levelled Churchyard" (1:196) and "Ah, are you digging on my grave?" (2:38) use the voice from the grave to mock the self-centered concerns of individuals. "Her Father" (1:273) and "The Moth-Signal" (2:111) use spectral voices to comment rudely and tauntingly on the romantic affairs of men and women. In both poems the ghost speaks only at the end; and in each poem the ghost's voice is a jarring intrusion into a dramatized human situation. Hardy's aesthetics of disjunction function here as the poet insists on the discordance between the timeless and the temporal.

A favorite motif of Hardy's is that the dead are better off than the living. In three poems Hardy has ghosts speak from under the sod to explain to the living that death is preferable to life. In all three of these poems the words of the ghosts have authority; the message that spectral voices deliver is conclusive. And it gains significance as it is repeated through Hardy's canon. In "Voices from Things Growing in a Churchyard" (2:395) several representative voices speak from the grave to deliver the message that all is well with the dead. The voices of the dead in "While Drawing in a Church-yard" (2:287) speak the same sentiments and conclude: " 'That no God trumpet us to rise / We truly hope.' " In "Jubilate" (2:257) the dead show as much with their dancing as they put into words; but their one-line message to the living, " 'We are out of it all!—yea, in Little-Ease cramped no more,' " confirms what Hardy's ghosts have said elsewhere.

In a number of poems the dead and the living converse; they speak to each other, frequently in a pattern of question and answer. "Night in the Old Home" (1:325) presents a speaker who is "A thinker of crooked thoughts upon Life in the sere" who questions "my perished people" and hears them advise him to:

"Enjoy, suffer, wait: spread the table here freely like us,
And, satisfied, placid, unfretting, watch time away beamingly!"

Here there is not a jarring disjunction between death and life. The words of the dead come in an easy conversational answer to the question of the living. "The To-Be-Forgotten" (1:181) follows a similar pattern as the living voice questions the dead and receives the dead's answer. In this poem, as in "Night in the Old Home," the spectral voices are not simply overheard by the speaker but their words come in response to the speaker's questioning; they form a conversation between life and death. The theme of "The-To-Be-Forgotten" is the same as that of "The Souls of the Slain": immortality is remembrance in the minds of the living. "The Dead and the Living One" (2:300) presents two ghosts and one living voice who, all three, enter into conversation. Here, again, the ghosts speak with authority and the mortal is naive. The poem closes with the female ghost's mordant laugh which is as conclusive as speech, and which serves the same function as the Ancient Briton's grin in "The Moth-Signal" and the words of the "cynic ghost" in "Her Father."

In Hardy's poetry ghosts can be victims as well as advisors. In "Spectres that Grieve" (2:37) the restless "phantoms of the gone" respond to a human's question, explaining that because they are misrepresented in the memory of mortals they must wander as "shaken slighted visitants" instead of enjoying the relief of death. The ghosts of "Family Portraits" (3:262), ancestors of the speaker, appear and act out a drama which, if completed, would explain the speaker's "blood's tendance." The fearful speaker interrupts and the ghosts withdraw with a reproach and a warning. In all these poems where the living and the dead converse it is the living who have questions and the dead who speak the answers; the condition of death appears to insure inviolability and authority.

But Hardy writes other poems in which the dead are as perplexed and uncomfortable as the living, even a few poems in which the living answer the questions of the dead. In "I rose up as my custom is" (2:94) and "The Woman I Met" (2:360) discontented ghosts appear to the living. In the first of these poems the ghosts receives a lecture from a living woman who has the authority within the poem. In the second a female ghost appears to the speaker; the ghost's purpose is not to make a pronouncement but to express feelings which she kept to herself when living. This ghost has a complex and vulnerable character. In "Something tapped" (2:202) a lonely and helpless ghost complains bitterly to the living; in "An Upbraiding" (2:282) an angry ghost berates a mortal; this ghost speaks its mind but its words carry no special authority; instead, these spectres reveal very "human" and intimate concerns. In similar poems the speaking ghosts are not greatly different from other personae; they reveal personalities like human personalities. These poems emphasize what the living and the dead have in common and grant no special insight to the dead. The female ghost of "The Monument Maker" (3:14) flirts with the sculptor as if she were alive; the ghostly speaker of "Not only I" (3:101) regrets the loss of life, something ghosts rarely do in Hardy's poems, and enumerates the various aspects of its temporal existence which are now "doomed awhile to lie / In this close bin with earthen sides." The speaker of "Regret not me" (2:106) assures the living that death is peaceful; nevertheless, the poem consists of a listing of the charming experiences of its life and, by implication, indicates the same sense of loss that pervades "Not only I."

Hardy also uses disembodied voices which are not the ghosts of individuals but disembodied intelligences which voice a poem's most conclusive words. "The Musical Box" (2:223) is one of the most important poems in the Hardy canon, a poem which identifies the precondition which must exist if humans are to enjoy happiness or satisfaction. And while the speaker of the poem is human, it is "a spirit" that enunciates the words which the speaker must grasp: " 'O value what the nonce outpours' " and again: " 'O make the most of what is nigh!' " In "The Clock of the Years" (2:278) the speaker and a "spirit" converse. The spirit is laconic; but he voices the wisdom of the poem. In a similar manner "At the Entering of the New Year" (2:415) uses a spirit to speak the words of authority within the poem. In both "There seemed a strangeness" (3:34) and "A Night of Questionings" (3:35) more talkative spirits, identified as "a Voice" and "the wind," philosophize on the human predicament. In all of these poems understanding, the answers to human questions, comes from a source somewhere between the human and the divine. A somewhat different use of the disembodied voice comes in two of Hardy's poetic fantasies: "Aquae Sulis" (2:90) and "The Graveyard of Dead Creeds" (3:33). In each poem the voice of an extinct religion is overheard and the imagined voices of the religions pronounce their own doom.

In the "Poems of 1912–13" Hardy makes direct use of a disembodied voice twice and twice more refers to "hearing" the voice of his deceased wife, Emma. The ghost of Emma speaks in "His Visitor" (2:57) as the spectre returns to Max Gate to observe and comment on the changes that have taken place. This ghost is different from Hardy's other phantom appearances; a different spectral sensibility exists here. Emma speaks of the domestic details of her old home; she comments on the everydayness and circumstantiality of things in a very specific, almost empirical, manner. This phantom refers to two shared lives: the very ordinariness of the items that hold her attention invoke a shared experience. Here the disembodied voice does not make pronouncements or offer insights; instead, her consciousness registers the concrete details of her household economy. Emma's spirit speaks again in "The Haunter" (2:55) to say that she is closer to her spouse now than when living. The pair were estranged when Emma was alive; but now, her ghost explains, "If he but sigh since my loss befell him / Straight to his side I go." This spectre talks about intimacy, the intimacy of death with life. The speaker of "Your Last Drive" (2:48), who is undoubtedly close to Hardy himself, addresses his words to a "dear ghost." He imagines the ghost speaking to him and quotes her words. What the phantom says is that, in contrast to the words of "The Haunter," a vast chasm exists between death and life; no separation can be more absolute:

> But I shall not know
> How many times you visit me there,
> Or what your thoughts are, or if you go
> There never at all. And I shall not care.

The speaker of "The Voice" (2:56) hears the sound of the dead: "Woman much missed, how you call to me, call to me." This poem lays equal stress on separation and intimacy: the speaker cannot quote her words, what the voice says is not fully articulated and the speaker even wonders whether the sound he hears is only the wind. And yet, "faltering forward," he cannot rid himself of the voice which, in one way, is even closer to him than the phantom of "The Haunter" who cannot make herself heard. The ghostly voices of the "Poems of 1912–13" are the voices of a highly individuated woman who Hardy knew intimately. This ghost is too much of an actual person to have the kind of authority possessed by the more ethereal presences who speak to humans from a spiritual realm. Even after her death, Emma was too human to possess the authority of a spirit.

The fact that Hardy used the disembodied voice so frequently is striking. It does seem to have allowed him to occasionally do in verse what he was used to doing in his fiction: offer commentary from an omniscient position. But this is only one of the functions of the disembodied voice. For a writer who was acutely aware of time and natural process, the voice of a spirit was one way to escape from that process and bring a timeless perspective to bear on human life. In the shorter poems, Hardy uses disembodied voices in at least three ways. The most familiar is the anonymous spirit who makes generalizing and ironic comments on human situations. Frequently, the anonymous spirits answer the direct questions of men and women, thus entering into a conversation with the living. The message that these anonymous ghosts have for humans is that the dead are content, that death is a relief, that the dead have no desire to return to life. These spirits speak with authority: wisdom is gained in death and humans can trust that the words that come from beyond the grave carry the authority of a spiritual world. Another type of ghost is fitful and bewildered. Death has not brought relief to these spirits and they wish to make contact with the living to have questions answered and situations resolved. The third use of the disembodied voice is in the "Poems of 1912–13," where the spirit of Emma Hardy visits her former home and her former husband apparently motivated by a simple, and almost human, need for companionship. This ghost is different from the others in that she has an individual personality not greatly different from the personality that was hers when alive. Emma's ghost does not offer understanding or make statements. It seems that she only wants to visit, to establish some kind of contact with her living husband, that loneliness may be her most urgent motivation.

Hardy, then, was fond of writing poems which employ the disembodied voice of a spirit or ghost. These poems are found throughout his canon; they are not clustered in any particular volumes of his verse. The ghostly perspective intrigued Hardy: in his autobiography he writes of regarding himself as a spectre "not solid enough to influence my environment" even in the midst of social visits. Hardy was both the advanced thinker and the poet of traditional vision. This traditional vision, his interest in the folklore of Wessex, made it easy for him to use spirits who speak words of authority to humans. On the other hand, his use of spirits to supply the answers to human problems may be an agnostic's way of indicating that there are no answers. Hardy's aesthetics of disjunction was a fundamental principle of his art, a mode he used throughout his poetry and fiction. This principle made it natural for him to conjoin two separate worlds—the world of the living and the world of the dead—for ironic effect. In the disembodied voice poems, the irony is a product of the difference between the two perspectives. On a less theoretical level, Hardy loved the odd and the unusual; he was fascinated by queer twists. A spectral perspective enabled him to exploit oddities and underline coincidences. Paul Zietlow and Frederick W. Shilstone have elucidated Hardy's use of various speaking voices throughout his poetry: Hardy's usual manner of composition was to create a voice not his own to speak in his poems which, he insisted, were "dramatic monologues by different characters" (1:235). The disembodied voices are one set of voices which recur again and again amongst the variety of personae in Hardy's canon.

Works Cited

Hardy, Thomas. *The Complete Poetical Works of Thomas Hardy*. Ed. Samuel Hynes, 3 vols. Oxford: Clarendon, 1982.
———. *The Life and Work of Thomas Hardy*. Ed. Michael Millgate. Athens: Univ. of Georgia Press, 1985.
Shilstone, Frederick W. "Conversing Stances in Hardy's Shorter Poems." *Colby Library Quarterly* 12 (1976): 139–48.
Weatherby, H. L. "Two Hardys." *Sewanee Review* 93 (1985): 162–71.
Zabel, Morton Dauwen. "Hardy in Defense of His Art: The Aesthetic of Incongruity." *Southern Review* 6 (1940): 125–49; rewritten with the same title for *Craft and Character*. New York: Viking, 1957.
Zietlow, Paul. *Moments of Vision: The Poetry of Thomas Hardy*. Cambridge: Harvard Univ. Press, 1974.

Hardy Ruins: Female Spaces and Male Designs

U. C. KNOEPFLMACHER

> . . . *I once inquired of her*
> *How looked the spot when first she settled there.*
> —Thomas Hardy, "Domicilium"
> (c. 1857–60)

> . . . *he found a "mine" in me, he said . . .*
> —Emma Hardy, *Some Recollections*
> (c. 1911–12)

The houses depicted in nineteenth-century British poetry differ substantially from earlier representations of a patriarchal seat in poems such as Marvell's "Upon Appleton House" and Pope's "Epistle to Burlington" as well as from the male mansions domesticated by female inhabitants in nineteenth-century realistic novels. In a century that separated an inner circle of female domesticity from an outer sphere of male traffic, the home became increasingly feminized, associated with childhood and hence with nurturance.[1] Yet a good many imaginative writers responded to this division by attempting to integrate gender opposites within a culturally defined feminine space. In *Jane Eyre*, for example, Ferndean replaces Thornfield Hall as a site in which an independent heroine can animate the paralyzed Rochester and enter a more equitable union. This integration, however, does not work in the same way for poets as it does for novelists; likewise, it works differently for men and women.[2] For Thomas Hardy, who preferred poetry to fiction, the recovery of the feminine was the propelling force behind his finest lyrics. Over his poetic career, Hardy wavered in his faith that the feminine, which he associated with the houses of childhood, could be recovered without the compromise of adult masculinity. Eventually, in his old age, he nonetheless managed to effect the "return to the native land" that Freud identified as a maternal "home" (Cixous and Clément 93).

U. C. Knoepflmacher, "Hardy Ruins: Female Spaces and Male Designs," *PMLA*, Vol. 105 (1990), 1055–1070. Copyright © Modern Language Association of America, 1990. Reprinted by permission of the Modern Language Association of America.

The structures of desire devised by Hardy's nineteenth-century poetic predecessors dramatize the difficulty of finding a feminine space capable of annulling gender and rendering sexual difference immaterial. By way of contrast, the patriarchal houses that novelists enlist as transformational spaces allow female occupants room enough to break down too rigidly gendered opposites. Just as Pemberley Hall crowns Elizabeth Bennet's efforts to soften Darcy's male pride (while simultaneously acting as a patriarchal corrective to her own prejudices), so are male mansions renovated when entered by Jane Eyre, Catherine Linton, Helen Huntingdon, Esther Summerson, and even Hardy's Bathsheba Everdene.[3] In Romantic and Victorian poetry, however, such a process of renewal and restabilizing remains far more problematic. Ruins, rather than living buildings, predominate in works in which a woman's abode, rather than a man's, becomes directly or indirectly associated with what Bachelard sees as a "dream-memory" of an original maternal envelope (15).

Romantic poetry all too often depicts a ruthless razing of the structures it persistently identifies with a feminine enclosure: the "purple-lined palace of sweet sin" that Keats's Lamia has devised for young Lycius cannot withstand the gaze of an older male realist; the "white walls" of the shelter where Byron's Haidee has transported her lover crumble after she, her unborn child, and her ultramasculine father die (*Lamia* 2.31; *Don Juan* 3.27.209).[4] One mode by which nineteenth-century male poets could sustain the intensity of their profound yearning for a return to a site free of strife was to link this threatened female space with death. In his influential poem "The Ruined Cottage" (eventually expanded into the first book of *The Excursion* of 1814), Wordsworth lingers on the decayed structure that once housed the female figure the Wanderer had regarded as "my own child" (line 500). The young poet, who has been "slaking" his thirst from a nearby well, soon finds the Wanderer's sad account of the last "tenant of these ruined walls" far more refreshing than any classical elegy bemoaning the disappearance of wood sprites or water nymphs (475–77, 916).

By having male teller and male listener jointly review "that woman's suffering" (922), Wordsworth strengthens their bond as well as his own poetic identity. The Wanderer's Margaret is cast as the alluring sleeper Cixous and Clément describe in *The Newly Born Woman*: "intact, eternal, absolutely powerless," she acts as an enabling presence for male dreamers, a second and "best mother" (66). The invigorated "old Man" grasps his staff with "sprightly mien," and Wordsworth's speaker, moved to bless Margaret "in the impotence of grief," can become more potent than before (965, 964). The inert female has provided male pilgrims with a starting point for their peregrinations: poet-son and Wanderer-father can now join other representative male selves, Solitary and Pastor, in public meeting places. The young speaker may profess a "brother's love" for the dead stranger who was like a daughter to the Wanderer. Yet the speaker is also her son. As the surviving foster child of both the Wanderer and Margaret, he proves hardier than the fragile figure ravaged by wifehood, widowhood, and "maternal cares" (858). His narrative thrives on her ruin.

Whereas Wordsworth's male selves reenter a maternal house only to egress, regrouped, as a strengthened masculine unit, Thomas Hardy struggles not to repress femininity in writings that self-consciously enlist—yet also subvert—the *Heimweh*, the profound homesickness, that his Romantic and Victorian predecessors had powerfully dramatized. Whether written at the outset or the end of his long career, a large proportion of his poems rely on an increasingly elaborate nexus of mother-feminine-house figurations to work out a gender opposition he would like to abolish. In his eagerness to annul gender, Hardy eventually devises lyrics and narratives that allow him to tap something like the fluidity recent critics have noted in Freud's essay "The Uncanny." Hardy's later poems demonstrate that femininity, as Shoshana Felman puts it, can act as more than a "snug container of masculinity," that it can, instead, enter and inhabit the masculine as much as the masculine can enter and inhabit the feminine (42). As we shall see, it was the empowering ghost of Emma Hardy that finally furnished Hardy with a means to bridge opposites. Though lost and obliterated, a *heimisch*, or "homelike," maternal place could animate a poetry in which the uncanny, or *Unheimliche*, becomes itself familiar, a "vibration of the *Heimliche*" (Cixous 545).

I

In *The Early Life of Thomas Hardy* (1928; rpt. in *The Life of Thomas Hardy*, 1962), attributed to Florence Emily Hardy but actually written by the subject himself, Hardy points his readers to the female place of origin of his younger, Wordsworthian self by reproducing a poem he composed sometime between the ages of seventeen and twenty. Screened from the public eye for nearly sixty years, "Domicilium" is itself a relic, much like Margaret's time-obliterated cottage. Like the Wanderer, the aged Hardy undertakes a revisitation. By returning to a setting that existed "nearly half a century before [his] birth," he can enlist these "Wordsworthian lines" for something more than their avowedly "naive fidelity" to a literal past (F. E. Hardy 4). For he not only restores a rural house of the 1790s but also returns to the time of Wordsworth's memorable perceptions of those maternal sister-selves placed near the ruins of Tintern Abbey or of Margaret's cot.

Still, as his reliance on the mask of Florence Hardy suggests, Hardy eschews a male guide such as the Wanderer to help him reconstruct what he calls, somewhat deceptively, a "paternal homestead." He refuses to silence those voices whose muting was necessary for Wordsworth to solidify a male poetic identity. Avoiding a male mediator like the one who interprets Doro-

thy's eyes as "gleams" of his own "past existence" in "Tintern Abbey"
(148–49), Hardy prefers to rely on a female mediator, "my father's mother,"
to help him explore his own origins (20).[5] It is the voice of this family
historian that takes over—at the exact midpoint of "Domicilium"—the
speech of the youthful male who has struggled to set the stage in the opening
three sestets.

Asked to recall the aspects of "the spot when first she settled there,"
the boy's grandmother integrates the human habitat with its surrounding
wilderness:

> Our house stood quite alone, and those tall firs
> And beeches were not planted. Snakes and efts
> Swarmed in the summer days, and nightly bats
> Would fly about our bedroom. Heathcroppers
> Lived on the hills, and were our only friends;
> So wild it was when first we settled here.
>
> (31–36)

By recalling the "uncultivated slopes" of the past (27), this artless speaker
undermines the cultivation of the would-be poet who has given the name
"domicilium" to what she, far more simply, calls "our house." Unlike
Wordsworth's Miltonic Wanderer, the grandmother is a witness who requires
no exalted correlatives. Beginning his narrative as a "man speaking to men,"
the young adult soon becomes a boy again, remembering how, awe-struck,
he had deferred to the authority of an ancient who still addressed him as
"my child" (25). Aware that "hardy flowers" flourish "best untrained" (8–9),
the youngster does not want his male training to distance him from the
Hardy woman who once flowered on this site. Eager to erase what separates
them, he allows her to close the narrative he began.

Despite his reliance on a female voice to finish his poem, the young
Hardy of "Domicilium" does not wholly reject the precedent of "The Ruined
Cottage." The grandmother's voice may receive far greater primacy than
Margaret's, which, when heard at all, is smothered by her two interpreters;
but by slipping into a second childhood and blending with the plants that
"lag behind the season," Margaret can serve as the agent of Wordsworth's
flickering desire to elude the adult, gendered identity his adult male personae
reluctantly accept (721). Yet even though the female speaker of "Domicilium" does not need to enact a death wish to break down the barriers between
self and not self, her unself-consciousness performs a similar function for a
male child conditioned to resist boundary confusions (Chodorow 106). In
addressing her son's son as "my child," this mother figure can condense two
generations into one. Although her identity remains far more social and
communal than Margaret's, her memories of a continuous past have the
same effect as the Wanderer's account of Margaret's dissolution into nature.

Margaret, in the few words accorded to her, remarks how "changed" she has become by her dislocation (765–67). As aware that "change has marked / The face of all things," Hardy's female speaker can at least sanction the yearnings of the adolescent who wants to cling to the child self she has nurtured (25–26). She belongs to an Ur-world in which binary oppositions— outer/inner, male/female, adult/child, artifact/nature—could still dissolve.

Yet "Domicilium" also inscribes the dialectic Hardy wishes to blur. Despite his nostalgic empowerment of a female voice, the autobiographer who reproduces this youthful discourse of desire only adds to the ironies already embedded in the text. However rapt and earnest, the child listener fails to avoid his inevitable transformation into the pretentious young poet who gives the verses their Latinate title. No impersonation can reclaim the pristine "spot" glimpsed by the grandmother. She is herself but a memory trace, having died and being "now / Blest with the blest" (20–21), as the speaker makes sure to inform us. Like Margaret, the grandmother remains a figuration of desire that must adapt itself, however reluctantly, to change. Her utterance thus anticipates the more self-conscious appropriations of female speech Hardy undertakes in "The Ruined Maid" (1866) or in the more pathetic "Tess's Lament" (1901). In the latter poem, the dairymaid— reclaimed from *Tess of the d'Urbervilles*—contends that "nettle, dock, and briar" have obliterated the warm and cozy spot she once shared with her lover (3.22).

In his inability to go beyond mere yearning, the Hardy of "Domicilium" cannot yet extricate himself from Wordsworth's bind. Eager to evoke the fusions he associates with a lost feminine space, the male artist nonetheless accepts his place in a circumscribed reality built on the very binaries he would gladly abolish.

II

Although Hardy would continue to covet the "spot" he had allowed the grandmother in "Domicilium," he now began to ironize the feminine and to endow the masculine with greater authority. While writing his prize essay "The Application of Coloured Bricks and Terra Cotta to Modern Architecture" (1863), the ambitious young architect was imitating Shelley, Browning, and Tennyson, poets he regarded as more intellectual and thus more adult than Wordsworth. The ironies that "Domicilium" minimizes dominate "Heiress and Architect" (1867), the highly patterned self-dialogue in which Hardy pits a ruthless male "arch-designer" against a sentimental (and Wordsworthian) female client. Their exchange allows Hardy to sharpen the tensions, still whimsically handled, in his first published piece of fiction, "How I Built Myself a House" (1865). There the unwary narrator, John, who wants a home built to the specifications he and his equally naive wife, Sophia, have set down, finds himself caught between her roomy prospects and an actual structure repeatedly "lessened" by practical constraints and by the "scientific reasoning" of the designer (Hardy, *Personal Writings* 163).

"Heiress and Architect" relies on a "decremental structure" to render a prospective house dweller's lessening scope of expectations (Bailey 108). The heiress of the title clearly stands for a soul who must confront an inheritance of material diminution and death. This unnamed "she" differs as much from the buoyant Sophia as the architect who acts as her instructor differs from Mr. Penny, the droll Dickensian consulted in "How I Built Myself a House." A brutal realist, the "he" of the poem programmatically destroys his client's illusions. As her "guide," he sets out to expose her defiance of "the rule" of laws he considers irrefutable. Her naïveté about life, he insists on showing, invalidates the various shapes into which she tries to enclose her desire for a place of her own. The reader is forced to share the pain of the heiress, whom Hardy subjects to an exorcism of a wishfulness he now identifies as feminine. At the same time, however, Hardy manages to induce an uncomfortably sadistic pleasure through the relentless process of reduction—and, ultimately, destruction—he carries out in the name of a realism he labels masculine.

The friction between the poem's "she" and "he" thus creates unsettling and unsettled conflicts: our emotional identification with the hopes and disappointments of the woman vies with our uneasy participation in the cruel, intellectual game by which her "cold, clear" male interlocutor systematically cuts her down. The division cannot be bridged. Despite its overschematic organization, stilted diction, and density of allusion, "Heiress and Architect" succeeds by the intensity with which Hardy rejects his own desire for fusion. Like Jude the Obscure, who is as enamored of Gothic tracery as the heiress is and as unable to find an enclosure for his idealism, the poem's "she" gradually yields to a process of disenchantment that approximates Hardy's own. Whether or not these verses specifically dramatize an ideological shift from "a 'Wordsworthian' to a 'Darwinian' point of view" (Bailey 108) ultimately matters less than Hardy's fashioning of an ironically handled gender dialectic that gives a new twist to the metaphoric yoking of houses, femininity, and death that recurs in Romantic and Victorian poetry.

Although the poem's "she" ostensibly takes the initiative by seeking out the advice of the "arch-designer" reputed to be of such "wise contrivance" (3), her action makes her his dependent from the very start. It is he who is given the first and last words in the ten-stanza poem. After citing the rules by which he expects the heiress to abide, he rejects each of the four types of building she asks him to design. Each structure proposed to house a variant desire is quickly exposed for its impracticability. In dismissing her requests with a brusqueness that borders on contempt, the architect not only exhibits his technical awareness but also displays his maturer grasp of "such vicissitudes as living brings" (10). He thus treats the heiress as if she were a child who must be admonished about the coming phases of life. Armed with the "facile foresight" that makes Milton's archangels superior to the innocents of Eden (32), this arch-designer is overly rigid. He may be skilled in architectural proportioning ("every intervolve of high and wide" [4]), but his lesson in fore-shortened expectations shows him to be culpably unbending.

The heiress first requests little more than the exposure to wilderness granted to the grandmother in "Domicilium." Yet she endows this building with palatial features more suited to the temperament of the "she" who had asked Tennyson to build her a pleasure home in "The Palace of Art." In "Domicilium," the wishful return to an untamed, pristine nature has been endorsed by a poet eager to slide back into boyhood; here, however, the heiress is rebuked for a childishness branded as self-indulgence:

> "Shape me," she said, "high walls with tracery
> And open ogive-work, that scent and hue
>   Of buds, and travelling bees, may come in
>   through,
>   The note of birds, and singing of the sea,
>   For these are much to me."
>   "An idle whim!"
>   Broke forth from him
> Whom nought could warm to gallantries:
> "Cede all these buds and birds, the zephyr's call,
> And scents, and hues, and things that falter all,
> And choose as best the close and surly wall,
>   For winters freeze."
>
> (13–24)

The contrasting visual shape of these two stanzas (the third and fourth of the poem) are maintained in the subsequent exchanges between the two speakers. The five-line stanzas given to the heiress are simpler in organization and rhyme scheme than the seven-line stanzas devoted to the architect's replies. His three four-syllable lines vie with the single six-syllable line that distills the heiress's wishes. These terse, shorter lines, which begin and end the architect's rebuttals, are his most dismissive. Typographically, they do not even align with the heiress's summarizing coda, thus reinforcing his disregard for her concerns. To accentuate this disregard, the architect's appropriations of the heiress's words become cruelly parodic. Her earnest reference to the "scent and hue / Of buds" turns into a hiss of derision: "*these* buds . . . / And scents, and hues, and *things* . . ."

But the architect's mocking transformation of the heiress's "*For* these are much to me" into his "*For* winters freeze" also suggests his prime mode of subversion. His use of "For" is strictly causal; hers betokens a denial of time's passage. The architect restructures his client's syntax by forcing sequence on what she has articulated as nonsequential. His curt "Cede" and "choose" are commands that, unlike her ambivalent "Shape me," stem from a confident knowledge of the shapes best suited to withstand the bitterness of winters. By way of contrast, the central verb in her first speech—"may come"—remains conditional, half-hidden among the nouns that come before and after. Such tentativeness captures the heiress's receptivity but also weakens her call for roomy interiors and "ogive" arches freely exposed to the outside.

The heiress's frank subjectivism allows the architect to scoff at her belief in a never-ending spring. He gruffly insists on the primacy of a depersonalized temporal order in which one season inevitably leads into the next. The "For" he wrests from her speech and retains to close off each of their next exchanges insists on the logic of this order. Having condemned her for misperceiving external nature, the architect proceeds to steel her against internal changes he also wants her to face. With morbid glee, he predicts a future made up of successive stages of degeneration: "For you will tire" (36) and "For you will fade" (48) give way to the calculated blow he inflicts in the poem's last line, "For you will die" (60).

Relentlessly pushed into giving up her yearning to blend with some form of otherness, the heiress decides that solipsism can permit her to escape the pains of disenchantment. "Some narrow winding turret, quite mine own" (50), she "faintly" hopes, might insulate her. Yet the unsparing architect is not about to relinquish the realism that Hardy sardonically exaggerates. Having repudiated every form of romantic relation, the architect now reminds the heiress of her material connection to the outside world. Her wish for a narrowly "winding" turret defies a last set of practical considerations:

> "Such winding ways
> Fit not your days,"
> Said he, the man of measuring eye;
> "I must even fashion as the rule declares,
> To wit: Give space (since life ends unawares)
> To hale a coffined corpse adown the stairs;
> For you will die."
>
> (54–60)

The coffin that is finally to house the heiress follows the "law of stable things," which she has previously ignored. A stable enclosure for his client's corpse has been the arch-designer's sole design.

That the "coffined corpse" was as preeminent in the mind of the poem's own designer is borne out by the illustration Hardy drew for "Heiress and Architect" on first publishing these verses in his 1898 *Wessex Poems*. Though horizontal in composition, the picture is printed vertically to fit the shape

of the book's pages.[6] To glimpse the contents of the rectangular enclosure, one therefore has to tilt the volume. Only then can the viewer see that the arighted rectangle frames still another rectangle and recognize that the attempt to reinstate a stable horizontal axis has in effect been anticipated by four figures steadying a box that would otherwise have to be inclined or even held perpendicularly. Portrayed as silhouettes, possessing extremities but no heads, the four figures are as incomplete as the similarly cropped, crosshatched coffin they carry. The composition accentuates a sense of mutilation: headless human beings (presumably male but curiously androgynous) carry a fragment containing the remains of a once vertical human being (made genderless by death). The drawing captures the poem's very mode, not just through the representation of a descending motion that corresponds to the "decremental structure" of the verses but also by the cropping of the four figures, who could stand for the architect's dismemberment of the heiress's four wishes. The sketch thus reinforces the poem's increasing sense of claustrophobia. The "uneven ground" of "Domicilium," which extended as far as the "distant hills and sky" (15, 12), has been pounded into a bit of human clay packed tightly into a box within a box. The spatial subversion that "Heiress and Architect" enacts, however, goes hand in hand with Hardy's literary deconstruction of all those Romantic and Victorian poems in which pleasure domes built by male poets are associated with a distinctly feminine or feminized imagination. Undeniably attracted to the structures of Romantic idealism, Hardy still valued the workings of Romantic irony. He now refused to partake in the buildup of lush details indulged, for example, by Shelley in *Queen Mab* or by Tennyson in "The Palace of Art."[7] Tennyson had been reluctant to "pull down" the overlavish structure he had built for the aesthetic "soul possessed of many gifts" ("To————. With the Following Poem ['"The Palace of Art"']"3). Even after he deferred to those reviewers who had deplored his imagination's insufficient "power over the feelings and thought of men" (Stevenson 136), Tennyson refused to raze an "effeminate" construct "so lightly, beautifully built" ("Palace of Art" 294). Hardy, by way of contrast, proved as intransigent as the architect who settles for the shape of a wooden coffin. Possibly remembering Tennyson's dedication to R. C. Trench, by then Bishop Trench, Hardy dedicated his own poem to A. W. Blomfield, a bishop's son and his genial employer. The dedication, as has often been noted, is deliciously ironic. For Blomfield had achieved his success as a fashionable architect by propitiating wealthy clients and by adapting himself to prevailing fashions. Hardy thus sets himself apart through the creation of Blomfield's truculent antitype—one clearly as reluctant to accommodate himself to feminine taste as Hardy remains resistant to a poetry that the mid-Victorians (including Tennyson) had come to regard as excessively "feminized" in its self-indulgence.

The progression in "Heiress and Architect" builds on the same "simile of human life" to which Keats resorted in a famous letter to J. H. Reynolds (3 May 1818) comparing "human life to a large Mansion of Many Apartments" (280–83). Keats's remarks have an obvious applicability to the poem in which the architect compels the "maid misled" (30) to confront dark passages that she, like Keats's Madeline or Lycius, would prefer to ignore. As the architect forces the heiress to wander through the "chambers" of her life, Hardy rehearses a succession of poetic genres that, he implies, have been rendered obsolete by what Keats, in his letter, calls the "advance of intellect." From her unreflecting absorption in nature (childhood), the heiress moves through socialization (adolescence), romance (sexual maturity), and solipsism (old age), before confronting death; each phase is associated with a type of poetry—pastorals (such as Wordsworth's), narrative verses, love lyrics (the "little chamber" of line 37 suggesting the Romantic sonnet), and elegies—and, finally, there is silence.

Such silencing fits the predisposition of the young poet, who did not publish his verses until he had exhausted his careers as an architect and a novelist. Yet Hardy's appropriation of the tropes of his favorite predecessors also suggests that, when he returned to poetry for the last three decades of his life, he was ready to see himself, like the heiress of this early poem, as the inheritor of assumptions and traditions he now imaginatively needed to relocate.[8] Hardy would overcome the binary oppositions shaping "Heiress and Architect" only after he had experienced the loss of a woman sharing his home. Emma Hardy's death enabled the old poet to exhume the femininity he had prematurely coffined.

III

When Emma Gifford Hardy died in November of 1912, three days after her seventy-second birthday, she left behind four completed works for the perusal of the man she had married in 1874. All these works were meant to signify the extent of her alienation from her husband. Printed by a Dorchester stationer, the volume of poems called *Alleys* (1911) and the exposition of the New Testament called *Spaces* (1912) were Emma Hardy's attempts to counter the unorthodoxy of the novelist who had turned poet after *Jude the Obscure* and *The Well-Beloved*. Like her unpublished fictional fragments, these rival efforts to catch the public eye had little effect on her widower. But her manuscript diary (which Hardy destroyed) entitled "What I Think of My Husband," containing "bitter denunciations, beginning about 1891 & continuing until within a day or two of her death,"[9] and *Some Recollections,* her vivid account of her life before their marriage, stimulated the emotional overflow that led to the eighteen poems he collected as "Poems of 1912–13" in *Satires of Circumstance* (1914), as well as to other memorializing verses both in that volume and in its sequels, *Moments of Vision* (1917) and *Late Lyrics* (1927).

Practically all the poems Hardy wrote in response to Emma Hardy's death reverse the progression traced in "Heiress and Architect" and still observed in verses such as "Memory and I," another allegory about thwarted desire.[10] The intense, unsophisticated longing for fusion that so provokes the irascible architect now activates the passionate lyrics of a septuagenarian. In "I Found Her Out There," the mobility denied to an heiress condemned to death in life is playfully and paradoxically granted to the lively female ghost whom the speaker now reclaims. This shade bears little resemblance to the "ageing shape" that Hardy found so difficult to confront during his wife's declining years. Resurrected by the intensity of her survivor's desire, the truant ghost is exhorted to return with the poet to the more elemental nature "Where she once domiciled" (38).[11]

The male speaker of "I Found Her Out There" is the exact inverse of the architect who had forced the childlike heiress to foresee her entombment. Instead, this speaker becomes freed himself by "the heart of a child" of the uncanny sprite he urges to desert her "loamy cell" (40, 41). The subdued breezes and "singings of the sea" desired by the heiress and derided by the architect (16) have swollen into liberating storm blasts shared equally by the old man and the female "shade" who,

> maybe,
> Will creep underground
> Till it catch the sound
> Of that western sea
> As it swells and sobs
> Where she once domiciled.
>   (33–38)

Stimulated by "the haunted heights / The Atlantic smites / And the blind gales sweep" (18–20), the wanderer finds "her" and experiences an epiphany. Hardy's speaker has traveled to the Arthurian ruins at Tintagel Head to expose himself again to the setting of the dead woman's girlhood. The visit confirms his belief that the spouse he has buried inland, so far away from these heights, can never become a quiet sleeper. Wakened by her memories, he can once more fuse with her by vicariously burrowing into her grave and sharing her presumed exultation at being released into the wild haunts of her adolescence. By relying once again on a dead female agent, like Wordsworth's Margaret or like the grandmother in "Domicilium," Hardy, though rooted in Dorset, can imagine a "spot" devoid of binaries and antagonisms. Having liberated the man who would no longer be an architect, Emma the dream child can restore the inheritance he had progressively denied to himself as much as to the real-life Emma Gifford. The femininity he has introjected frees this male heiress from having to coffin a child heart.

That Hardy was the first to recognize the perversity of the paradoxes involved in this imaginative process of gender reconstitution seems amply evident from his other Emma poems (as well as from his fictive foreshadowings in novels like *The Well-Beloved*). He knows that the ghost he seeks out, addresses, impersonates, and causes to speak is but an aspect of himself. On reading Emma's diaries, Thomas unquestionably became aware of his own culpability. He saw himself as she had perceived him, as the jailer of the bride he had immured in Max Gate, where she had been brought under false pretenses. For his own part, Thomas also had felt betrayed. Unable to bear the older Emma's lost resemblance to the bride he had idealized, he punished her by allowing her the dubious status of co-dweller in his house. His choice of the Vergilian subtitle "Veteris Vestigia Flammae" for the first series of Emma poems suggests his ability to reverse the roles of betrayer and betrayed that he had assigned earlier. He could see himself as Aeneas and cast Emma as the wronged Dido. But it was the rekindling of those vestigial flames that mattered. The "woman much missed," now reborn as a trusting child, was more than a guide to Cornwall's romance. She could now once again fill the long-silent Max Gate with remembered song and sound and movement. She could bestow on Thomas precisely what the architect had denied to the heiress.

In the Emma lyrics of *Satires of Circumstance* and *Moments of Vision*, the dramatic motions stirred up by a dead woman's "shade" help to refeminize the house in which she had been imprisoned. Her own powers are now respected; her airs are preeminent. Even at its most querulous, her voice is allowed a full hearing. For Hardy recognizes the importance of femininity to the continued unfolding of his imagination. He has never until now understood his bond to this "faithful phantom," who prides herself on following him so "alertly" wherever "his fancy sets him wandering" ("The Haunter" 4, 3).

When the ghost fussily complains about the slightest changes in the appearance of the home her architect-bridegroom had designed for her so very, very long ago, her devotion is still stressed:

> The change I notice in my once own quarters!
> A formal-fashioned border where the daisies
>   used to be,
> The rooms new painted, and the pictures
>   altered,
> And other cups and saucers, and no cosy nook
>   for tea
>   As with me.
>   ("His Visitor" 6–10)

Whereas the "man of measuring eye" in "Heiress and Architect" delighted in altering his client's quarters, the man who has dared to repaint walls and relocate decorations obviously fears the reproach of one who asks him to remember "my rule here" (13). The servants hired since her death know nothing about her rule, but her widower feels compelled to carry out her wish that nothing be disturbed. Small wonder that the second Mrs. Hardy privately demurred about this ghost's stranglehold: "I may not alter the shape of the garden bed, or cut down or move the smallest bush, any more than I may alter the position of an article of furniture."[12]

Although Thomas had blamed Emma for the cooling that had marked the later years of their marriage, he could not bear to think of her as "cold, iced, forgot," like the "pretty plants" she had once tried to keep alive ("The Frozen Greenhouse" 22, 21). Her death thus led him to implant a warm domestic hearth at the center of the "domicilium" he had periodically escaped. He had once stressed the "cold, clear view" of the manly realist "whom nought could warm to gallantries" ("Heiress" 8, 20). Now, however, he heaps gallantries on one to whom he attributes the heiress's yearning for a warm relationship with a sustaining other. Comforted by the words of the voluble ghost who lives within his brain and by memories of the sound of her piano music, he dreads above all her removal into the "roomy silence" of her cemetery home. The threat of separation, which informs most of the Emma poems, is as frightening for the old man as for a small child.

Like a mother who intimidates her child by playing on this fear, the ghost in "His Visitor" prefers the privacy of the grave Hardy obsessively reopens in *Satires of Circumstance*:

> So I don't want to linger in this re-decked
>   dwelling,
> I feel too uneasy at the contrasts I behold,
> And I make again for Mellstock to return here
>   never,
> And rejoin the roomy silence, and the mute and
>   manifold
>   Souls of old
>
>   (16–20)

Unwilling to be forsaken by one who prefers the "manifold" company of other dead souls, the speaker decides to partake in her reunions. In one of the finest lyrics in *Moments of Vision*, "During Wind and Rain," he places himself among the Gifford "Elders and juniors" whom Emma had herself recalled. Remembering her nostalgic account of the last house she shared with her family in Plymouth before being forced to leave the community in which she had spent her first nineteen years, Thomas appropriates Emma's moments of symbiosis and separation.

"During Wind and Rain" conflates details scattered over many pages in *Some Recollections*. Drawing on the description of Bedford Terrace, the "pleasant home" that proved to be his wife's last secure haven, Thomas relies on the hindsight by which Emma regarded this building as full of "curious omens" betokening death and dispersal for a family soon to fall from "so high" an eminence (*Some Recollections* 30–32).[13] The "They" of the poem are deliberately left unidentified. Blended through their music, the members of this domestic group lack individuality:

> They sing their dearest songs—
> He, she, all of them—yea,
> Treble and tenor and bass,
>   And one to play,
> With the candles mooning each face. . . .
>   Ah, no; the years O!
> How the sick leaves reel down in throngs!
>
> (1–7)

Who *are* "he" and "she"? The lack of specificity allows the speaker, who is acutely aware of severance, to insert his own presence among the singers. The "nameless" singing opens an "elsewhere" for a man "capable of becoming a woman" (Cixous and Clément 93, 98). Stranded in a different era by the passage of many years, he nonetheless can insinuate himself into this alien, vanished household and regard it as if he were there. Despite its insistence on separation and change, "During Wind and Rain" thus reconstitutes a "he" and a "she" among "all of them." Through a time warp, ruin and wholeness are simultaneously perceived; dispersion and integration can somehow coexist:

> They change to a high new house,
> He, she, all of them—aye,
> Clocks, and carpets and chairs
>   On the lawn all day,
> And brightest things that are theirs. . . .
>   Ah, no; the years, the years;
> Down their carved names the rain-drop ploughs.
>
> (22–28)

The scattered material objects on the lawn—with the clocks taking an ominous precedence in the list of a household's "brightest things"—will become permanently dissipated when a single day is replaced by "the years." Yet, as the last line shocks us into recognizing, the animated occupants of the building have long ago become inert objects themselves, reduced into names on tombstones. Only the single raindrop, so like the tear of a single mourner, can restore movement, stirring and plowing up lives that have crumbled into clay.

In combining his sense of abandonment by his wife with her recorded pangs of separation from Bedford Terrace, Hardy makes the "he" and "she" of the poem stand for more than the parents whom Emma Lavinia Gifford was forced to leave behind. They also represent the aged poet and the young "she" he imaginatively joins by adding his own lyric to the song that had once united "all of them." But his vicarious entry into another's family romance suggests that he is processing a much earlier separation. Long before Emma's death, Thomas had fashioned a powerful poem associating the interior of a house with an ecstatic self-annulment through music. Though more compact than "During Wind and Rain," "The Self-Unseeing," which Hardy published in 1901 in his largely elegiac *Poems of Past and Present*, is strikingly similar.[14] In "The Self-Unseeing," just as in "During Wind and Rain," past and present are blended as well as kept apart. But the "I" who becomes a child again, dreamily at one with the smiling "She" who observes him swaying to the music of a dead "He," is a Hardy who needs no surrogate to express his profound yearning for the lost maternal shelter he wants to preserve.

In "The Self-Unseeing," the revisited Hardy home at Higher Bockhampton is presented metonymically in the first of the poem's three quatrains. The "ancient floor" still "is"; but the "former door / Where the dead feet walked in" has been relocated (1, 3–4). The poem never identifies the owner of those feet as Hardy's father, who had died in 1892. Nor does it make clear that the ancient floor is still occupied by Hardy's octogenarian mother, Jemima Hardy, with whom he may well have shared his memory of the epiphanic moment the poem celebrates. Thus, when the second stanza opens by recalling, "She sat here in her chair, / Smiling into the fire" (5–6), it seems plausible that the speaker still has before him the same woman who, now in her old age, joins her son in remembering how she smiled while watching the child entranced by the music of the father-fiddler who "stood there, / Bowing it higher and higher" (7–8).

Like the change to a "high new house" in "During Wind and Rain," the upward motion of the violin presages a fall from such heights of ecstasy. Yet this family unit can no more anticipate change than the Giffords can. Indeed, when the young mother smiles at her husband and at the boy who is his namesake, she helps to fuse the trio in a moment of self-forgetfulness. In "During Wind and Rain," a "he" and "she" could merge with "all of them." In "The Self-Unseeing," the "I" of the poem comes into being by recalling his oneness with the "we" presided over by the approving mother. In the last stanza, adult self-consciousness and the intoxicated self-obliviousness of the swirling boy coalesce:

Childlike, I danced in a dream;
Blessings emblazoned that day;
Everything glowed with a gleam;
Yet we were looking away!
(9–12)

The poem's last line insists on a paradox. Only by refusing, like the heiress, to look at the future, can this trio avoid the foresight that might warn them that fathers die, that mothers—like floors—become "hollowed and thin," that boys grow into men subject to disenchantment. And yet the house of memory survives, its foot-worn floors still as visible as the sturdy peasant woman who hobbles across them. Dead male feet can therefore be resurrected into the living feet of poetry—a poetry that for the mature Hardy must repossess and reprocess the child's freedom of movement within a female space.

IV

After Hardy finally took his first wife to meet his mother in 1876, he kept "a complete silence" about the encounter, "and to the end of his life he never commented on the relationship between the two women" (Gittings, *Later Years* 7).[15] Yet little documentation about that relationship seems required. If my reading of some of the poems in the previous section is valid, the death of Emma Hardy allowed her husband to indulge in emotions that, though more suited to the loss of a mother, were kept in abeyance when Jemima Hardy died in 1904 at the age of ninety, a ruin of the once vital woman whose hold on him her son regarded with considerable ambivalence (Gittings, *Young Thomas* 24–25, 48–49).

It seems significant that the death of the matriarch who had been the "real guiding star of [Hardy's] early life" (Gittings, *Later Years* 118) inspired no creative outburst such as that occasioned, a decade later, by Emma's demise. "After the Last Breath (J. H. 1813–1904)," the single poem that directly memorializes Jemima Hardy in *Time's Laughingstocks* (1909), is stately and formal, a restrained tribute offered by a public "we." Even the poem that precedes it, "Night in the Old Home," avoids the I-you relation of the Emma poems. A speaker hears the voices of his family's many ghosts while visiting the now deserted house at Higher Bockhampton. Yet the mother is only one among the chorus of shades who advise the mourner to adopt their own "satisfied, placid, unfretting" mood.

The grandmother celebrated in "Domicilium," Mary Head Hardy, fares much better in *Time's Laughingstocks*. The decay of this maternal figure, who was already sixty-eight when Thomas was born, never agitated the time-

conscious boy who had slept at Higher Bockhampton in the bedroom next
to hers. "One We Knew (M. H. 1772–1857)," which clearly acts as a
pendant to the poem memorializing Jemima Hardy, treats the grandmother
as a fertile source for endless anecdotes and tales. Placed in the same position
as the mother in "The Self-Unseeing," the woman who stares at a fire is
directly credited as someone capable of mothering a poet-novelist's imagination:[16]

> With cap-framed face and long gaze into the
> embers—
> We seated around her knees—
> She would dwell on such dead themes, not as
> one who remembers,
> But rather as one who sees.
>
> She seemed one left behind of a band gone
> distant
> So far that no tongue could hail:
> Past things retold were to her as things existent,
> Things present but as a tale.
>
> (25–32)

It seems noteworthy that this "she" should be hailed for possessing the
very qualities of imagination that shape poems such as "During Wind and
Rain" and "The Self-Unseeing," in which Hardy recalls vanished scenes not
as one who remembers but as one who sees. The female shades who stimulated
Hardy's imagination were, like the living women in his life, versions of the
mother he could not afford directly to impersonate or appropriate. The man
who confessed, in his middle seventies, that "he thought he had never grown
up"[17] could present himself as the rapt listener of the grandmother who
addresses him as "my child" in "Domicilium" or as the truant chided by
the motherlike ghost of Emma Hardy. More important, he imposed the
house of his youth, the cottage at Higher Bockhampton where his mother
continued to live, on the female structures of his poetry. Even the too narrow
staircase of "Heiress and Architect" stems from a memory of the old home,
"where the stairs were too narrow to save space" (Bailey 108). Had the boy
once fantasized how a coffin would have to be edged down those stairs?
Whether superimposed on Max Gate or on the Gifford residence of Bedford
Terrace or reduced into much smaller containers—graves, coffins, drawers,
and lockets containing female mementos of the past—a Bachelardian dream-
memory of a primal space, violated yet reconstituted, underlies the design
of a host of Hardy's finest lyrics.

Yet if Hardy's oneiric houses helped him dramatize his sense of eviction
from the primal refuge of a mother's body, his poems often try to repossess
or translate a maternal abode. "Her Death and After," the early short story

in verse that remained one of his favorites, depicts such a repossession. The narrator seeks a "gate" to lead him into the "tenement" where "one, by Fate, / Lay dying that I held dear" (3–6). Surveying the "piteous shine" of the rooms in which he finds a young mother on her deathbed, the speaker hears the cry of her baby daughter, soon to be orphaned (16). The dying woman admits that her visitor would have made a better father than the man she married: "Would the child were yours and mine!" (40). Eager to adopt her offspring after he hears of the degradation of "the lame lone child" (61), the speaker arranges to meet the dead woman's husband by the ruined earthworks near Dorchester's churchyard. He avoids the "hallow sod" of the dead woman's tomb and prefers to face his rival against the back-drop of the "haggard" arena where old "Pagan echoes" still reverberate from "hollows of chalk and lime" (74, 78, 80). To reclaim the child, he concocts a fiction, professing to have fathered her. He offers the husband a choice: a duel or the gift of the little girl. Soon he is greeted by a "little voice" that comes to his "window-frame": "My father who's not my own, sends word / I'm to stay here, sir, where I belong" (119, 121–22).

What belonged to an entombed mother now belongs in the house of one who has replaced both parents. Yet the speaker who can restore a lost symbiosis is also painfully aware of the price he has had to pay, "for I'd harmed the dead, / By what I said / For the good of the living one" (128–30). The irony is bitter. The desexualized love between adult and child requires the sexualization of the dead mother, defamed as an adulteress. In the drawing Hardy devised for "Her Death and After," the topography accentuates this conflict. Beyond the churchyard where a pure mother is entombed loom the pre-Roman earthworks that were converted into a "Cirque of Gladiators" (76). In Hardy's rendering, this structure, near whose walls the sexual rivals meet, resembles a giant orifice, a place of origination and exit from life.

The mother Hardy associates with his own creativity becomes a focal point for the tug-of-war between a childlike desire for sustained fusion and an adult insistence on the necessity of detachment. This conflict is evident in the curious poem "In Childbed," which Hardy placed immediately after his rather stiff memorial to Jemima Hardy in *Time's Laughingstocks*. Whereas in "Her Death and After" the male speaker replaces the young mother who died in childbirth, Hardy here animates the "spirit" of a dead mother who addresses a "me" who is her daughter and who has herself just given birth to a child. The dead mother chides her daughter's "innocent maternal vanity" almost as sternly as the architect had checked the heiress's desire to retain some form of symbiosis. The young mother's joyful oneness with her infant, the dead woman insists, will eventually fade: "Yet as you dream, so dreamt I / When Life stretched forth its morning ray to me" (17–18). In this all-female poem, however, the younger woman escapes the heiress's disenchantment. Cradling her own child (whose gender remains unspecified), she refuses to process the "strange things" uttered by her ghostly parent.

In this quasi-Blakean Song of Experience, Hardy adopts the point of view of both mothers: his own offspring, his poetry, he seems to imply, originates in a symbiosis that "time unwombs" (9). The unwombing or distancing that his ironic poems and fictions obsessively re-create always vies, however, with a yearning to recapture the oneness of the "weetless child," a self-unseeing creature, cradled in its mother's arms. Although such weetlessness, or unknowing, gives license to Hardy's characteristic irony, it also propels the desire that activates his lyrics. The "infant or thoughtless Chamber," as well as the "Chamber of Maiden Thought," can never be wholly vacated in the house of Hardy's poetry.

Despite their philosophizing and intellectualizing, Hardy's poems persistently tap the rudimentary emotions I have tried to capture in this essay. The child "who thought he had never grown up" vies with the old man who delights in abstract formulations. The anger and yearnings of this child surface in unexpected places. Much has been written, for instance, about Hardy's Immanent Will and its operation in a poem like "The Convergence of the Twain," which, J. O. Bailey categorically states, "is not a personal lament; it is a philosophic statement" (266). But Hardy's treatment of the female hull of the *Titanic* allows him to find still another primal space in which an "unwombing" and the animation of new life can simultaneously occur.

Like the "maid misled" in "Heiress and Architect" and like the ruined maidens of Hardy's fiction, the ship on her maiden voyage will be undone by her unforeseen contact with an icy and "sinister mate" ("The Convergence of the Twain" 19). The violation by this growing monster floods the ship's steel chambers and opens the interior to "rhythmic tidal lyres" (6). Though ruined, however, the female wreck also becomes a habitat for new forms of life:

> Over the mirrors meant
> To glass the opulent
> The sea-worm crawls—grotesque, slimed, dumb,
>   indifferent.
>
> . . . .
>
>   Dim moon-eyed fishes near
>   Gaze at the gilded gear. . . .
>   (7–14)

As in "Heiress and Architect," so also here, Hardy evinces a sadistic delight in a grim process of denigration. The looking glasses that reflected the "vaingloriousness" of jeweled Edwardian ladies (15) now mirror dumb and elementary forms of life. The ship has become a huge coffin. The fall from high to low, the move from interiority to exteriority, noted in the poems I discuss earlier, is dramatized here as well.

Yet the invasion by crude marine creatures of this Titan's shattered interior also carries an effectual pleasure that goes beyond the aggressive desire to appropriate an immense womb.[18] These fetal creatures, though grotesque, facilitate our return to something primal, forgotten, "unweeting." Couching on the "stilly" floor, the ship who is a "she" has ceased to be an enclosure for civilized adults. Instead, she cradles childlike creatures at an earlier evolutionary stage. She has herself descended to an earlier state of being after her "consummation" with her mate (33). Like the ghost of a rejuvenated Emma Hardy, she can become one who stills, a nurturer. The fish who sway in the "rhythmic tidal lyres" within her are as oblivious to human "vaingloriousness" as the young boy who had swayed to music in "The Self-Unseeing." For this mother hull is herself a "domicilium," a spot for new life and for the generation of poetry.

Notes

1. The two most famous Victorian representations of the feminine domestic ideal are Coventry Patmore's *Angel in the House* (1854–62) and John Ruskin's "Of Queens' Gardens" (1865). Earlier writers such as Sarah Ellis and Sarah Lewis, however, had already upheld the privatization of domestic space. The ambiguities and contradictions of sexual difference marking out separate spheres in this period have been amply analyzed by contemporary critics; see, for example, Armstrong, Auerbach, Christ, Davidoff and Hall, Gilbert and Gubar, Houghton, Poovey, and Welsh.

2. The great difficulty faced by a female child in establishing ego boundaries in a patriarchal culture allows some feminists to argue that a girl's relation to the unconscious, the body, and maternal rhythms is closer than a boy's (see Chodorow). While differing in their fundamental philosophical and political programs, French feminist critics such as Hélène Cixous, Catherine Clément, and Julia Kristeva nonetheless posit that poets, female or male, are "complex, mobile, open" in allowing the opposite sex "entrance" into them (Cixous and Clément 84–85). Kristeva, without relying on a theory of feminine language, demonstrates

how male writers, predominantly modernist poets like Mallarmé and Baudelaire, allow the semiotic "chora," linked to the mother's body, to speak through their writing (93–98). Poetry, closer to song and pure rhythm, she argues, is less controlled than prose by the symbolic strictures of syntax.

3.   Still, Gothic enclosures are far more unstable than the houses found in the traditional novel of manners. Decaying (like Wildfell Hall) or razed (like Thornfield), such buildings display a " 'ruined' architecture" that cannot be mended (Gordon 231). Thus, Hareton and the second Catherine must forsake the Heights for the Grange, while Esther Summerson must found a second Bleak House. For the transgressive qualities of the Gothic, see Jackson, Sedgwick, and Wilt, among others.

4.   Quotations from the poems of Byron, Keats, Shelley, and Wordsworth are taken from Perkins.

5.   Whereas James Gibson prints "Domicilium" as the first item in *The Complete Poems of Thomas Hardy*, Samuel P. Hynes places it first among the *Uncollected Poems*, volume 3 of *The Complete Poetical Works of Thomas Hardy*. Citations of Hardy's poems are taken from Hynes and identified by line.

6.   Inserted between the fourth and fifth stanzas of the poem (i.e., after the architect's "For winters freeze" and the heiress's second request), the drawing appears on page 213 of *Wessex Poems*.

7.   Hardy read *Queen Mab and Other Poems* in London in 1866. For a helpful overview of his lifelong interest in Shelley, see Bartlett.

8.   The idea of relocation or translocation, itself derived from Shelley, dominates Hardy's tributes to Shelley and Keats, "Shelley's Skylark" (1887) and "The Selfsame Song" (1922), poems in which he "houses" their images and words. Hardy's self-positioning in spaces once occupied by his Romantic predecessors is especially effective in "Rome: At the Pyramid of Cestius near the Graves of Shelley and Keats" (1900) and in the powerfully evocative "At Lulworth Cove a Century Back" (1920).

9.   Letter from Florence Dugdale to Edward Clodd, 16 Jan. 1913 (qtd. in Bailey 24). Ever protective of her husband, the woman Thomas wedded a year after Emma's death worries that he will wind up "believing" his first wife's accusations.

10.   Placed near the end of *Poems of Past and Present* (1902), "Memory and I" also introduces a series of decremental structures and culminates with a picture of female decay.

11.   Although Emma Hardy's first "domicilium" was in Devon (which her widower also revisited), she lyrically recorded her later move from Plymouth to the "invigorating air" of North Cornwall. "I Found Her Out There" clearly recalls her description of the "winter waves and foam reaching hundreds of feet up the stern" and the "strong dark rocks with the fantastic revellings" of the marine birds (*Some Recollections* 38, 42). The same setting acts as a backdrop for the unpublished novel *The Maid on the Shore*, which Emma wrote early in her marriage and which Thomas preserved.

"I Found Her Out There" represents a sharp departure from the four previous poems in the carefully crafted sequence of "Poems of 1912–13." In "The Going," "Your Last Drive," and "The Walk," Emma's mourner is temporally bound to her last days; in "Rain on a Grave," he is spatially anchored. Now, however, by returning to the scene of their courtship, he can wrest her (and himself) from a bondage to time and space. She is again the young woman who describes their growing attachment in their drive to Tintagel and Trebarwith Strand and other coastal places: "We grew much interested in each other and I found him a perfectly new subject of study and delight, and he found a 'mine' in me, he said" (57–58). The ghost liberated in "I Found Her Out There" is "mined" in later poems in the sequence, such as "The Haunter" and "The Voice."

12.   Letter from Florence Emily Hardy to Rebekah Owen, 5 May 1916 (qtd. in Bailey 299).

13.   As Evelyn Hardy and Robert Gittings were the first to recognize, Hardy not only

drew on these and other details in his wife's descriptions but also chose to stress the downpour she regarded as an emblem of her final separation from her Plymouth childhood: "never did so watery an omen portend such dullnesses, and sadnesses and sorrows as this did for us" (E. Hardy 37, 68).

14. So similar, in fact, that Carl Weber mistook it for a poem about Hardy's first wife and included it in his arbitrarily constructed chronological cycle of 116 Emma lyrics (158).

15. Michael Millgate speculates that Hardy's delay in "putting himself, or his wife, squarely within his mother's orbit" stemmed from shame over his class origins. He notes that Jemima Hardy disapproved of "this deliberate avoidance of 'home' " and refused to meet the couple in any house other than her own (176–77).

16. Following Winnicott, Perry treats the mother as the other whose first domestication of space later triggers the adult mind's "energy for inner exploration" (7). In *Playing and Reality* Winnicott explains how "mental images" of the mother are reactivated in periods of transition (15, 96–97).

17. Florence Hardy to Alda, Lady Hoare, 7 Apr. 1914. Florence Hardy was among the maternal figures in her husband's life. Writing to Lady Hoare on 9 Dec. 1914, she claimed that her feelings for Hardy were like those of "a mother toward a child with whom things have gone wrong." (Both letters are quoted in Gittings, *Later Years* 159.)

18. In discussing the so-called femininity phase or femininity complex undergone by boys in early childhood, Melanie Klein notes how the frustrated desire to appropriate the mother's "organs of conception, pregnancy, and parturition" lead the son to "destructive tendencies whose object is the womb" (189–91). By resolving his identification with the mother, the adult male not only enhances his relation to other women but also manages to sublimate "the desire for a child and the feminine complement which play[s] so essential a part in men's work" (191).

Works Cited

Armstrong, Nancy. *Desire and Domestic Fiction.* New York: Oxford UP, 1987.

Auerbach, Nina. *Woman and the Demon: The Life of a Victorian Myth.* Cambridge: Harvard UP, 1982.

Bachelard, Gaston. *The Poetics of Space.* Boston: Beacon, 1960.

Bailey, J. O. *The Poetry of Thomas Hardy: A Handbook and Commentary.* Chapel Hill: U of North Carolina P, 1970.

Bartlett, Phyllis. "Hardy's Shelley." *Keats-Shelley Journal* 4 (1955): 15–29.

Chodorow, Nancy. *The Reproduction of Mothering: The Psychoanalysis of Gender.* Berkeley: U of California P, 1978.

Christ, Carol T. "Victorian Masculinity and the Angel in the House." *A Widening Sphere: Changing Roles of Victorian Women.* Ed. Martha Vicinus. Bloomington: Indiana UP, 1977. 146–52.

Cixous, Hélène. "Fiction and Its Phantoms: A Reading of Freud's *Das Unheimliche* (The 'Uncanny')." *New Literary History* 7 (1976): 525–48.

Cixous, Hélène, and Catherine Clément. *The Newly Born Woman.* Trans. Betsy Wing. Minneapolis: U of Minnesota P, 1986.

Davidoff, Leonore, and Catherine Hall. *Family Fortunes.* Chicago: U of Chicago P, 1988.

Felman, Shoshana. "Rereading Femininity." *Yale French Studies* 62 (1981): 19–44.

Freud, Sigmund. "The Uncanny." Trans. James Strachey. *New Literary History* 7 (1976): 619–45.

Gilbert, Sandra, and Susan Gubar. *The Madwoman in the Attic.* New Haven: Yale UP, 1979.

Gittings, Robert. *Thomas Hardy's Later Years.* Boston: Little, 1963.

———. *Young Thomas Hardy.* Boston: Little, 1975.

Gordon, Jan. "Narrative Enclosure as Textual Ruin: An Archaeology of Gothic Consciousness." *Dickens Studies Annual* 11 (1983): 209–38.

Hardy, Emma. *Some Recollections by Emma Hardy.* Ed. Evelyn Hardy and Robert Gittings. London: Oxford UP, 1961.

Hardy, Florence Emily. *The Life of Thomas Hardy: 1840–1928.* London: Macmillan, 1962.

Hardy, Thomas. *The Complete Poems of Thomas Hardy.* Ed. James Gibson. London: Macmillan, 1976.

———. *The Complete Poetical Works of Thomas Hardy.* Ed. Samuel P. Hynes. Vols. 1–3. New York: Oxford UP, 1982–85.

———. *Thomas Hardy's Personal Writings.* Ed. Harold Orel. Lawrence: U of Kansas P, 1969.

———. *Wessex Poems and Other Verses.* New York: Harper, 1898.

Houghton, Walter. *The Victorian Frame of Mind: 1830–1870.* New Haven: Yale UP, 1957.

Jackson, Rosemary. *Fantasy: The Literature of Subversion.* New York: Methuen, 1981.

Keats, John. *The Letters of John Keats, 1814–1821.* Ed. H. E. Rollins. Vol. 1. Cambridge: Harvard UP, 1958.

Klein, Melanie. "Early Stages of the Oedipus Complex." *Love, Guilt, and Reparation and Other Works: 1921–1945.* New York: Dell, 1975. 186–98.

Kristeva, Julia. "Revolution and Poetic Language." Secs. 1–12. Rpt. in *The Kristeva Reader.* Ed. Toril Moi. New York: Columbia UP, 1986. 89–136.

Millgate, Michael. *Thomas Hardy: A Biography.* New York: Oxford UP, 1985.

Perkins, David, ed. *English Romantic Writers.* New York: Harcourt, 1967.

Perry, Ruth. Introduction. *Mothering the Mind: Twelve Studies of Writers and Their Silent Partners.* Ed. Ruth Perry and Martine Watson Brownley. New York: Holmes, 1984. 3–24.

Poovey, Mary. *Uneven Developments: The Ideological Work of Gender in Mid-Victorian England.* Chicago: U of Chicago P, 1988.

Sedgwick, Eve Kosofsky. *The Coherence of Gothic.* London: Routledge, 1986.

Stevenson, Lionel. "The 'High-Born Maiden' Symbol in Tennyson." *Critical Essays on the Poetry of Tennyson.* Ed. John Killham. New York: Barnes, 1960. 126–36.

Tennyson, Alfred, Lord. *The Poems of Tennyson.* Ed. Christopher Ricks. London: Longmans, 1969.

Weber, Carl J., ed. *Hardy's Love Poems.* By Thomas Hardy. London: Macmillan, 1963.

Welsh, Alexander. *The City of Dickens.* Oxford: Clarendon, 1971.

Wilt, Judith. *Ghosts of the Gothic: Austen, Eliot, and Lawrence.* Princeton: Princeton UP, 1980.

Winnicott, D. W. *Playing and Reality.* London: Tavistock, 1971.

Hardy's *The Dynasts*: 'words . . . to hold the imagination'

KENNETH MILLARD

The Dynasts occupies an anomalous position in Hardy studies; while his standing as a poet has improved in the later part of the twentieth century, this revaluation has yet to reach his epic work on the Napoleonic Wars. The poem has been called "the indispensable culmination of his work"[1] and "the final fruit and major event of his creative life,"[2] but *The Dynasts* receives no thorough treatment in Donald Davie's *Thomas Hardy and British Poetry* (1973), in Tom Paulin's *Thomas Hardy: The Poetry of Perception* (1975), or John Bayley's *An Essay on Hardy* (1978), and criticism seems impervious to the belief that Hardy "took pride in it as the greatest of all his literary achievements."[3] *The Dynasts* belongs to the stage in Hardy's career when he had repudiated fiction and was devoting his whole attention to poetry; Part First was published in 1904, Part Second in 1906, and Part Third in 1908; *The Dynasts* represents a major contribution to the character of Edwardian poetry. The poem has often been considered in the context of Hardy's career; this chapter hopes to show that it is useful to regard the poem in the context of its period, as part of a response to the problem of poetry in the early twentieth century, which Hardy shared with Housman, Thomas, and the Edwardians. It also tries to show the relation of *The Dynasts* to Hardy's other poetry, in a move towards "the unity and wholeness of Hardy's vision, regardless of the genre in which he chose to write."[4]

In choosing the Napoleonic Wars of 1805–15 as the subject of his major poetic work Hardy put his imagination at the service of history. This decision necessarily limited the scope of artistic creation before he began, for "he did not here create out of his own imagination that material with which he worked."[5] Moreover, Hardy is not at liberty to shape his material for his idiosyncratic purposes but strives throughout for historical accuracy, to the extent that "Whenever any evidence of the words really spoken or written by the characters in their various situations was attainable, as close a paraphrase was aimed at as was compatible with the form chosen" (Preface). Hardy's eagerness to achieve historical verisimilitude involved him in extensive researches, such that, as he wrote to Henry Newbolt, "In the *Dynasts* I was obliged to condense so strictly that I could not give a twentieth part of the detail I should have liked to give."[6] Hardy compensates for these omissions and compressions by demanding from the reader some prior knowledge of the historical background; his submission to historical precedent is so complete that he must in part abdicate conventional authorial responsibilities: "the subject is familiar to all; and foreknowledge is assumed to fill in the junctions required to combine the scenes into an artistic unity" (Preface). The collaborative effort calls for a knowledge of the major historical events, a requirement which is sometimes onerous. This is especially true of Hardy's presentation of affairs in Spain in Part Third, which necessitates a familiarity with Spanish history of the early nineteenth century. This is a difficulty with the poem "taking its unity simply from the actual logic of historical events."[7] The degree to which the action of the poem is prescribed by historical precedent acts as a curb to imaginative indulgence; in *The Dynasts* imagination is subjugated to rigorous empirical constraints. The scope of historical record which the poem compasses serves to qualify severely the possible hazards of imaginative freedom.

The pressure of historical precedent is felt throughout the poem, in the formal structure with its brief and quickly moving scenes, and in the smallest details where the poet, in footnotes, needlessly explains of a minor character "that both her children grew up and did well" (3. i. iv). Such notes are included to support the sense of historical authenticity, and reveal Hardy as a writer unwilling to relinquish the fruits of his research for the sake of artistic economy. The intrusiveness of his historical sense is felt when he unnecessarily comments, "The writer is able to recall the picturesque effect of this uniform" (3. ii. i); or that at one point "the writer has in the main followed Thiers" (I. ii. ii); or when he informs the reader that "The remains of the lonely hut . . . are still visible on the elevated spot referred to" (I. ii. v); or when he comments that the Gloucester Lodge "is but little altered" (I. iv. i). The pointlessness of these asides becomes obvious when he provides a footnote for the rose allegedly given by Napoleon to Queen Louisa of Prussia, to the effect that the gift "is not quite matter of certainty" (2. i. viii), and when he portrays Madame Metternich's rejection of Napoleon's offer of marriage with the qualification "So Madame Metternich to her husband in reporting this interview. But who shall say!" (2. v. i). These obtrusive and irrelevant notes (and there are many) are of little interest except as a guide to Hardy's faithful reproduction of historically accurate detail. They hinder the progress of the narrative and interrupt "that 'willing suspension of disbelief' " which Hardy had called for in his Preface. The poet's submission to prescribed authority is indicative of an anxiety for the trustworthiness of imagination and the effort to produce an historically sound record is such that imagination fulfils a lesser role than elsewhere in Hardy's works. As one critic expresses it, "The more history has to say the less chance has imagination . . . to get a word in."[8] In the thoroughness of its submission to historical precedent *The Dynasts* is, in a sense, an indictment of the faculty of imagination.

In an early scene in Part First, Pitt outlines an important distinction for *The Dynasts*:

> To use imagination as the ground
> Of chronicle, take myth and merry tale
> As texts for prophecy, is not my gift,
> Being but a person primed with simple fact,
> Unprinked by jewelled art.
>
> (I. i. iii)

Is *The Dynasts* a work of "imagination" or "chronicle," of "myth" or "prophecy," of "simple fact" or "jewelled art"? Pitt argues for an honest relationship between speaker, subject, and audience; he asks that communication should not simply draw attention to the orator and his art. His speech is an attack on Sheridan's empty rhetoric, a mere "device / Of drollery . . . Mouthed and maintained without a thought or care / If germane to the theme, or not at all." Sheridan's facility is exposed at the Pavilion at Brighton when the Prince of Wales finds that he cannot repeat the eloquence of an earlier speech: "What shall I say to fit their feelings here? / Damn me, that other speech has stumped me quite!" (2. iv. vii). The Prince, too eager to satisfy his audience's demands, calls on Sheridan for an appropriate metaphor, and as he rehearses it, the following exchange takes place:

A NOBLE LORD: *(aside to Sheridan)*
Prinny's outpouring tastes suspiciously like your brew, Sheridan. I'll be damned if it is his own concoction. How d'ye sell it a gallon?

SHERIDAN: I don't deal that way nowadays. I give the recipe, and charge a duty on the gauging. It is more artistic, and saves trouble.

(2. iv. viii)

The products of imagination are open to abuse, and Sheridan's rhetoric serves as a warning that eloquence is not necessarily a measure of sincerity. His corruption of that which is "artistic" is reminiscent of Touchstone's argument in *As You Like It*, that "the truest poetry is the most feigning" (III. iii. 17). Sheridan's cynical manipulation of imaginative devices confirms Hardy's endorsement of Pitt's belief in "simple fact."

The word "fact," acting as a synonym for the empiricism of *The Dynasts*, occurs only a few times in the poem, and chiefly in close succession in Part

First. Nelson greets Collingwood's interpretation of the French Armada's feint to the West Indies with "So far your thoughtful and sagacious words / Have hit the facts" (I. ii. i). Collingwood's suspicions are entirely borne out by subsequent events. Similarly Decrès's report to Napoleon of Villeneuve's inaction is expressed by the words "featless facts" which, the action confirms, are indisputable, incontrovertible, and undeniable. The other important use of "facts" comes from Villeneuve himself, who faces numerous possible contingencies:

> Rather I'll stand, and face Napoleon's rage
> When he shall learn what mean the ambiguous lines
> That facts have forced from me.
>
> (I. ii. ii)

Villeneuve learns that "facts," when crowded upon one another, demand selection and interpretation, and here originate the "ambiguous lines" of his text. As one critic expresses it, "those facts have to be interpreted, and interpretation is a conversional process by which facts become metaphors."[9] Villeneuve's words are a lesson in exegesis, showing that empiricism alone is inadequate and that interpretation begins at an early stage, when "facts" are to be reconciled and acted upon. The attendant ambiguity disrupts and subverts Pitt's notion of "simple fact." Hardy's poem cannot but elucidate and interpret, yet it is the function of his historical material to hold imagination in check, to prevent it from designing "ambiguous lines." Of Pitt's speech on the death of Nelson, the Spirit of the Years says:

> For words were never winged with apter grace,
> Or blent with happier choice of time and place,
> To hold the imagination of this strenuous race.
>
> (I. v. vi)

Pitt's speech captivates a nation, but his eloquence springs from the aptness of his historical subject, Nelson, and in so doing yokes imagination to "fact." In this sense the word "hold" carries connotations of restraint, of not allowing free rein.

Imagination in *The Dynasts* is consistently characterized as dangerous and untrustworthy. During the scene at a London club (2. v. iv) there are three pointed references to the speciousness of composed words: Josephine "had learnt her speech by heart, but that did not help her"; Pitt's speech in Parliament was "a brilliant peroration" but "it was all learnt beforehand, of course"; and the debate to which Pitt contributes is "only like the Liturgy on a Sunday—known beforehand to all the congregation." Each of these orations is disparaged because it is not spontaneous and sincere but contrived and premeditated for particular dramatic effect. This distrust of imaginative stratagems extends to the common people of Wessex who burn an effigy of Napoleon. A rustic has walked miles to witness the occasion, but he is distraught upon discovering that it is not Napoleon himself but a "mommet" or representation, and he indignantly exclaims, "Then there's no honesty left in Wessex folk nowadays at all!" (3. v. vi). The poem allows the rustic's complaint a good deal of credence—he had thought that the Emperor had been captured,

> and brought to Casterbridge Jail, the natural retreat of malefactors!—False deceivers—making me lose a quarter who can ill afford it; and all for nothing!
>
> (3. v. vi)

The distress caused by the substitution of an artistic likeness for the real thing is permitted, even here, a serious expression. The syntax of speech is used so that the accusation "False deceivers" reflects on both "malefactors" and the locals responsible for the jape, thus equating that which is evil and criminal with an innocuous practical joke. This strongly moral treatment brings to mind Auden's criticism of *Twelfth Night*, that it was written "in a mood of puritanical aversion to all those pleasing illusions which men cherish and by which they lead their lives."[10]

Hardy's anxiety for the honesty of language is articulated by King George III who, in his madness, is comforted by a doctor with the news of the English victory at Albuera:

> He says I have won a battle? But I thought
> I was a poor afflicted captive here,
> In darkness lingering out my lonely days
>
> .   .   .   .
>
> —And yet he says
> That I have won a battle! Oh God, curse, damn!
> When will the speech of the world accord with truth,
> And men's tongues roll sincerely!
>
> (2. vi. v)

The capacity of a mere figure of speech to inflict acute personal anguish parallels the hardship suffered by the rustic of Casterbridge, who discovers the consequences of artistic deception. These incidents share a profound and obsessive suspicion of casual affectation which is consistently portrayed throughout *The Dynasts*; Hardy confirms this interpretation with an anonymous gentleman's aside on King George's outburst: "Faith, 'twould seem / As if the madman were the sanest here!"

The portrayal of imagination and the various shapes it finds in *The Dynasts* only rarely takes the form of an affirmation. Chiefly the poem recognizes the autonomy of language as a self-sufficient system, and it is this autonomy wherein the danger lies. This is a modern characteristic which Hardy shares with other Edwardian poets. The poetry of Edward Thomas can be seen as a series of negotiations with the intractable nature of language, his faith in names supplying a measure of security to an otherwise uncertain linguistic world. Similarly Henry Newbolt's totemic incantations evince an uneasy disparity between language and things, and Housman's verse is consistently undercut by the poet's awareness of its duplicity as a linguistic construction. For one critic the effect of this is to erode the *"sense of meaningfulness* associated with poetic rhetoric," and the ultimate consequence is to "produce a mental stillness so complete that no voice disturbs it."[11] This interpretation of what Thurley believes is a uniquely English style receives assent from the poetry of Hardy, Edward Thomas, and Housman, and at times from Brooke and Newbolt too, each of whom creates a verse which rests on the absence of an identifiable speaking persona. This is the Thomas of "Lights Out," the Brooke of "Fragment," and the lyrical Newbolt who wrote "Commemoration" and "Messmates." Thomas Hardy's shorter poems would require a separate analysis here, but a poem such as "Afterwards" is notable for its ability to extinguish the personality of its author, the man "who used to notice such things." Hardy's poems often enact a drama of self-erasure in which the writer is "dissolved to existlessness" ("The Voice").

The most demonstrable expression of imagination as an independent faculty in *The Dynasts* is the Will which creates all things, Its "Eternal artistries in Circumstance / Whose patterns" are the source of every action and every thought in the human drama. The Will represents the ultimate creative freedom or poetic sublimity which, without vision or reason, spins out Its web indulgently, arbitrarily, and without constraint of any kind. The Will governs all human lives, "moving them to Its inexplicable artistries" (3. i. i). But although It is supreme, It is not transcendent but "Immanent":

> Thus do the mindless minions of the spell
> In mechanised enchantment sway and show
> A Will that wills above the will of each,
> Yet but the will of all conjunctively;
> A fabric of excitement, web of rage,
> That permeates as one stuff the weltering whole.
>
> (3. i. v)

The Will is a creative principle which is not intelligent but unconscious, not omniscient but inherent, and the "Phantom Intelligences" are merely the choric aspect of the Will. Like the voices of Hardy's poem "The Subalterns" they are powerless to influence events. The cosmic scope of the Will is such that Its perspective casts even dynasts of Napoleon's power as "Like meanest insects on obscurest leaves" (3. vii. ix). This is brutal in its diminution of the protagonist's stature, and it is part of the immense artistic challenge Hardy sets himself in *The Dynasts* to maintain this overview convincingly and yet conceive scenes of human life which by their urgency will affirm (albeit momentarily) the value and status of their subjects. It is in this achievement that the poetry of *The Dynasts* consists.

The Will of *The Dynasts* is not completely without purpose; the last lines of the poem herald the sound of "Consciousness the Will informing, till It fashion all things fair!" (After Scene). This apparently belated confidence in the power of evolutionary meliorism has been criticized on the grounds that Hardy added it as a platitudinous afterthought, but, apart from the fact that such a technique is not characteristic of Hardy, the idea of awakening consciousness is consistently dramatized throughout the poem. When Gevrillière approaches Fox with the plan to assassinate Napoleon, he is rebuffed in the belief that,

> we see
> Good reason still to hope that broadening views,
> Politer wisdom, now is helping him
> To saner guidance of his arrogant car.
>
> (2. i. i)

This is not simply poor judgement. Fox astutely observes the operation of consciousness in others, and the absence of it in Gevrillière: "The man's indifference to his own vague doom / Beamed out as one exalted trait in him" (2. i. i). Fox's conviction in the power of noble virtue leads him to believe that Napoleon will be cured by benevolent forces. Fox rejects the assassination plan in the considered opinion that Napoleon will, in the end, see sense.

The evolving self-knowledge of the Will is reflected in that of the human characters who are Its "outshaping," and in this way *The Dynasts* should be seen as a drama of consciousness. The self-consciousness exhibited by some of the leading figures is a measure of that imagination which they share with the Will, it is an expression, in small, of the creative principle of Hardy's universe, one which can never be complete but which constantly reaches towards poetic sublimity. Nelson is distinguished by the broadness of his perspective, and a measure of his intelligent perception is registered in his analysis of the man who shoots him:

> He was, no doubt, a man
> Who in simplicity and sheer good faith
> Strove but to serve his country. Rest be to him!
> And may his wife, his friends, his little ones,
> If such he had, be tided through their loss,
> And soothed amid the sorrow brought by me.
>
> (I. v. iv)

This is both generous and shrewd; Nelson understands perfectly the equivocal vicissitudes of war. He is not distracted by personal antagonism towards his adversaries but sees the role of the individual within the larger scheme. This ability is an intimation of the cosmic perspective of the Will. Before the battle at Trafalgar, Nelson is worried by "Strange warnings . . . That my effective hours are shortening here." Collingwood dismisses such fears and expresses the confidence that the Admiral has a charmed life, but Nelson will not be patronized:

> I have a feeling here of dying fires,
> A sense of strong and deep unworded censure,
> Which, compassing about my private life,
> Makes all my public service lustreless
> In my own eyes . . .
> He who is with himself dissatisfied,
> Though all the world find satisfaction in him,
> Is like a rainbow-coloured bird gone blind,
> That gives delight it shares not. Happiness?
> It's the philosopher's stone no alchemy
> Shall light on in this world I am weary of,
>
> (I. ii. i)

Nelson's self-consciousness, enabling him in a detached manner to distinguish between his private and public lives, acts as a momentary intimation of the ultimate detachment of the Will. His creative impulse in coining the image of the "rainbow-coloured bird" is a sudden recognition of his own place as part of the Will's anatomy, and therefore of his imminent death. In the drama of consciousness, Nelson is endowed with a glimpse of the Prime Mover at the moment It conceives his demise; Nelson dies fulfilling his role with consummate efficiency: "I'm satisfied. Thank God, I have done my duty!" (I. v. iv).

The key to the theme of self-consciousness in *The Dynasts* lies with the unlikely figure of hapless Villeneuve, whose first words reveal his imaginative turn of mind: "Do I this / Or do I that, success, that loves to jilt / Her anxious wooer for some careless blade / Will not reward me" (I. ii. ii). Following immediately upon Nelson's speech about the "rainbow-coloured bird" Villeneuve's petulant despondency is intended as an illustration of that kind of leader "who is with himself dissatisfied" and who has consequently lost his military vision. One critic of the poem remarks that "Free and effective action always becomes more difficult if a person allows an image of himself to come between him and what has to be done."[12] Villeneuve suffers from a consuming self-concern which inhibits direct and emphatic action; his intense preoccupation with how his behaviour might appear to others prevents him from executing his duty. In Morrell's words, "Concern for this image of himself, in his own and others' eyes, destroyed his ability to act freely and effectively in the service of France."[13] Villeneuve uses imagination as a way to self-assessment, but unchecked it turns to self-indulgence.

Villeneuve's self-consciousness does not only inhibit action, it contributes directly to his death. Hardy accompanies Villeneuve's suicide with two important images of self-awareness. As he paces up and down the room at Rennes "He sees himself in the glass as he passes," and addressing himself in the mirror he exclaims:

> O happy lack, that I should have no child
> To come into my hideous heritage,
> And groan beneath the burden of my name!
>
> (I. v. vi)

Villeneuve projects his reputation through subsequent generations by means of the metaphor of progeny, and he rejoices that no image of himself, "no child," shall keep alive his ignominy. That he addresses himself in such a direct way is indicative of the advanced and deluding self-consciousness from which he suffers. This view is given support by Decrès's opinion of Villeneuve, and by the manner of its expression:

> Yet no less
> Is it his drawback that he sees too far.
> And there are times, Sire, when a shorter sight
> Charms Fortune more.
>
> (I. iii. i)

Villeneuve's consciousness is, paradoxically, too wide; he is aware of so many contingencies that he becomes incapable of committing himself decisively to any single one. Decrès remarks that a limited vision is unclouded by irrelevant possibilities, and the metaphor of role-play is extended:

> A headstrong blindness to contingencies
> Carries the actor on, and serves him well
> In some nice issues clearer sight would mar.
> Such eyeless bravery Villeneuve has not;
> But, Sire, he is no coward.
>
> (I. iii. i)

Villeneuve's defect was not cowardice but fear of appearing a coward. The image of the actor is a good one; Villeneuve was too conscious of an audience to play his part effectively. He is self-conscious to the point of becoming incapacitated. In the context of the debate about imagination in *The Dynasts*, Villeneuve's morbid self-consciousness is a further warning against the dangerous excesses of creative indulgence. This is further evidence that it is the purpose of Hardy's style in the poem not to allow imagination free rein. His poem is composed of "words . . . to hold the imagination."

Napoleon too is obsessed with the idea of progeny, but he is unique among the players of the drama. When Maria Louisa is suffering the pains of childbirth, Napoleon appeals to the physician's sense of professional identity, and asks him to suspend his self-consciousness:

> Fancy that you are merely standing by
> A shop-wife's couch, say, in the Rue Saint
> Denis.
>
> (2. vi. iii)

Napoleon has the key to effective and successful action, and at the point of emergency he knows better than to contemplate the wider ramifications; circumspection must be curtailed for urgent action to take place. Only the correct measure of consciousness facilitates action in accord with the consciousness of the Will. Napoleon's consciousness must be at a minimum for the forces of the Will to work through him. As one critic said of another prominent leader, "Wellington does not take the successes personally. It is less important for him, the agent, to be upheld than for the impersonal principle to be borne out."[14] This is true; in the larger scheme of things, individuals are irrelevant.

Napoleon is exceptional because he shows some understanding of his relationship to the Will, and because his leadership is egotistical: he serves not France but his own ambition. The Spirit of the Years says of Napoleon, "He's of the few in Europe who discern / The working of the Will" (2. i. viii), and Napoleon confirms this by speaking in a metaphorical language redolent of the Spirits themselves: "We are but thistle globes on Heaven's high gales / And whither blown, or when, or how or why / Can choose us not at all!" (2. ii. vi). English statemen are the agents of their country, but Napoleon is the instrument of the Will, and, crucially, he is aware of this:

> The force I then felt move me moves me on
> Whether I will or no; and oftentimes
> Against my better mind . . . Why am I here?
> —By laws imposed on me inexorably!
> History makes use of me to weave her web.
>
> (3. i. i)

Yet despite his military successes, the progress of Napoleon's career in *The Dynasts* is constantly hampered by his increasingly exaggerated sense of his own importance. he never loses his awareness of the Will, but he comes to overestimate his individual value: "Instead of *doing*, he becomes conscious of *being*."[15] Napoleon's errors are the result of a growing obsession with his own image, and his self-indulgence, like that of Villeneuve, takes the form of contemplating immortality, securing a hold upon the time in which he cannot live:

> I must send down shoots to future time
> Who'll plant my standard and my story there.
>   (2. v. i)

What elsewhere Napoleon calls "The launching of a lineal progeny" (2. i. viii), and what Josephine describes as "this craze for home-made manikins" (2. ii. vi), is a vanity the magnitude of which exceeds his real importance. Napoleon is doomed when his self-consciousness reaches a certain pitch, at the Tuileries: "My thanks; though, gentlemen, upon my soul / You might have drawn the line at the Messiah. / But I excuse you" (2. vi. iii). Napoleon confesses the ludicrous inflation of his self-esteem as his end draws near: "To shoulder Christ from out the topmost niche / In human fame, as once I fondly felt, / Was not for me" (3. vii. ix). The connectedness of the themes of self-consciousness and imagination is illustrated when Napoleon parades his troops before a portrait of his son:

> Yes, my soldier-sons
> Must gaze upon this son of mine own house
> In art's presentment!
>   (3. i. iv)

This incident, "a pathetic egocentric lapse just before the whole tide of the disastrous Russian campaign turns against him,"[16] identifies the fatally corrupting agency of imagination and the various forms it takes: the picture is "a portrait of the young King of Rome playing at cup-and-ball, the ball being represented as the globe" (3. i. iv). Here, art and gratuitous self-indulgence become synonymous. Free of empirical constraints, imagination is dangerously uncontrolled.

Napoleon is a distinctively Edwardian hero, that is to say, not a hero at all in the traditional sense, but one who is neutered by the conditions of his existence like those other Edwardians, Axel Heyst and Mr Polly. This is not only because his every action is set within the cosmic context of the Will which by Its scope diminishes all human activity. As early as Part First, Act One, Hardy writes that "The Emperor looks well, but is growing fat" (I. i. vii). This inauspicious adumbration comes surprisingly early in the campaign. Considering Hardy's over-zealous attention to historical detail elsewhere, *The Dynasts* is often curiously reluctant to concede to Napoleon the achievements which history proves undeniable. The poem undercuts the Emperor's progress with disparaging asides, such as that at Astorga which sketches "his unhealthy face and stoutening figure" (2. iii. ii). It is a demeanour which later "bears no resemblance to anything dignified or official" (2. iv. ii). At the banks of the Nieman on the march to Moscow, Napoleon "shifts his weight from one puffed calf to the other" (3. i. i). The Emperor's physical degeneration is the counterpart to his spiritual descent, as if he is flawed by indulgence of both mind and body. Hardy is correct to characterize Napoleon with a tyrant's necessary ruthlessness; at the Satschan Lake he orders the massacre of two thousand fugitives "with a vulpine smile" (I. vi. iv). It is curious how often French successes under Napoleon's direction are presented not from the victor's point of view but from that of the defeated, a perspective which hardly allows Napoleon his hour of glory. In his final soliloquy in the wood of Bossu, he says:

> Great men are meteors that consume themselves
> To light the earth. This is my burnt-out hour.
> (3. vii. ix)

Napoleon is depicted throughout the course of *The Dynasts* as if in a "burnt-out hour," and this is characteristic of the Edwardian period's loss of faith in heroic models.

The real hero of *The Dynasts* is not Napoleon but England. In his Preface Hardy complains of "the slight regard paid to English influence and action throughout the struggle" by previous European writers, and Hardy's poem can be seen partly as an attempt to rectify what he felt was an imbalance in the presentation of the role of England in subduing the French dictator. The dual purpose of *The Dynasts* has been succinctly identified by C. A. Garrison: "Hardy's reasons for dramatising these events are corrective: to right the wrong impression of England's part in the wars . . . and to destroy the concept of a heroic Napoleon."[17] The poem begins in a sense with Napoleon's defeat, by England at Trafalgar (the culmination of the early action), and although Napoleon dreams throughout of conquering England, Hardy has already shown the hollowness of these rhetorical boasts. Napoleon's most cherished ambition can never be fulfilled. Hardy might have concurred with Pitt that England's role was to "save Europe by her example" (I. v. v), or with the Prince Regent in the belief that Napoleon "owes his fall to his ambition to humble England" (3. iv. viii). England occupies the central place by virtue of Napoleon's obsessive tirades against her, and by his assertion that "The English only are my enemies" (I. iv. v). This historical distortion is instructive.

Unlike some Edwardian patriotic verse *The Dynasts* does not advocate war but enumerates "the foul obscenities of carnage,"[18] yet the poem shares with Newbolt, Austin, Watson, Masefield, and Edward Thomas in a major explication of the theme of England. *The Dynasts* is a presentation of history in a patriotic vein which might be usefully compared with Thackeray's *Vanity Fair* (1847–8), a work which leads to the same historical event without celebrating it. As an Edwardian patriotic poem *The Dynasts* is usefully considered in the context of contemporary efforts to give a single unified expression to the subject of "England."

The self-deception of Villeneuve and Napoleon is the result of an overimaginative concern for their own reputations. The critic Geoffrey Thurley has commented on this form of creative activity:

> Self-deception is certainly incompatible with the writing of poetry, but we need not necessarily conclude that the object of poetry is therefore self-knowledge. The idea of self-knowledge might be quite irrelevant to the aims and purposes of a great poet. He may quite simply, have something *more important* to communicate, something which needs to be able to take its own honesty and integrity for granted. To posit self-knowledge (as irony) as an end may ultimately be corrupting and stultifying.[19]

This is precisely what happens to Villeneuve and Napoleon; each of them is consumed by the desire to know only himself to the exclusion of the world in which he moves. In so doing he denies the governing perspective of the Will, and this proves fatal: self-knowledge cannot suffice as an end in itself. This is the origin of the distrust of imagination in *The Dynasts*; Hardy fears that it may be a way to self-delusion.

Such was the situation in the early twentieth century that Edwardian poetry was largely unable "to take its own honesty and integrity for granted" but set out to discover and affirm its identity and voice. This verse is exploratory rather than didactic. The poetry of Hardy, Housman, and Edward Thomas is often concerned with the fragility of human personality and the elusiveness of that language which purports to express it. It is the severe impersonality of their treatment of the self, the formal externalization of Thomas's "The Other," and the fictive indeterminacy of 'A' Shropshire "Lad," which prevents their verse from falling into what Donald Davie has called "various kinds of sterile self-congratulation."[20]

This discourse of checks and balances, the tendency to attach the imagination to empirically verifiable fact, is a common Edwardian characteristic which can be traced in the syntax of Edward Thomas, in Henry Newbolt's use of historical material for poetry, and in Housman's anxiety about the corrupting potential of imagination. John Masefield's depiction of physical action serves a similar purpose in restricting the excesses of creative indulgence. Each of these poets submits their imaginative impulse to external phenomena and to the rational structures of argument. Geoffrey Thurley has argued that this is a distinctively English procedure: "Leavis's emphases upon self-knowledge, humility, modesty and integrity *in fact* have had the effect of limiting the scope of the poetic imagination."[21]

These epithets apply almost perfectly to the poetry of Edward Thomas, as they might to Philip Larkin. A more recent critic has defended this kind of verse as "the poetry of equipoise"[22] and identified Wordsworth, Hardy, Betjeman, and Larkin as its chief exponents. But does *The Dynasts*, in its epic scope, rise above the limiting strictures of empiricism? Does the poem express a faith in imagination sufficient to allow it access to the realm of great poetry?

Imagination is not possessed exclusively by the commanding figures of *The Dynasts*, the creative leap made possible by the use of a metaphor is accessible to all, to the servant for example, who asks, "Dost know what a metaphor is, comrade? I brim with them at this historic time!" Upon receiving an imperfect reply, he continues:

> Your imagination will be your ruin some day, my man! It happens to be a weapon of wisdom used by me. My metaphor is one may'st have met with on the rare times when th'hast been in good society. Here it is: The storm which roots the pine spares the p-s-b-d. Now do ye see?
>
> (3. iv. iii)[23]

The distinction of this kind of imaginative activity is that it enables the speaker to understand the larger scheme of things directly; he learns something not just about himself but about the nature of the world in which he lives. Imagination is not always a route simply to self-knowledge but to the servant's broader "wisdom." This amounts to a contradiction of Hynes's argument that "Metaphor is a mode of knowing, and since man cannot know, he can speak only in flat, discursive, unmetaphorical language."[24] Even the anonymous citizens of Vienna are capable of highly developed metaphorical expression:

> Ere passing down the Ring, the Archduke paused
> And gave the soldiers speech, enkindling them
> As sunrise a confronting throng of panes
> That glaze a many-windowed east façade:
> Hot volunteers vamp in from vill and plain.
>
> (2. iii. v)

This extended metaphor is proof that the imagination can operate in a liberating fashion in *The Dynasts*, enabling even the lesser figures to make creative connections between different kinds of experience and so take a small step towards the unifying perspective of the Will. Imagination here is not purely self-reflexive (serving to develop simply the individual's sense of personal identity), and it is not disablingly internalized. The metaphor is evidence of a genuinely expanding consciousness, and since imagination is not quantitative, this constitutes a leap of faith, and in the context of *The Dynasts*, poetic faith. Other similar imaginative connections are made by the gentleman who says of the subduing of Napoleon, "Yet this man is a volcano / And proven 'tis, by God, volcanoes choked / Have ere now turned to earthquakes!" (I. i. v); by Castlereagh who says, "I know no more what villainy's afoot / Or virtue either, than an anchoret / Who mortifies the flesh in some lone cave" (2. iv. vii); by Villeneuve's officer who says of the English fleet, "Their overcrowded sails / Bulge like blown bladders in a tripeman's shop / The market-morning after slaughterday!" (I. v. i); and by Napoleon, who describes "toadstools like the putrid lungs of men" (I. iv. v). There are very few uses of metaphor in *The Dynasts* and most, but not all, are attributed to the leaders who succeed by virtue of their imagination.

The theme of self-consciousness in *The Dynasts* is reflected by the poem's self-consciousness of artistic form. *The Dynasts* is notable for the dispersal of its authorial voice through the medium of stage directions, dumb shows, and various Spirit voices. Rather than a central governing omniscient persona, the poem has a variety of commenting phantoms, and their unresolved debate constitutes the second level of the drama. Critics have argued that the Spirits Sinister and Ironic represent the voice of Hardy, simply because they express a consistently ironic view.[25] But other remarks are commensurate with the Hardy of the Wessex novels: "all joy is but sorrow waived awhile" (2. ii. vi); "Nature's a dial whose shade no hand puts back" (2. ii. vi). These comments are uttered by Josephine and Napoleon respectively. At the Commons, Pitt warns, "Times are they fraught with peril, trouble, gloom / We have to mark their lourings, and to face them" (I. i. iii). This might be Hardy also, the Hardy of "In Tenebris II": "if way to the Better there be, it exacts a full look at the Worst." Likewise Moore's stoicism might be claimed as the true expression of the author's point of view in *The Dynasts*.[26] The search for a single authorial persuasion in *The Dynasts* is a fruitless one; it is a special formal characteristic of the poem that there is none, and this is not surprising given that the poem is a "drama." This is to concur with Harold Orel, who writes that "We cannot say for a certainty which speeches of the Spirits in *The Dynasts* represent Hardy's personal doctrine."[27] More than any other of Hardy's works, *The Dynasts* is at pains to disguise authorial intention, as well it might, coming after the *Tess* and *Jude* débâcles. The debate between the Spirit of the Pities and the Spirits Sinister and Ironic is the central interpretative dialogue, but it is one which the author restrains from definitively resolving. This is the reason for the poem's impression of being remote and inaccessible, the reader is given no clear and reliable directions.

However, this is not to say that there is no point of view in *The Dynasts*; a strong controlling influence is exercised by the poem's "dumb shows" which place the scenes before the reader's attention in a distinctive manner: "A moving stratum of summer cloud beneath the point of view covers up the spectacle like an awning" (2. ii. v). The guidance of the reader's vision by means of precise optical arrangements is a highly developed technique, used to determine what is seen and how: "The eye of the spectator rakes the road from the interior of a cellar" (2. iii. i). This mode of authorial direction is oblique, but nevertheless governs the arrangement of the reader's perspective:

"The town, harbour, and hills at the back are viewed from an aerial point to the north" (2. ii. iii). This visual positioning is not static but free-moving, and the mobility thus afforded is the real omniscience of the poem. It is embodied by the ranging "eye" which dictates a series of optical movements:

> The north horizon at the back of the bird's-eye prospect is the high ground stretching from the Bisamberg on the left to the plateau of Wagram on the right. In front of these elevations spreads the wide plain of the Marchfeld . . . In the foreground the Danube crosses the scene . . . immediately under the eye, is the Lobau . . . On this island can be discerned . . . Lifting our eyes to discover . . . we perceive . . . A species of simmer which pervades the living spectacle.
>
> (2. iv. ii)

This intensely visual technique suggests a stylistic continuity between *The Dynasts* and Hardy's novels, "the recurrent motif of spying in his fiction,"[28] but more importantly, in its physical detachment it parallels the Spirits' mode of perceiving. The powerlessness of the Spirits to influence the course of events corresponds to the formal restraint from authorial speech, and despite both provinces of interpretation, the drama proceeds regardless. Detachment endows a clear-sighted view of the whole picture, but it deprives the beholder of the power to act. This is true in Hardy of both physical detachment, removed from the point of action, and of temporal detachment, represented by powerless hindsight.

As the young Maria Louisa and her ladies leave Vienna by coach, "they glance at the moist spring scenes which pass without in a perspective distorted by the rain-drops that slide down the panes, and by the blurring effect of the travellers' breathings" (2. iv. i). Louisa's perspective is caught up in the human interpretative processes of perception and in the very qualities of the scene she views. Although she is in a position to take action, she lacks the clear-sightedness which facilitates action in accordance with the Will. Her vision is clouded, literally, by the very fact that she is human; Louisa's perspective cannot be disentangled from the obscuring effect of "the travellers' breathings." The imperfection of the young ladies' view has something in common with that of the artist of Hardy's lyric "The Figure in the Scene" who sketches in the rain:

> But I kept on, despite the drifting wet
> That fell and stained
> My draught, leaving for curious quizzings yet
> The blots engrained.

The way in which artistic representations are marred, or their "perspective distorted," by the inherent imperfections of the scene they depict, contributes (paradoxically) to their fidelity. Hardy's visual style includes a provision to the effect that each is conditioned by the mode or the circumstances of perception. In other words, the poem makes an important allowance for human frailty in the act of seeing, "both what they half create / And what perceive" (Wordsworth's "Tintern Abbey").

The formal structure of *The Dynasts* alternates between the two perspectives illustrated above: one has the power of clear vision but no ability to act, and the other has the power to take action but is unsighted. The achievement of the poem is the convincingly sustained presentation of both views despite one another; it represents an opposition between the impersonal process of historical evolution and the human suffering of which that process is composed. John Bayley has expressed the belief that the two spheres are "isolated from each other, so that each can be enjoyed and reflected on in a manner appropriate to its own nature,"[29] but I would argue that it is in the very struggle between the divergent positions that the poetry of *The Dynasts* consists. At the bridge of the Beresina for example, where thousands of French are drowned in the freezing water, the poem focuses not upon the vast Grand Army's disintegration, but on the attendant women and their final gestures of desperation:

Then women are seen in the waterflow—limply bearing their infants between wizened white arms stretching above; Yea, motherhood, sheerly sublime in her last despairing, and lighting her darkest declension with limitless love.

(3. i. x)

The sight of women carrying their children at arm's length above the consuming waters is an appallingly vivid image of human suffering and the struggle with adversity, one which acquires its significance partly by its opposition to the cosmic drama. The scene is quickly counterpointed by an expression of nature's eternal endurance: "darkness mantles all, nothing continuing but the purl of the river and the clickings of floating ice" (3. i. x). Once the desecration is over, the waters progress unperturbed.

The best example of this technique is the discovery by the Russians of the remnants of Napoleon's Grand Army:

They all sit
As they were living still, but stiff as horns;
And even the colour has not left their cheeks,
Whereon the tears remain in strings of ice.—
It was a marvel they were not consumed:
Their clothes are cindered by the fire in front,
While at their back the frost has caked them hard.

This macabre group of corpses, perished in extremities of heat and cold, provides a pictorial set piece which momentarily arrests the conduct of narrative and history and defies the perspective of the Will, whose interpolations argue that these scenes are without importance. Such portraits of human suffering are static close-ups set in opposition to the ranging omniscient movements elsewhere; this technique exchanges the panoramic sweep for an intimate focus which can accommodate the smallest of details, contrary to imposing spectral directions. Like the poems of Wilfred Owen, these cinematic "stills" slow down the progress of events as a means of exercising a degree of control over them, and to concentrate the visual attention with an intensity which evokes compassion. Within the context of *The Dynasts* these are moments of epiphany, what Edward Thomas called "moments of everlastingness," which evince an abiding faith in human character, and in the force of poetry to convey them.

A greater artistic success than C. M. Doughty's *The Dawn In Britain* (1906) or John Davidson's *Testaments* (1901–8), *The Dynasts* is the major poetic work of the Edwardian period, giving shape and focus to the character of English pre-war verse. For Abercrombie writing in 1912, *The Dynasts* "attains to something that the age of Tennyson and Browning quite failed to effect,"[30] and it is the distinctively modern impetus of the poem which separates it from its Victorian predecessors and aligns it with the twentieth-century verse of Hardy's contemporaries.

Notes

1. R. A. Scott-James, *Thomas Hardy* (1951), 35.
2. A. Chakravarty, *The Dynasts and the Post-War Age in Poetry: A Study in Modern Ideas* (1938), 11.
3. H. Orel, *Thomas Hardy's Epic-Drama: A Study of The Dynasts* (Lawrence, Kan., 1963), 102.
4. H. E. Gerber and W. E. Davis, *Thomas Hardy: An Annotated Bibliography of Writings about Him* (1973), 18.
5. W. R. Rutland, *Thomas Hardy: A Study of His Writings and Their Background* (1938), 291.
6. H. Newbolt, *My World As in My Time: Memoirs* (1932), 283.
7. L. Abercrombie, *Thomas Hardy: A Critical Study* (1912), 185.
8. J. C. Bailey, *The Continuity of Letters* (Oxford, 1923), 234.
9. W. E. Buckler, *The Poetry of Thomas Hardy: A Study in Art and Ideas* (1983), 120.
10. W. H. Auden, *The Dyer's Hand* (1963); paperback edn. (1975), 520.
11. G. Thurley, *The Ironic Harvest: English Poetry in the Twentieth Century* (1974), 34.
12. R. Morrell, *Thomas Hardy: The Will and the Way* (Singapore, 1965), 78.
13. Ibid., 79.
14. S. Dean, *Hardy's Poetic Vision in* The Dynasts: *The Diorama of a Dream* (Princeton, NJ, 1977), 130.
15. Morrell, *Thomas Hardy: The Will and the Way*, 79.
16. Ibid., 79.

17. C. A. Garrison, *The Vast Venture: Hardy's Epic-Drama* The Dynasts (Salzburg, 1973), 86.

18. H. C. Duffin, *Thomas Hardy: A Study of the Wessex Novels, the Poems, and* The Dynasts (3rd edn., Manchester, 1937), 265.

19. Thurley, *The Ironic Harvest*, 25.

20. D. Davie, "A Voice from the Fifties," *Times Literary Supplement* (8 Aug. 1975), 899.

21. Thurley, *The Ironic Harvest*, 25.

22. G. Harvey, *The Romantic Tradition in Modern English Poetry: Rhetoric and Experience* (1986), 8.

23. The "p-s-b-d" is a piss-a-bed, a folk name for the dandelion.

24. S. Hynes, *The Pattern of Hardy's Poetry* (Chapel Hill, NC, 1961), 166.

25. "It is the Spirit Ironic who attacks war as absurd, and so speaks for Hardy on this point." J. O. Bailey, *Thomas Hardy and the Cosmic Mind: A New Reading of* The Dynasts (Chapel Hill, NC, 1956), 71.

26. "Moore's success . . . reminds us of the type of action to which Hardy gives, perhaps, final emphasis." Morrell, *Thomas Hardy: The Will and the Way*, 82. But W. F. Wright believes that "Villeneuve is in philosophic outlook most like the poet himself." W. F. Wright, *The Shaping of* The Dynasts: *A Study in Thomas Hardy* (Lincoln, Nebr., 1967), 170.

27. Orel, *Thomas Hardy's Epic-Drama: A Study of* The Dynasts, 24–5.

28. J. H. Miller, *Thomas Hardy: Distance and Desire* (1970), 7.

29. J. Bayley, *An Essay on Hardy* (Cambridge, 1978), 229.

30. Abercrombie, *Thomas Hardy: A Critical Study*, 188.

Index